Retrieving Origins and the Claim of Multiculturalism

Retrieving Origins and the Claim of Multiculturalism

Edited by

Antonio López & Javier Prades

Translated by

Mariangela Sullivan

WILLIAM B. EERDMANS PUBLISHING COMPANY
GRAND RAPIDS, MICHIGAN / CAMBRIDGE, U.K.

Originally published as *All'origine della diversità: Le sfide del multiculturalismo,*
ed. Javier Prades, by Guerini e Associati, 2008.

Published 2014 by
Wm. B. Eerdmans Publishing Co.
2140 Oak Industrial Drive N.E., Grand Rapids, Michigan 49505 /
P.O. Box 163, Cambridge CB3 9PU U.K.

Library of Congress Cataloging-in-Publication Data

All'origine della diversità. English
    Retrieving origins and the claim of multiculturalism /
    edited by Antonio López & Javier Prades ; translated by Mariangela Sullivan.
        pages   cm
    ISBN 978-0-8028-6990-6 (pbk.: alk. paper)
    1. Multiculturalism. 2. Multiculturalism — Religious aspects. 3. Cultural pluralism.
    4. Cultural pluralism — Religious aspects.   I. López, Antonio, 1968-
II. Prades, Javier, 1960-   III. Title.

BD175.5.M84A4513   2014
261 — dc23

                                                                2014027609

www.eerdmans.com

Contents

Preface

Anyone reflecting on large-scale social changes, particularly those changes that are both rapid and global, would do well to keep in mind the lesson recalled by Nobel Prize winner Alexis Carrel: many observations and a little reasoning are necessary conditions for reaching the truth. So it is for multiculturalism: it is crucial to first gather information in order to offer explanations for it, or to orient its turbulent unfolding. Although this method may seem obvious, it is nevertheless glaringly absent from many discussions on the topic of multiculturalism.

The massive presence of immigrants in Europe; their ethnic, cultural, and religious diversity; their integration into the daily life of our societies; their participation — or at least the beginnings of their participation — in the democratic life of our nations. . . . Before all such considerations it is important to recognize that we find ourselves faced with a historical process that is still underway. The making of history is linked to an intersection of freedoms: that of God, that of men, and that of evil. This is why it has a "non-deducible" quality, the causality of which cannot be fully mastered. We must go along with history in order to perceive its profile. This does not mean that the historical occurrences, situations, causes, and processes brought to life by these elements are the fruit of a fatal design, or of blind chance. From the moment the Son of God became flesh, died, and was raised for our salvation, the unavoidable reality of the factor of liberty, with its three elements, emerged in the consciousness of man in such a way that it can never again be erased.

To get to the "roots of diversity," that is, "to pass beyond multiculturalism," it is necessary to know, interpret, and orient it. These arduous objectives can be pursued only by a personal and communal individual willing to live as a protagonist in society, even to the point of risking his or her own freedom.

The various essays on the theme of multiculturalism that make up this book, organized into three sections (legal and social sciences, philosophical sciences, and theological sciences), seek to respond to these three objectives. They offer a key to reflection that can accompany the consciousness of the peoples of the wealthy West as it faces the process of hybridization of civilizations.

I feel it is necessary to insist on the category of witness, with all its theoretical richness (Prades). The Truth, which is so because it is personal and alive, always calls man's freedom to the stand — Truth wants freedom as a witness. The witness conceives of himself as a mere instrument of the truth to which he testifies. In giving testimony he discovers his true visage. This attitude is the guarantee of radical openness and a willingness to grant to the living truth the right to manifest itself at any time. For this reason witness is never given once and for all. The human being is called to testify to the truth here and now, in this precise historical circumstance, which is neither that of yesterday nor that of tomorrow. From this perspective, it is clear that the truth, because of its universal nature, always appears "in the form of the concrete universal — that is, of the universal value . . . of a determined and particular realization" (Botturi). Therefore, there is no way to know and recognize the truth apart from the free and considered encounter between witnesses, both personal and communal. This is the only way to orient the ongoing process of hybridization of civilizations toward the good life.

The reader will find herein numerous and valuable suggestions both for grasping the radical issues posed by the encounter between cultures (just think of the issue of the positive nature of difference) and for overcoming proposals that are incapable of offering solutions, or at least of opening up passable avenues. In particular, the authors agree on the necessity to "move beyond multiculturalism."

Our age is starved for men and women able to furnish proof, with convincing reasons and in all the environments of human existence, that the mixture of peoples happening today is not a death sentence, but rather the loving design of the Father. Far more convincing than the fatalistic *sic placitum* (therefore, he decided) of Virgil (*Aeneid* 1.283) is the *beneplacitum Patris* (it pleases the Father) of Irenaeus (*Adversus haereses* 4.26.2). Christians, out of pure mercy, can testify to this.

†Angelo Cardinal Scola

Introduction

Antonio López

This book explores the philosophical, legal, and theological roots of Western multiculturalism, that is, of the relatively peaceful coexistence of different cultures within a liberal society. Western societies, in both Europe and North America, conceive themselves as relatively well-ordered constitutional democracies within which a plurality of races, philosophies, religions, and cultures can and do coexist. They thus claim to provide a space open to the coming together of different cultures. The historical development of Western societies seems to have made the coexistence of different worldviews and lifestyles a fait accompli. Men and women from different nations seeking, among other things, religious freedom, economic prosperity, political refuge, adequate education, or peaceful coexistence migrated and continue to migrate to Europe or to North America. However, the coexistence of different cultures is more than the outcome of a migratory process. It is not only an instantiation of the capacity Western liberal societies have for *tolerating* a vast plurality of worldviews, opinions, lifestyles, and cultures; but it is also, in a second and deeper sense of the term, an instantiation of their capacity to *generate* this plurality. Therefore, "multiculturalism" is not something that has befallen the West. It is rather an expression of the very nature of liberal culture. In this way, "multicultural" is not to be taken for granted as a neutral description of our contemporary liberal societies. It is also actively generated by liberal culture as such. In this light, rather than preoccupying ourselves with offering insights on how to best order cultural dialogue, we can go deeper, as do the authors contributing to this book, by questioning the very reality of "multiculturalism" itself. Do the fundamental presuppositions of a liberal society truly support and preserve the full reality of different cultures in peaceful, fruitful coexistence? Thus, the book's goal, positively stated, is to open access to what is other than oneself and one's own culture so that the encounter with this other can actually take place and be fruitful. To better understand the uniqueness of this work, we must first elucidate some traits of the anthropology that undergirds our Western liberal culture. Though much by necessity must remain unsaid in these brief opening remarks, the reader will be able to consider this culture more deeply through the rich reflections that this book offers. Afterward, I will specify the originality of the book — namely, its aim to bring a Christian anthropology to bear on both the truths and misconceptions of the encounter of cultures — and offer an outline of its content.

American society is liberal in a way that Europe is not. The former is a technological society with a pragmatic understanding of the human being and truth, a society therefore in which thinking and acting receive their form and content in terms of making. The latter is a society whose historical memory precedes the age of progress and whose rejection of God has an ontological depth unfamiliar to American religiosity. The European liberal culture is a fruit of the reaction to the peculiar mixture of secular and religious functions that the Church incurred when, following the barbarian invasions, she had to take social and political functions proper to kings and other political authorities. American culture has never known this mixture. Unlike European liberal culture, it began to shape itself on a land that was considered utterly open to man's untethered exercise of freedom and that was historically unfamiliar with any form of unbalanced relation between the political and the religious spheres. Therefore, Europe's political liberalism carries within itself a rejection of the Church's authority, and so includes a rejection of its teachings about God and man that had previously informed the European worldview. Despite these differences, however, both the American and European versions of liberal society perceive human beings as individuals who are defined primordially by their own freedom, and both conceive of freedom not as the capacity to embrace the truth but as the unrestricted exercise of choice — this, of course, takes a concrete historical form in America that is foreign in Europe. This liberal anthropology believes that every thing comes after a human choice and is determined by it: work, leisure, family relations, gender, even our own bodies. The perception of freedom as the capacity to determine itself through choice represents therefore the architectonic criterion of liberal culture. This criterion makes it very easy, on the one hand, to perceive other cultures as the fruit of human choices and, on the other hand, to remain unaware of the overarching liberal framework that interiorly shapes every human expression in its own image. Since culture is the ordering of social life in light of a potentially all-encompassing worldview or criterion, the way a liberal society organizes itself is both the outcome and the promoter of this culture whose ordering criterion is free choice. This is one of the main reasons why in liberal societies the task of the state is to create a neutral space in which different groups have access to numerous possibilities for self-realization. The state, whose scope and extension is limited by society itself, is responsible for securing the peaceful and prosperous coexistence of its members, who organize themselves freely according to their own traditions, upbringings, and sensitivities. Within Western democracies, especially in North America, any human being can find a space to live, associate, deepen and foster his or her own culture, and embrace freely his or her preferred religious identity. At the same time, this political framework prides itself on pursuing, preserving, and promoting individual freedom (mainly of conscience and of religion), equal dignity, and self-evident rights. Liberal society therefore governs itself through a juridical state, and its specific legal, judicial, economic, and institutional parameters tend to be seen as self-given, that is, democratically determined by the collective will of individuals whose equal dignity is defended and gradually redefined by the state.

Liberal anthropology and its cultural expression reach into the theological, for, being finite, the human being cannot account for his human and social existence without explicit or implicit reference to the absolute. What man thinks of himself and of society reflects what he thinks of the absolute, God. If the human person is understood on the basis of undetermined freedom of choice, it is because God is considered to be an apersonal and monadic being. The God of liberalism determines itself freely and sees relation with the other as strictly secondary to itself. This God dwells alone in the sheer exercise of its absolute freedom. Obviously, much needs to be said to adequately ground this claim, and the reader will find many rich insights in the following essays to help him ponder the extent of this claim. It suffices to indicate here that liberalism is both theologically and anthropologically anarchic. Liberalism holds that both God and the human being have no beginning, no principle *(an-archic)* except their own (absolute or finite) freedom. Paradoxically, anarchy — understood as the capacity to fulfill oneself out of one's own resources — becomes the governing and ordering principle of liberal society that hides itself behind innumerable expressions of human creativity and choice.

It is possible to perceive without much trouble three different and related implications of the liberal perception of freedom. First, every concrete exercise of determination — whether the expression of an individual or of a whole culture — remains private, that is, enclosed within the self. Human actions and opinions can never reach the status of the universal and hence remain within the parameters of liberalism itself. Opinions and actions image the liberal framework by presenting themselves as apparently original and confined to their immediate range of influence. Second, since every difference (gender, cultural, religious, political, etc.) is the expression of the same abstract freedom, each difference is ultimately seen as indifferent, that is to say, as not essentially different from the others and hence as irrelevant. Thus, despite all its activity, liberal society leads to an insurmountable stasis in which no choice is really effective. Concretely speaking, this means that a liberal society will be able to host within itself different cultures and religions only if they remain private, that is, irrelevant, and hence harmless, to the all-encompassing anarchic horizon. Within a liberal society one can be, for example, Buddhist, Jewish, Muslim, Protestant, or Catholic — provided one's religiosity is freely chosen. Pushing further the message that Lessing conveyed so forcefully in his play *Nathan the Wise,* we can say not only that there are no moral, existential differences between the major religions, but that these religions are ontologically identical. Liberal societies contend that religions are different expressions of the same private, formal, and abstract exercise of freedom. Third, since there can be only one ultimate principle, the coexistence of different totalizing worldviews is a priori ruled out. Liberalism, apparently allowing the coexistence of different cultures, traditions, and religions within itself, de facto prevents and seeks to eliminate the existence of any culture, tradition, or religion that does not fold itself to liberalism's self-understanding. In this sense, the novelty of liberalism does not rest in its simply allowing cultures to exist freely within itself, its fostering their individuality, or its absorbing them into a dominant form as did the European totalitarianisms of the twentieth century. Rather, liberalism's novelty resides in recreating in its own image every human expression (social, political, economic, cultural, religious) that falls within its horizon, while at the same time supporting the illusion that such contentless human expression still preserves its own integrity. Hence, rather than describing the unity that liberal culture generates as integralistic, relativistic, or multicultural, it would be more adequate to account for it in terms of a self-concealing totalitarian worldview.

Approaching the encounter between multiple cultures in a single society, as this book does, is therefore a fascinating and delicate task that requires us to be aware of the language used in carrying out this task. This will prevent us from replacing the full horizon within which the cultural encounter occurs with a partial interpretation of it. The cultural liberal framework has indeed affected the language we use to describe the coexistence of cultures. The language of "identity" and "difference," used to designate the other (individual or culture) and the relation with it, has been replaced with that of "equality" and "diversity." In liberal societies, "identity" rings too strongly of unchangeable nature and predetermined physiognomy. "Equality" therefore has taken the place of "identity." "Equality," however, indicates something else altogether than identity. It regards a purely formal similarity. Consequently, moderns have problems understanding why race, gender, religion, social status, or political proclivities are not in fact qualities of equal character for defining a human person. In the modern mind, each characteristic is equally subservient to the singular understanding of human freedom as self-determination; just as religion and politics are freely chosen and informed by the human being, so the body and one's gender are at the disposal of one's own freedom, whose creative and modifying power is enhanced by modern sciences. Liberal culture no longer sees that identity regards the nature of the human person inasmuch as it is given to the human being with the task of becoming oneself by responding in history to the antecedent call of the original giver. "Difference," we mentioned, is explained in terms of "diversity." Yet, if we attend to the etymology of the words, this account is inaccurate. "Difference" indicates a common reality borne by one and the other in a way that is mutually irreducible: the same reality is "carried" by the one "apart from," that is, as "other to," the other *(differre)*. In this sense, for example, gender difference indicates the same human nature possessed in a way that is irreducible to the other gender, and cultural differences — which, however, do not belong to human nature in the same way as gender does — refer to various ways of ordering social life, ways which, however, are fruit of the engagement of the same human nature with the ultimate mystery as this engagement unfolds in varying historical, sociological, and geographical circumstances. "Diversity," instead, regards multiplicity and change *(divertere)*. Hence, whereas "difference" regards what the human person is, "diversity" regards the external aspect, not the essence, of man. Cultures are different and thus are actively open to each other and to the truth precisely because they are rooted in the same human nature as it relates to God and to others. When, instead, cultural difference is interpreted in terms of "diversity," cultures are perceived as ultimately irrelevant variations of the same notion of culture and hence remain static and closed in themselves, unable to encounter and enrich each other.

With all this, we do not wish to suggest that the terms "diversity" and "equality" are to be disregarded. We simply indicate that, on the one hand, in order to see the other for what it is, one must see it in both its external and internal aspects. If we see otherness only in formal terms, what the other *is* would be irrelevant to human interactions and endeavors. Put differently, in the modern, liberal framework the other is not seen for what it is, and hence it will always be at the service of society's most powerful ideology. On the other hand, we want the reader to notice that the substitution of diversity for difference and equality for identity is the expression of an anthropology whose architectonic principle is freedom as absolute self-determination. It is fitting, then, that one of the main characteristics of this book is its awareness of the increasingly pressing need to regard the encounter with the other person and with other cultures with fresh eyes.

Retrieving Origins and the Claim of Multiculturalism posits anew the question regarding the encounter and coexistence of cultures. This book gathers, along with articles collected later, the essays presented at three seminars held in Milan and Treviso (Italy) during the academic year 2007-2008 and organized by the Foundation for Subsidiarity. Rev. Javier Prades organized the seminars and is the editor of the Italian edition of this book. The richness of this work that the reader will most readily note is its interdisciplinary nature. More important, however, is its attention to the origins of human nature and experience. The authors build their reflections upon an understanding of otherness that takes its bearings from their shared metaphysical and anthropological assumption: human original experience speaks of a universal human nature and discloses what it means to be human, and to relate to others and to God. Furthermore, while the authors come from different Christian traditions and religions, the large majority of them are brought together also by the conviction that the Christian faith enables rather than hinders an authentic approach to the longstanding debate on multiculturalism. What brings them together in the first place, however, is not an agreement on a set of ideas but a friendship. This friendship is in itself the lived ground that enables them to reflect on the encounter with other cultures in a concrete and poignant way. The claim of the book then is that the Christian faith and the common metaphysical foundation revealed by original experience enable all people to see the other for what he is: an intersection of eternity and singularity, as well as a freedom oriented to and always already in search of the truth. The "other" is fundamentally given to himself and hence free. We are free because we are, anthropologically and ontologically speaking, gift — not because we exist as individuals who must each define what he is. We are given to ourselves within a communion of persons and entrusted with the task to search for and, in the relationship with others, to embrace our personal and unique destiny. As created in gratitude, man's freedom is always already a response to this antecedent and enabling original, divine gratitude. Thus, unlike liberalism's purely formal understanding of freedom and of otherness, this view of the other allows us to see again its essence and its intrinsic openness to and search for the infinite, ever-greater truth. Grounding this understanding of the other and its freedom, the anthropology and theology that undergird the following essays can, on the one hand, strengthen what is true in our Western liberal culture. These truths include, inter alia, the aims to protect all human beings, especially those who cannot defend themselves, in their dignity as free and rational subjects; to protect freedom of religion and of conscience; to let society effectively limit the extent of the state so that there may be true dialogue and peaceful community; to preserve a non-ideological separation of church and state; and to defend a non-ideological secularity of the state. On the other hand, however, the theology and anthropology offered here aim to correct what in Western liberalism is ambiguous, and so to bring our contemporary culture to a more mature expression of social life ordered in light of the truth of man's nature.[1]

The last unique aspect of this volume that I would like to highlight is that it gathers contributions from both European and American authors. While the latter think about and examine the theme of the coexistence of cultures within the liberal context sketched here, the former ponder this same theme within the specific form of the European liberal state. The book therefore will allow readers from both sides of the Atlantic to understand each other more deeply.

The essays have been organized into three different sections corresponding to the authors' disciplines: philosophy, law, and theology. The first part, "Perceiving Otherness, Understanding Difference," examines the philosophical presuppositions operating in and ordering the encounter of cultures. Francesco Botturi outlines the different theoretical accounts of multiculturalism and proposes the category of "recognition" as a means through which to overcome the difficulties intrinsic to multiculturalism. Carmine Di Mar-

---

1. See David L. Schindler, *Ordering Love: Liberal Societies and the Memory of God* (Grand Rapids: Eerdmans, 2011), p. 73.

tino shows how an adequate understanding of man's "original experience" enables us to discover both what the human being is and the ground thanks to which different cultural expressions can encounter each other. Pierpaolo Donati offers a sociological reflection whose goal is to put into question the presumed neutrality of the state. Costantino Esposito explores the relation between multiculturalism and nihilism and the bond that unites fundamentalism with relativism. Antonio López offers an account of our technological culture in order to bring forth the difficulties it presents for perceiving the other as other and to propose wonder as a path to affirming the other for what it is.

The second part, "Ordering Social Life," approaches multiculturalism from a legal perspective. Marta Cartabia's essay wonders whether and in what sense human rights represent a minimum common denominator that is able to allow peaceful social life. Lorenza Violini presents the juridical problems inherent in the libertarian form of multiculturalism. Joseph Weiler's contribution allows us to better perceive the danger that a totalitarian culture represents for his Jewish culture, which remains a minority within modern liberal societies.

The last part, "The Recognition of God as the Ultimate Ground," theologically deepens this fascinating question. Msgr. Javier Martínez elucidates the attitude that the Church should adopt before multiculturalism and its philosophical ground, modernity. Whereas Massimo Borghesi examines the phenomenon of the encounter among cultures as it unfolded in the second half of the twentieth century and the role that Christianity is called to play in that unfolding, Stanley Hauerwas presents a theological exploration of the American difference with regard to Europe as it can be seen in both societies' understandings of war. John Milbank studies what the increasing presence of Islam in England represents for an adequate conception of pluralism. Javier Prades approaches the theme of the encounter and dialogue between different religions through the perspective of the Christian witness to truth. Finally, David L. Schindler offers an examination of the specific nature of American liberalism and its veiled totalitarian ordering of social life. The book offers many rich vistas and insights into the very pressing question of the coexistence of different cultures within Western societies. It is the hope of the editors that these reflections will offer new light to help the reader perceive more accurately the question of the encounter of cultures in our society and to render the Christian proposal more intelligible.

PART I

PERCEIVING OTHERNESS, UNDERSTANDING DIFFERENCE

Recognition and Culture: Toward a Model of Intercultural Subjectivities

Francesco Botturi

The phenomenon of multiculturalism represents a crisis for the liberal democratic tradition in two ways: first, inasmuch as it erodes the national base of modern statehood, and second, inasmuch as it calls into question the individual attribution of rights. It is typical of multiculturalism (at least as it has unfolded in Western Europe) to bring to the social scene cultural identities based on ethnicity, in which a person's dual membership (cultural and ethnic) shapes the relationship between subjective identity and citizenship in a new way. The claim to an identity and the (potential) identity conflict become relevant depending on both the new differences between cultural and ethnic identities, which do not belong to the traditional ways of mediating interests, and on the more densely communitarian character of ethnic, and often religious, belonging. We should not underestimate the fact that multiculturalism adds to the preexisting internal threat to the democratic state's national base, and to the strong regional ties that were typical of the Old Continent.

Multiculturalism in its entirety constitutes the crisis facing modern universalism. As Caniglia has said, the social model carried by multiculturalism is "a radical detachment from modernity and its fundamental principles. With its appeal to cultural particularism and the communitarian dimension, multiculturalism appears to mark a strong break with universalist, egalitarian, and emancipation ideologies, which are at the center of the modern project."[1] Multiculturalism goes especially against the Enlightenment-

---

1. Enrico Caniglia, "Il multiculturalismo come forma sociale del postmoderno," in *Mul-*

FRANCESCO BOTTURI

modern social idea of eliminating any references to differences, traditions, and memberships in order to reach a universal condition, guaranteed by the state, that gives freedom to the individual.

Therefore it comes as no surprise that for political, and, in particular, liberal thought, the multiculturalist phenomenon has become an urgent and unsettling question, toward which one's position is ultimately regulated by one's understanding of universalism. According to the function one attributes to the recognition of universal value in the cultural, social, and political spheres, different theoretical positions are taken and different solutions to the issues arising out of multiculturalism are proposed.

Multicultural Models

The most typical models seem to confirm this variance according to one's understanding of universalism.[2] (1) The *pure multiculturalist thesis (differentialist* and/or *communitarian)* transforms the multicultural situation into a coexistence project for different ethnic, religious, and cultural traditions based only upon recognition of their right to exist. This extreme model is a minority position in the relevant literature, but is culturally widespread despite being theoretically and practically problematic.[3] Multicultural policies understood in this way favor the value of cultures and the anthropological dignity they express, but renounce every criterion of universality that is at

---

ticulturalismo o comunitarismo?, ed. Enrico Caniglia and Andrea Spreafico (Rome: LUISS University Press, 2003), p. 39.

2. For an analytical review of the theories of multiculturalism, see Vincenzo Cesareo, *Società multietniche e multiculturalismi* (Milan: Vita e Pensiero, 2000); and Vincenzo Cesareo, "Multietnicità e multiculturalismi: Problemi e sfide per la convivenza sociale," in *Per un dialogo interculturale,* ed. Vincenzo Cesareo (Milan: Vita e Pensiero, 2001), pp. 27-64. For a more specific discussion, the content of which I assume here, see Paolo Gomarasca, *I confini dell'altro: Etica dello spazio multiculturale* (Milan: Vita e Pensiero, 2004), including the related bibliographical information.

3. See Enzo Colombo, *Le società multiculturali* (Rome: Carocci, 2002). The "multiculturalist" solution finds direct legitimization in "differentialist" philosophies; see Gilles Deleuze and Félix Guattari, *A Thousand Plateaus: Capitalism and Schizophrenia* (Minneapolis: University of Minnesota Press, 1987); and Rosi Braidotti, *Nuovi soggetti nomadi* (Rome: Luca Sossella, 2002). See also the proposal coming from a differentialist interpretation of multiculturalism in Maria Laura Lanzillo, "Noi e gli altri? Multiculturalismo, democrazia, riconoscimento," in *Multiculturalismo: Ideologie e sfide,* ed. Carlo Galli (Bologna: il Mulino, 2006), pp. 81-108.

once an internal bond and a criterion for judging the cultures themselves. This model necessarily expresses a relativistic vision of cultural identities, which does not prove to be well-adapted for transforming factual coexistence into a joint social and political life — a transformation for which communication between cultures is indispensable.

Indeed, the sociopolitical applications of this model have led (particularly in England and the Netherlands) to the mere juxtaposition of communities, a passive coexistence that slides towards a potentially conflictual estrangement between communities; the marginalization of weaker communities and the (self-)segregation of more cohesive ones; the exaltation of authoritarian power surrounding the heads of communities; the constitution of uncontrollable, hidden powers; protected forms of illegality; and so on.

(2) *The integrationist model* takes the opposite approach, but shares the same particularistic assumption as pure multiculturalism. The opposition consists in the supposition that cultural identities are fully communicable and capable of assimilation, such that it is desirable in principle, and under certain conditions, feasible, to achieve the ultimate integration of minority or weaker cultures into stronger ones, where "stronger" indicates, in concrete terms, the one that holds the majority in the country of immigration.

Here it is clear that absence of cultural universality has an ambivalent meaning and is like a bistable function, open to opposite effects. In the integrationist model this absence works against the preservation of difference and toward a monocultural solution of coexistence, on the assumption that, in the absence of a universal culture capable of encompassing different ones, cultures can regulate themselves according to factual priorities or prevalence of power.

(3) Unlike these first two models, two others work from the assumption of a universality that regulates the various cultures, but each in a very different way from the other, and each with grave problems. First of all, the neo-mercantile interpretation of multiculturalism, including *corporate multiculturalism,* understands multiculturalism as a variegated component of the global market and its commercial order. Here, the immense multicultural plurality is perceived as the experimental scope of an unprecedented and promising economic universalism, in which every difference can find its peaceful placement. Technical, mercantile universality has a power of external unification, which does not bring the various cultures it meets along the way into communication, but does take them out of isolation and puts them into contact with one another. This universalism's value is a symptom of a universalist false consciousness, because it refers to a universality of tech-

5

nology, commerce, and finance. These represent an aspect of universality that is both incomplete and dangerously abstract: we can already see how the universalism promoted by globalization encourages reactive processes of cultural identification, which in turn can tend toward a localism that is abstract, or to a symmetrical universalism that is fanatical.[4] When this is the case, the unprecedented techno-practical unification of the world risks being accompanied by an equally unprecedented cultural fragmentation, with unforeseeable results.

(4) The second universalist model operates in the political sphere: it is the *secular model of universality*. To compensate for the lack of unity in the purely multiculturalist hypothesis and the lack of respect for identity differences in the integrationist hypothesis, the possibility of maximum ethnocultural pluralism and its regulation is presented on the condition of maximum neutralization of cultures' public relevance. This neutralization is exemplified in the French paradigm of *laïque*[5] citizenship, which proposes the guarantee of republican coexistence in the form of a smallest common denominator, with regard to which cultural differences are subject to the fate of a paradoxical, alienating privatization. The laïcité model, therefore, seems to be a good example of recourse to an abstract universality, which is equivalent to cultural neutrality. It is theoretically weak, and its outcomes are highly problematic with respect to the historical expectations of cultures.

(5) As mentioned above, the liberal political tradition — thought to be the most universalist and at the same time the most open to the problem of difference — is strongly called into question by multiculturalism, which forces liberal democracy to question its own intrinsic universality, or more precisely, its capacity to undergird the political synthesis of ethical-legal universality and cultural particularity. At base, the self-critique of contemporary liberalism caused by the multicultural phenomenon questions the individualistic assumption and its tendency to subsume the new cultural subjectivities. It therefore demands a holistic inquiry into liberal political subjectivity, especially regarding its capacity to wed singularity with sociality, particularity with universality.

Practically speaking, the debate within neoliberalism is headed toward

4. See Benjamin Barber, *Djihad versus McWorld* (Paris: Desclée de Brouwer, 1996).

5. See the report on which the French law on public religious behavior was modeled, Commissione Francese Stasi, *Rapporto sulla laicità: Velo islamico e simboli religiosi nella società europea*, (Milan: Libri Scheiwiller, 2004). See also Marcel Gauchet, *La religion dans la démocratie: Parcours de la laïcité* (Paris: Gallimard, 1998); and Michel Troper, "French Secularism, or Laïcité," *Cardozo Law Review* 21 (2000): 1267-84.

an *intercultural model* through the consideration of whether the individual rights tradition is capable of including legal recognition of collective cultural identities.

Charles Taylor ("hospitable liberalism") and Will Kymlicka ("liberal culturalism") move in the direction of passing beyond the individualistic interpretation of rights, on the basis of recognizing the intimate bond between liberty and culture, towards an idea of citizenship differentiated according to group belonging. Jürgen Habermas holds that the coexistence of multicultural groups does not require protection of collective rights, because each individual already owns rights of cultural belonging.[6] His proposal opens up an anthropological perspective that should be further investigated. The value of Habermas's analysis lies in the introduction of an intersubjective dimension of identity as a principle of renewal for the theory of individual rights; while the limit of the analysis lies in the still-merely-procedural nature of its theory of intersubjectivity.

Recognition and Culture: Honneth and Benhabib

In my view, a twist occurs in the debate when the focus shifts to the anthropological category of "recognition," already in use in the debate. To reflect on recognition as a means of personal and social relation creates the possibility of understanding in a new way, and in a single take, subjective identity and cultural reality. The most important authors on this topic are Axel Honneth and Seyla Benhabib. The former takes up the category of recognition from Hegel, with the specific intention of finding a connection between universalist claims of an individualistic strain, and communitarian claims marked by a particularistic contextualism. The category of recognition is, according to Honneth,[7] the most appropriate for the critical discussion of

6. Will Kymlicka, *Multicultural Citizenship: A Liberal Theory of Minority Rights* (Oxford: Oxford University Press, 1995). See Matteo Bellati, *Quale multiculturalismo? I termini del dibattito e la prospettiva di W. Kymlicka* (Milan: Vita e Pensiero, 2005), with a comprehensive bibliography; Charles Taylor, "The Politics of Recognition," in *Multiculturalism: Examining the Politics of Recognition,* ed. Amy Gutmann (Princeton: Princeton University Press, 1994); Jürgen Habermas, "Struggles for Recognition in the Democratic Constitutional State," in Gutmann, *Multiculturalism.* Concerning clear opposition to cultural rights, as conflicting with the idea of liberal pluralism, see Giovanni Sartori, *Pluralismo, multiculturalismo e estranei: Saggio sulla società multietnica* (Milan: Rizzoli, 2000).

7. Axel Honneth, *Lotta per il riconoscimento: Proposte per un'etica del conflitto* (Milan:

the liberal tradition's monological identity, because it affirms the individual subject's relational identity, understood as structural and intrinsic. It is important here that we understand recognition not simply as an enrichment of existence between people, but as a basic need and therefore also a desired and fundamental good of the human person.

The recovery of the category in Honneth comes about with the strong influence of George Herbert Mead,[8] from whom he receives tools for analyzing the processes of social recognition, as well as a certain ambiguity about the nature of subjective identity. This ambiguity relates to the potential (contradictory) reduction of identity to a mere social product, to the effect of socialization — as though recognition did not also require a capacity to receive and develop identity, which presupposes that an identity is already in play. But Mead offers tools for a reading of Hegel from a social psychologist's perspective that enrich the empirical analysis, even if they weaken the philosophical claim of Hegel's argument: socialization derives from an awareness of the meaning of action through the introjection of its effect in the other. In this way, identity is articulated in the function of the "Me," the object of normative social control; and of the "I," as a creative component; or in the internalization of normative external expectations and the assertion of one's own uniqueness in relationship with another.

Honneth believes it is possible to focus on the Hegelian anthropology of recognition, removing it from the mortgage of its fundamental combativeness and instead harmonizing it with a proposed ethic. This ethic brings the metatraditional and transcultural universalist dimensions of ethical rule together with the teleological dimension of self-realization as a particular ethic of the good life. It is what Honneth calls the "formal concept of ethical life," which responds to the double need for universality and particularity highlighted by contemporary social and multicultural relationships. What, interestingly, characterizes Honneth's argument is finding in recognition the focal point of anthropological identity, of social relationship and moral experience together: the subjective identity is relational, inasmuch as it is interwoven with the network of its recognitions, in which interaction finds

---

il Saggiatore, 2002); translated from the German by Joel Anderson as *The Struggle for Recognition: The Moral Grammar of Social Conflicts* (Cambridge: Polity Press, 1995). See Lucio Cortella, "Etica del discorso ed etica del riconoscimento," in *Libertà, giustizia e bene in una società plurale,* ed. Carmelo Vigna (Milan: Vita e Pensiero, 2003), pp. 225-48.

8. See George Herbert Mead, *Works of George Herbert Mead,* vol. 1, *Mind, Self, and Society: From the Standpoint of a Social Behaviorist,* ed. Charles W. Morris (Chicago: University of Chicago Press, 1934).

both the sense of a valid normativity beyond historical-social contexts, and the particular ethicalness of the good life. In the second place, characteristically, Honneth thinks of recognition in an analogical way: it is available in its central function at the intersubjective level, that is, in the wide range of human love; at the legal level; and at the level of social cooperation.

Benhabib also takes up recognition as a condition of identity, wondering how, to use Taylor's expression, a "policy of recognition" may constitute a response to the problem of relations between cultures. That is, since the inter-individual phenomenon is insufficient to indicate the adequate collective forms of recognition, what are the specific conditions of practicability of political-level recognition and of a multicultural policy?[9] Benhabib's response — in its ethical portion — points in the direction of a "deliberative democracy," which is essentially characterized by a binary approach to politics (institutions and public life) that strongly validates civil society, understood not only as a place of arbitration of conflict, but also as a place of initiative and spontaneous self-organization, of debate and renegotiation. "It is in the public sphere, situated within civil society," according to Benhabib, "that multicultural struggles have their place" in the framework of a public ethic founded on the "principles of universal respect and egalitarian reciprocity."[10] The principles can be realized through a variety of legal and political systems, that is, they allow for a variety of normative implementations; yet all such implementations express at the political-institutional level the criterion of recognition as the foundation of the political itself.[11]

However, the new insistence of Benhabib's argument concerns the relationship between a policy of recognition and culture — culture that today has become "the indicator and differentiator of identity" as well as the object of requests for political and legal recognition. So what is the relationship between culture and recognition? What is recognized when recognition is turned toward cultural identity? And what kind of recognition encompasses cultural

---

9. Cf. Seyla Benhabib, *La rivendicazione dell'identità culturale: Eguaglianza e diversità nell'era globale* (Bologna: il Mulino, 2005), pp. 77-87; originally published as *The Claims of Culture: Equality and Diversity in the Global Era* (Princeton, NJ: Princeton University Press, 2002).

10. Benhabib, *Claims of Culture*, p. 106.

11. "My claim is that this emphasis on the resolution of multicultural dilemmas through processes of will- and opinion-formation in civil society is most compatible with three normative conditions: *egalitarian reciprocity, voluntary self-ascription,* and *freedom of exit and association.* I maintain that these norms expand on the principles of universal respect and egalitarian reciprocity central to discourse ethics." Benhabib, *Claims of Culture*, p. 106.

identity? With these questions it is possible to express this point of view's new contribution to the multicultural question: Benhabib's perspective is more focused on the *thing* that is in play, which is not first of all political, social, or legal, but cultural, and therefore also relational and related to identity.

Strong or "mosaic multiculturalism" (as Benhabib calls it), that is, the multiculturalist and relativist view, assumes that human groups and cultures are clearly circumscribable entities, endowed with fixed identities and stable outlines; whence the idea that respect for cultures consists in absolutely equal consideration of them, yet sees them as irreducible and ultimately incommensurable realities. Ultimately, respect for and recognition of cultures coincide with the impossibility of making a value judgment about them, and, paradoxically, with their isolation. But even when such notions of respect do not have multiculturalist rigidity, Benhabib observes that "faulty epistemic premises" are widespread in the way cultures are considered: for example, that cultures constitute "clearly delineable wholes," that they correspond one-to-one with population groups, and that this lack of correspondence is not a specific political problem.[12] This way of seeing things is extrinsic to the real life of cultures, which contain different dynamics because in reality each culture is made up of actions, of narratives and judgments. Cultures are interwoven with actions and interactions, by means of narratives that together form a *fabric* that expresses attitudes and value orientations. This means that cultures are "dynamic constructions of identity," constantly in the act of developing and therefore "creations, recreations, and negotiations of imaginary boundaries between 'we' and 'the other(s).'"[13] Benhabib proposes "interactive universalism," meaning that the identity and otherness of others becomes well-known only through their own narrations, that universal community only comes about through interactive exchange, and that, more deeply, interaction is intrinsic to the way cultures are.

Universal and Particular

Benhabib's perspective calls for careful reflection and further refinement,[14] but in my view it points in the right direction, allowing us to

12. Benhabib, *Claims of Culture*, p. 4.
13. Benhabib, *Claims of Culture*, pp. 8, 64.
14. See requests and proposals for in-depth analysis of the idea of *recognition*, aimed at the multiculturalist debate, in Pierpaolo Donati, *Oltre il multiculturalismo: La ragione relazionale per un mondo comune* (Rome: Laterza, 2008), particularly chapter 3, "Promesse e limiti del multiculturalismo: Quale riconoscimento delle differenze culturali?"

avoid the alternative between, on the one hand, a universalism that is a priori and formal, external to the various cultural and religious identities, and on the other hand, a particularism of the differences that is relativistic and without a principle of unity. These two concepts divide the scene counterproductively, such that multiculturalist policies oscillate between a recognition of identities independently by qualitative evaluations of merit, and an extrinsic regulation of them based on principles, rules, and procedures. The link between actual historical subjects and the criteria of their possible coexistence is an elusive one. As Michael Walzer says, "The necessary character of any human society: universal because it is human, particular because it is a society." In other words, the universality of human forms always appears in and through the particularity of their historical development. "To recognize this," Walzer continues, "means accepting at once *minimalism* and *maximalism,* the *subtle* (of minimal and universalist morality) and the *frequent* (of maximal and particularist morality), a universal morality and a relativist one. It suggests a general understanding of the value of life in a particular place, and above all in one's own place and country."[15]

More precisely, the link is inseparable between universal and particular, the one with the other in each human cultural reality. We might say that every culture is an expression of the universal human culture, which manifests itself only in historically determined cultural forms. Therefore culture has anthropologically structural conditions that, in their always-particular, historical effectuations, are universal.

If in anthropological relationships transcultural universality and contextual particularity are inseparably unified, we must conclude that the anthropological universal expresses itself in the form of the concrete universal — that is, of the universal value (universally understandable and significant, translatable and communicable) of a determined and particular realization or, more precisely, of a singularity. Indeed here, considering individuals, actions, and entire cultures, "the paradox stands that the more the realization is *singular,* the more its value is universal: the example of a work of art is representative; it is maximally participatory in the measure of its being maximally unrepeatable in having found its own singularity."[16]

15. Michael Walzer, *Thick and Thin: Moral Argument at Home and Abroad* (Notre Dame: University of Notre Dame Press, 1994), p. 8.

16. See Francesco Botturi, "Universalismo e multiculturalismo," in *Universalismo ed etica pubblica,* Annuario di etica 3, ed. Francesco Botturi and Francesco Totaro (Milan: Vita e Pensiero, 2006), p. 126 (our translation).

In conclusion,

1. It is the nature of culture to be like an organism that lives by relationships, contacts, and metabolic exchanges with other cultures. These exchanges come from the need for reciprocity in recognition. There is, then, between cultures and recognition, an intimate, physiological connection, which measures the pathology of those situations in which cultures close in on themselves (generating inevitable explosions or implosions). This structure of culture — which finds its analogical manifestation in historical cultures — is the foundation of their possible interaction (interculturality).

2. It is the process of anthropological interactivity that brings about an expression of universal values and meanings, and, just as with individuals, interaction between cultures brings common fundamental goods to light. For this reason the possibility of interaction is not bound to preemptive recognition of universal common goods; on the contrary, it is precisely communicative interaction that brings about the discovery and acceptance — according to the rhythm set by the circumstances — of universal value commonalities, as is the case with human rights. Therefore the common or universalistic elements cannot reveal themselves if not in their encounter and collision, mixture and detachment, in time. We can dismiss a priori the idea that universality is the sum of cultures or that it corresponds to their "reduction" to some neutral, undifferentiated lowest common denominator. Rather, the universality of cultures will be, on the one hand, an ideal of fullness, that is, the ideal harmonization of all their equally possible truths. On the other hand, universality will be the historical reality of the result of their encounter or clash, their integration or separation — that is, the reality of the forms of their coexistence. The result of this — an outcome not foreseeable a priori — is what Alasdair MacIntyre calls the "dialectic of traditions."

3. Only in this concrete, historical framework is it possible to appreciate the effort to define the axiological conditions (rights) and procedural conditions (rules) for the comparison between cultures, thus avoiding the grave misunderstanding of confusing these conditions with a universal prerequisite for cultures themselves. Indeed, the conditions of comparison have the task (typical of the state) of defining cultures and guaranteeing them the qualified (never neutral) space for the coexistence of cultural universals. The creation and the guarantee of that space is the task of impartial public institutions (but these are not indifferent;

they operate according to universal principles that are already historically shared at more authoritative institutional levels). Thus, as Benhabib asserts, when institutions carry out this task, the "struggle for the
recognition of cultural differences and the contestation for cultural narratives can take place without domination."[17]

17. Benhabib, *Claims of Culture,* p. 8.

The Encounter and Emergence of Human Nature

Carmine Di Martino

The "Need" for Multiculturalism

The term *multiculturalism,* as we are all well aware, does not stand for a matter of fact, but for a cultural and institutional-political model geared toward the management of diversity in a multiethnic society — like the one that has come into being in the Western world over the past decades. The model first emerged in the Anglo-Saxon world in the 1970s, and went on to become diffuse throughout Western countries. It proposes equality and non-discrimination (*in primis* racial discrimination) of individuals and groups, in acknowledgment of the equal dignity of all citizens and all ethnicities, independent of their language, culture, or religion. Determined to protect the diverse ethno-cultural identities present in society, the multiculturalist model therefore promotes and incentivizes initiatives taken into consideration because of their explicitly ethnic basis. Its catchphrase is "equal opportunity." Nothing is more attuned, or so it seems, to respect for the identity of the other, to a perfect secularism of the state, to the democratic spirit, or to opposing the assimilatory violence of a militant and invasive state that would impose on foreigners or visitors its own language, values, or cultural horizon.

Nevertheless, in its concrete actualization, multiculturalism has paradoxically revealed the opposite face. Not only has it failed to live up to the hoped-for results for which it was designed — that is, it has not assured tolerance, peace, and an orderly coexistence in which ethno-cultural differences are assembled and protected. On the contrary, it has nourished and deepened conflicts, exacerbated initial divisions, and provoked greater seg-regation. The same goes for the opposite, French assimilationist model. As Donati observes, "Since being adopted as official policy in several countries, the ideology of multiculturalism has generated more negative than positive effects (social fragmentation, separateness of minority groups, and cultural relativism in the public sphere). As a political doctrine it seems ever more difficult to put into practice. Today, in its place, we speak of *interculturality*."[1] In fact, practically speaking, Canada and Australia, each of which has been in some way the place of advanced putting-into-practice, are abandoning multiculturalism, and Great Britain and the United States have begun to seriously question it.

The intention of this chapter is not to conduct a sociological or political study, but rather to interrogate ourselves about the meaning and roots of the multiculturalist perspective and the reasons for its insufficiency. The chapter attempts to show how these reasons lie in multiculturalism's premises. To simplify as much as possible, multiculturalism bears within itself, more or less explicitly, a dual theoretical postulate: (a) it resolves individualities within collective, ethno-cultural identities, imagining cultures as solid, per-fectly defined, and impenetrable; (b) it asserts the absolute otherness and incomparability of cultures,[2] according to which each one is unique and different from all the others, intrinsically auto-referential, and irreducibly idiomatic; values, moral norms, and customs that characterize cultures have autarchic consistency, but cannot be assessed through the categories rele-vant to external cultural worlds. From the multicultural viewpoint — which even in name is born from a request (at once ethical and epistemological) for the recognition and respect of the other, that is, of non-Western cultures wrongly considered by an old, exclusionary, and eurocentric anthropology to be "non-cultures" — historical-cultural worlds cannot or ought not com-municate between themselves, and one cannot legitimately inquire whether each culture is more or less true. Indeed the very category of "truth" dimin-ishes particularity since it belongs to a predetermined origin. In considering cultures there is no room for "more" or "less" (truth, value, etc.), but only "equal," which is another way to say, looking beyond the intentions of mul-ticulturalism, that cultural differences are purely indifferent: cultures all have

1. Pierpaolo Donati, *Oltre il multiculturalismo: La ragione relazionale per un mondo comune* (Rome: Laterza, 2008), part 4 (our translation). Here the author gives a detailed account of the several forms taken by multiculturalism and of its outcomes.

2. Cf. Carmine Di Martino, "La convivenza tra culture," in *I diritti in azione,* ed. Marta Cartabia (Bologna: il Mulino, 2007), pp. 491-506.

the same value inasmuch as they are ultimately all equally unfounded, that is, lacking in any value that transcends their pure factuality.

If these remarks are close to the mark, one should not wonder that the consequence of the multiculturalist model is an absolutization of ethnic and cultural differences. The model does nothing more than to realize the reduction of the individual both to collective identities and to the exteriority and juxtaposition between cultures that are inherent in its theoretical premises. Its implicit ideal is the mere coexistence of unrelated entities, of things extrinsic to one another, that is, of separate systems perfectly "equi-valent" and incomparable among themselves. Such systems have nothing to communicate or exchange; they cannot enter into relationships, but can only collide.[3] Therefore multiculturalism ends up being ultimately, in its apparent heterogenesis of ends, a multiplier of estrangement, that is, the first step toward hostility and conflict.

All of this being said, let us take a closer look. Multiculturalism — this is my thesis — is not a single interpretative model among many, is not a local episode, but represents the end point and the somehow coherent expression of a chosen path, followed only within the West, which underwent a marked acceleration over the last century and has brought to the fore what anthropologists have called "cultural relativism." In this sense multiculturalism brings with itself a profound need, which we shall now illustrate.

Throughout the twentieth century, Western culture, philosophical or not, battled mightily against the idea that the West is a "peak," a culmination, an entelechy of humanity and of reason. A radical historicization of our rationality — brought about by motivations and a specific, long path that we cannot reconstruct here — has been carried out: we, as Westerners, are just one of the possible examples of rationality; we have nothing that allows us to think of ourselves as superior to other cultures. Our evidences, our truths — despite being ever proposed as "universal" — belong to an essentially particular point of view (just as every other point of view is essentially particular), and they are all to be redirected to the interior of the borders of this definite and entirely *historical* perspective.

The philosophy of the twentieth century has primarily carried out this recontextualization of culture (of Western culture in general, and of Western

---

3. In the discussion on these questions it is useful and necessary to consider the positions of Jürgen Habermas and Charles Taylor. The fundamental tenets of their thoughts are well explained in Charles Taylor, *Multiculturalism and "The Politics of Recognition": An Essay with Commentary,* ed. Amy Gutmann (Princeton, NJ: Princeton University Press, 1992).

philosophical culture in particular), calling into question any claims of "truth" or "universality," beginning with its own. What dominated was a statement of the perspectival character of all knowledge: it is nothing but the product of delimited, finite, historically-bound perspectives. No culture — with its contents — can claim to have a universal validity that surpasses the historical world and the life practices that give rise to and constitute it. Nietzschean perspectivism has become our truth. Following the direction indicated first by Nietzsche and then by Heidegger, the philosophical production of an entire century — if we consider the continental thread, although American pragmatism also took a similar direction — was dedicated to a prompt deconstruction of "metaphysics," which is another word for philosophy inasmuch as it claims to grasp and state that which truly is, reality as it is, and therefore to grasp the principle, the cause, the foundation of being, identifying it from time to time in different ways (by choosing from the primary elements of Thales to the Nietzschean Will to Power). Philosophical rationality has always sought the foundation, the ultimate explanation, the conditions of possibility; it has always meant tracing back to evidences and universal truths, regardless of the results attained and the continuous corrections and retractions in which this rationality has consisted. It springs from the search for truth about the world and being in general, and has never been anything else. Now, the process of historicization of Western rationality signals the end, so to speak, of the metaphysical claim to tell the truth about humankind and about the world.

And we too, in an unprofessional way, have become or find ourselves being — willy-nilly — faithful disciples of Nietzsche and Heidegger, perhaps without even knowing who they are. For us too the truth has been absorbed into history: only viewpoints exist — perspectives with their respective finite interpretations — and nothing beyond them. All of this is in some way taken for granted, before even reflecting on it. We have internalized the historical approach, and we are suspicious of every "reality" that proposes itself as universal, that is, as a structural dimension that is not determined by a historical perspective. Think, for example, of sexual difference's "being overcome" by the classification of "gender": what is at stake today, on the human level, is the presumed definitive resolution of the structural level into the historical perspective; sexual identity itself becomes an interpretation, a mere historical and social product. All of this is clearly visible when we look at ethical issues. From that angle it seems clear that perspectivism, historicism, and the hermeneutic of equivalence of interpretations represent an obvious way forward, an almost obligatory style of thought: heading in a different direction entails a sort of resistance, means going against the grain. Under this "obligation," the questions put to us in such an uncomfortable way in our time (those having to do with life and death, the meaning or non-meaning of existence, and issues from cloning to euthanasia, as well as sexuality and the difference between humans and animals, etc.) neither can nor must have answers on the plane of common or universal rationality. Only a single principle, from any philosophical point of view, is recognized and steadily held, namely, the equivalence of different interpretations and the freedom to subscribe to them all. Ultimately, each interpretation self-authenticates, no longer needing to pass through the sieve of a common rationality. Only technical-scientific rationality is common, and it does not address any of these questions.

The process of radical historicization that occurred within Western culture is deeply tied to the way of understanding its relationships with other cultures. To go a step further, metaphysics (and philosophical rationality itself) began to be seen as the basis of Western imperialism. From a certain moment in our recent history on, a way of talking — a rhetoric, even — has been imposed concerning the alliance of logocentrism and ethnocentrism. Metaphysical rationality took the stand of the accused, guilty of having promised, in a certain structural sense, by its very nature, the various forms of world domination by the West. A great deal of contemporary hermeneutic efforts were consequently geared towards showing the "noncentrality" of European culture, towards radically relativizing it. For some decades — and still today — the critique of metaphysics, of logocentrism, of eurocentrism, and of ethnocentrism has been the distinctive feature of the most prestigious philosophical reflection, at least in the world of continental Europe.

The effects of such a position on the relationship with other cultures is undeniable: every attempt to inquire about, understand, or define another culture from criteria immanent to Western rationality represents a disguised form of colonialism. Asking the other to account for the reasonableness of his practices, values, or customs, rather than merely taking note of them, is the first sign of a chauvinistic awareness of superiority and a totalitarian will to homogenize. Cultures are universes of meaning comprehensible only to their own members, and they cannot be evaluated by any external categories. For example, a particular way of conceiving and treating women will be controversial or "not true" for us, but could be true and legitimate for others, and is ultimately incapable of being judged from our point of view: it has *its own* truth, that is, its historically conditioned, particular, and determinate reasonableness, and this is enough. In this respect, "cultural relativism" represents both the other face, or the inevitable implication of, Nietzschean perspectivism and the deconstruction of metaphysical rationality. It provides — as this paper intends to bring to light — the theoretical basis of the multiculturalist model: it radically calls into question universality of any kind, which in this model becomes socially unacceptable. It should not escape notice that "cultural relativism" is obviously an entirely Western theory itself, which cannot but make the claim that it is universal.

This is, however, only half of the truth. We find ourselves dealing today not only with the finiteness of interpretations (with "the disassembled, or anyway disassembling, world of restless identities and uncertain connections")[4] but with another universalism, which imposes itself even before any self-critical consideration of philosophy: the universalism of tele-techno-science. Even the most ferocious anti-Westernism speaks the language of techno-scientific universalism and practices the technological *medium* (or would intend to do so). People can be Western or Eastern, and of any religion they please, but they must have Internet and the atomic bomb — that is, the techno-science that constitutes the most advanced frontier of Western rationality. And if we limit ourselves to looking within our own boundaries, we realize that a person may have an opinion on everything, but not on the doings of science; for the very fact that science *is,* the fact of its occurring in time, is the happening of truth. Beyond a pure rhetoric of ultimate or penultimate ends and ethical limits, scientific practice claims to be and is recognized as apodictic.

Singular and Universal

In short, multiculturalism does little more than to condense within itself a path already followed to its end. Its doctrine reflects and enacts the attempted liquidation of the universality and quest for truth proper to metaphysical rationality. In this resides its "necessity," its character that is anything but localized or random.

Nevertheless, as described above, multiculturalism is worn out, fails to withstand the test of facts, and reveals itself to be weak precisely where it

4. Clifford Geertz, "The World in Pieces: Culture and Politics at the End of the Century," in *Available Light: Anthropological Reflections on Philosophical Topics* (Princeton, NJ: Princeton University Press, 2000), p. 226; originally published as *Welt in Stücken: Kultur und Politik am Ende des 20. Jahrhunderts* (Vienna: Passagen Verlag, 1996).

believes itself to be strong, that is, in managing diversity and assuring tolerance through a systematic deactivation of value judgment. Rather than smoothing conflicts, multiculturalism, precisely by virtue of its hypotheses, becomes a structural factor that nurtures them. Indeed, multiculturalism undertakes to govern the public sphere via a merely procedural ("indifferent") recognition of differences, declining on principle to make any inquiries into truth (which have become theoretically *incorrect*) and imagining that ethno-cultural identities, with their contents and life practices, can grow and coexist without coming into contact or mutually evaluating one another. In this vision, each identity can reach for itself toward ever-greater influence without entering into competition with other identities, because they all move in profoundly divergent directions, both with respect to one another, and with respect to the guiding principles of the legal and governmental order (which, obviously, is never lacking). But if the ideal of multiculturalism is to construct a social and political space populated by parallel universes bound to remain forever parallel, impermeable, and incapable of evaluation, it can only succeed under two paradoxical conditions: (a) the total isolation of every ethnic group/religion/culture (which means designing the perfect quarantine of social space); or (b) the systematic sterilization of identities, a sort of desertification of religions and cultures.[5] It is easy to see that such a model constitutively bears incurable tensions, and is entirely insufficient to the task of addressing the looming situation.

In brief, it is the failure of multiculturalism that compels us to call again into question frameworks of thought that had seemed well established. If what this essay has laid out is true, escaping from the paralysis of multiculturalism (and from the shoals of the opposite, assimilationist model) means calling into question the relativistic dogma of the "incomparability of cultures" and re-proposing universality (that is, a dimension or a *universal structure of human experience*) in a new and sophisticated way. To conceive of social space as the shared-life and interaction of cultures — as the "interculturality" which is increasingly referred to today — instead of as the place of mere cohabitation without relationships or communication indeed implies a need to rethink the condition of possibility of *encounter* between them.

To this end, Husserl's reflection on the relationship between the "familiar world" and the "foreign world" is helpful. Bumping into a different historical humanity, with its culture and system of values, I may come across

5. Carmine Di Martino, "La convivenza tra culture," in *I diritti in azione,* ed. Marta Cartabia (Bologna: il Mulino, 2007), pp. 491-506.

20

objects whose use is unknown to me, habits whose original motivations and final goals elude me, signs and linguistic expressions that I do not understand. I find myself faced with a historically and environmentally defined world, replete with its many objects, real and ideal, its beliefs and its certainties of being — all completely familiar to the individuals within it, but profoundly foreign to myself. "I simply cannot understand their ways of relating to this world, or understand this same world as they understand it, or understand how this world is for them, how these people are to one another, and so forth. *And nevertheless I understand them and we understand each other as humans.* We have in our vital relationship a layer adequate to that purpose."[6] Therefore, everything that is still so foreign, still so incomprehensible, has *a kernel of comprehensibility,* without which it could not be experienced at all, not even as foreign. There is a common threshold which allows us to understand "one another inasmuch as we are human."

What compels us to accept this common *kernel?* The incontrovertible fact that the possibility of understanding is always open — even starting from an unfathomable distance. It is only from this fact that we can give reason for the incomprehension, unknowing, and misunderstanding. As Derrida sharply commented, for Husserl "no cultural identity presents itself as the opaque body of an untranslatable idiom, but always, on the contrary, as the irreplaceable inscription of the universal in the singular, the unique testimony to the human essence and to what is proper to man."[7] It is as though the relativistic-multiculturalist approach shifted the burden of proof: it must be demonstrated *that there is* a universal dimension of experience, that is, an "elementary experience," common to all individuals. This approach supposes that such a universal dimension is a pure myth, since apparently there is no structural universality that cannot be explained by historical-cultural contingencies of life practices, as Rorty would say. But the burden of proof should lie with the opposite position: it should have to be demonstrated that *there is not* a ground of identity, that a common kernel does not exist, since experience attests to the fact that understanding has always happened and continues to happen — the translation is underway between individuals belonging to different historical and environmental worlds. And if there is meeting, exchange, and translation, there is a common point. Even when

6. Edmund Husserl, *Zur Phänomenologie der Intersubjektivität: Texte aus dem Nachlass, dritter Teil, 1929-1935,* Husserliana 15, ed. Iso Kern (Dordrecht: Martinus Nijhoff, 1973), p. 625 (our translation).

7. Jacques Derrida, *The Other Heading: Reflections on Today's Europe,* trans. Pascale-Anne Brault and Michael B. Naas (Bloomington: Indiana University Press, 1992), p. 73.

we speak of untranslatability, we necessarily do so on the basis of a translation that has always been done and remains to be done, at once possible and impossible, effectively possible precisely because it is impossible in an absolute sense, and therefore always open.

The theoretical weakness of multiculturalism — or more precisely, of the "cultural relativism" that lies at its root (without forgetting the results that this relativism has assured for philosophical and anthropological reflection) — paradoxically resides in its incapacity to conceive of difference (between cultures as between individuals). Difference exists only in reference to identity; a pure difference is not at all different from non-difference. To think of diversity as *ab-solute* would be to cancel it out: the manifestation and recognition of the diversity of the other, of his or her infinite otherness — as we would say using the lexicon of a certain philosophy of Lévinasian strain — structurally implies a primary identity. In the minimal terms of an I-you relationship, this means that the other must take the form of an "ego," an ego like myself, because he appears as "alter" without his otherness becoming mixed up with that of the other things in the world. As Derrida observes, again commenting on Husserl, "If the other was not recognized as ego, its entire alterity would collapse."[8] Blinding ourselves to this ultimate "identity" (whether understood as it is here in Husserlian terms as the form itself of egoity, or in another way) entails the impossibility of giving an explanation for what happens: the appearance of plurality and multiplicity, of the difference of individuals, humanity, and cultures. Before giving these things content, however, we can understand this identity as that *possibility* revealed by *the happening* of encounter with the other as *that which was already there,* perforce at work. To put it into the dry style of a formula: if the encounter happened, it must have been possible. Therefore, every time an *encounter* takes place between the familiar world and the foreign one, between individuals of different cultures, we see a new testimony to the "universality" of that threshold that makes possible both encounter and understanding. Universality is always at work — "it operates anonymously," as

8. Jacques Derrida, "Violence and Metaphysics," in *Writing and Difference,* trans. Alan Bass (Chicago: University of Chicago Press, 1978), p. 125. In this essay dedicated to Lévinas's thought, Derrida shows the necessity of following the Husserlian phenomenological approach in order to maintain the otherness of the other asserted by Lévinas: "If the other were not recognized as a transcendental alter *ego,* it would be entirely in the world and not, as ego, the origin of the world. To refuse to see in it an ego in this sense is, within the ethical order, the very gesture of all violence. If the other was not recognized as ego, its entire alterity would collapse," p. 125.

Husserl would say — waiting for neither reflection nor argumentation, neither the recognition of mankind nor its deliberation, before going into effect. It can be denied, but never suppressed. It involves a minimal-universal threshold of humanity whose existence must be presumed in order to explain what has always, in fact, occurred.

To highlight the essential point of this discussion: what is universal is not culture, which is always particular — although every culture has, even when it does not intend to embrace it, an intrinsic vocation to propose itself as universal — but rather *humanity*. That is to say, what we originally and effectively have in common with the other is not in the first place to be found at the level of worldviews, values, and norms, but rather at that non-deducible threshold revealed precisely in the encounter between distinct individuals who are incarnate and historically determined. This threshold is the condition of encounter, and is what we have called "humanity." On this we can speak, within our cultural horizon and in our own language, of a nucleus of *evidences, needs, and original dispositions* by which every human being is a person like each of us, and by which reciprocal understanding is always possible in principle. In addition to being called again to that ever-questioning and ever-understanding openness to the world — as we would say in Heidegger's language — that characterizes human being and presides in the constitution of all culture, in speaking of this nucleus we are above all referring to the incommensurability of those needs for meaning, justice (beyond the law), fulfillment (what Husserl called "being directed in an infinite dimension toward 'perfection,' toward true self-preservation," that is, toward "real being"), relationship with the other, and for sharing.[9] These needs characterize the humanity of humankind and guide our openness to the world. It may seem incredible to find in the work of an author like Jacques Derrida, considered by many to be the champion of a philosophy of difference that leads toward radical nihilism and relativism, an insistent reference, particularly in the work of his final years, to a "universal dimension of experience,"[10] the recognition of which would alone open the space for a tolerance that "would respect the distance of infinite alterity as singularity."[11] Contrary to a widespread misconception, the simple assertion of this *universal* dimension of experience lays the foundation for respecting the *singu-*

9. Husserl, *Zur Phänomenologie der Intersubjektivität*, p. 378 (our translation).

10. Jacques Derrida, "The Deconstruction of Actuality: An Interview with Jacques Derrida," *Radical Philosophy* 68 (Fall 1994): 36.

11. Jacques Derrida, *Acts of Religion*, ed. Gil Anidjar (New York: Routledge, 2002), p. 60.

larity of the other, its infinite alterity and difference. Not to recognize this universal dimension, on the other hand, constitutes the very principle of violence and does not allow for distinction between the *alterity* of another human being and that of a thing.

Encounter and Reason

If "universal" does not first of all refer to this or that culture, but to the event of the human, it is important to note that this reference is always made from within a determinate culture. That is, the universal structure of experience is at once *within* and *beyond* every culture, at once transcendent and immanent: *trans-immanent,* we might say. The "trans-cultural" is never an abstract, disembodied generality, available in a kind of autonomous transparency. An anecdote that Heidegger borrows from Hegel is illustrative: "Someone wants to buy fruit in a store. He asks for fruit. He is offered apples and pears, he is offered peaches, cherries, grapes. But he rejects all that is offered. He absolutely wants to have fruit. What was offered to him in every instance *is* fruit and yet, it turns out, fruit cannot be bought."[12] What the metaphor means is that the "human nature" only appears within this or that culture, according to this or that historical signification. Here we find ourselves in an indefinite field of revelation, of expression, and therefore of modification. Indeed, this ultimate structural *identity* always occurs within determinate shapes and meanings; it can unfold in very different and even apparently opposite ways. This means that it is constitutively assigned to multiple, incessant, and always still-to-come emergences, to a recognition and a translation that are, on principle, always open (which allows, at the same time, the possibility of better and worse, progress and regress).

That structural identity is manifested only in determinate forms provides a key to understanding "interaction" between cultures (which, along with clash and elimination, has occurred throughout the history of humankind). If it is true that every culture represents a universe of meanings, values, and ways of living in which that possibility called "human nature" finds expression by historicizing itself; if each culture constitutes a way of embodying those original needs and dispositions that allow us to mutually rec-

---

12. Heidegger narrates the episode in his essay *Identität und Differenz* (Pfullingen: Günther Neske, 1957); translated by Joan Stambaugh as *Identity and Difference* (Chicago: University of Chicago Press, 2002), p. 66.

ognize one another as human beings (even in the difference between our backgrounds); then the encounter between cultures — each one of which is, in its own way, "the unique testimony to the human essence and to what is proper to man" — can open the way for a new emergence of the original identity. Do we not owe to encounters not only the development of our "self," but also the introduction to every new happening in life? In the relationship between cultures this means not only that, in the encounter with the other (the other culture, the other "inscription of the universal in the singular") the needs and dispositions that make up the human being reveal themselves as the same (as an identical element in its different modes of manifestation and apprehension), but also that entering into relationship with the ways and responses of the other, with the other's figures of meaning, can provoke a reconfiguration of our own awareness, and in this way can make the "unprecedented" occur. The encounter with the other (in all senses of the word) calls forth the meaning of our own experience of the world, precisely in that it poses alternatives. Even the mere desire to persevere in belonging to one's own culture (which in a certain sense is never "one's own," as it always comes from "the other") takes on a different meaning, since it entails (even implicitly) an option and a judgment (the mere "I will keep on doing what I'm doing" is a value judgment). The encounter with others — which, in order to be an encounter, requires a living self-awareness — opens the possibility for self-criticism as much as for a stronger adhesion to one's own tradition. Speaking of "interaction" in this way, we do not propose a plan of worldwide syncretism or globalization of meaning (which would end up becoming just another form of hegemony, of forced universalization). Rather we mean, on the one hand, to assert that the emergence of the universal structure of experience does not occur at the expense of certain cultures — as though they had to proceed by subtraction, abstracting from their concreteness — but occurs because of them; and on the other hand, to recognize that cultures and religions are essentially comparable. If there is interaction, there is comparability, and therefore the possibility and even the duty to critique, even if this cannot take place according to pre-established criteria.

Every culture, like every religion, is on principle susceptible to being judged by that same original human disposition that presides over its emergence and that characterizes, according to different degrees of awareness, the profound essence of every subjectivity. It is the universal structure of experience, incessantly emergent in the encounter with the other, that operates as an out-and-out critical principle of every culture and of its figures, as a deconstructionist request implicitly at work within every system. In experiencing others and the world, every subject is as much defined by his own culture as he is ultimately irreducible to it: not in the sense that there exists such a thing as a man isolatable from culture (that is, one able to live outside of a determinate history or culture), but rather in the sense that he carries within himself the possibility to diverge from and overcome his own culture. For this reason, after having necessarily inherited his culture, he may decide to abandon it in favor of another. The human being is never without culture, but reserves toward it a power of "escape," by which (for other reasons) Merleau-Ponty defined the human being,[13] and which is founded on the trans-immanent structure of human nature. This structure is at once the unceasing origin and the internal, untamable criticism of every culture; it is the opening of the culture which, as such, cannot be absorbed by it. The structure of human nature is the critical principle that allows us to say "yes" and "no," to question what is worse and what is better, to identify ourselves and to take our leave — in brief, to be critical, that is, open to ulteriority. It is with regard to this original and nondeducible threshold, beyond the determinations in which it manifests itself, that not everything is equivalent and that there can and ultimately must be value judgments, correction, critique and self-critique, straining toward the future — all within this or that culture as well as in the relationship between cultures.

Such critique regards, first of all, the interaction with cultural horizons that are different from our own. Faced with the rise of ethics and religious beliefs oriented toward a direction that is antithetical to the values we consider undeniable, we must ask ourselves: in what sense can we think of our values as "undeniable"? Only as habits as old as they are ungrounded? Do our customs and lifestyles have reasons, and more reasons than those of others? Or are we simply attached to them because they are ours — we like them, and so we want to defend them? The problem is clear: we can speak about "reasons," and not only of habits and tastes, only if a comparison is operating between particular styles and that universal structure of human being that represents their root, however it is expressed. If it were not this way, we would have to consider every system of values to be fully legitimate, regardless of its contents and its consequences. To follow through on the point, we would have limited ourselves to considering, for example, (past and future) practices of cannibalism and human sacrifice merely as different

---

13. Maurice Merleau-Ponty, *Phenomenology of Perception,* trans. Colin Smith (New York: Routledge, 2002), p. 198.

morals, heterogeneous with respect to ours, justifiable in their own contexts and not able to be judged on the basis of our cultural categories.

In the second place, the problem regards, even more importantly, what happens within Western societies. Today we are challenged in various ways by a remarkable number of issues: the use of human embryos, cloning, euthanasia, abortion as a fundamental human right, gender identity classification, pedophilia, incest, human-animal equality, and so on. In the name of *what* will we take a position, any position? Can we refer ourselves to something more than feelings and personal dispositions or idiosyncrasies? Or, put in a more contemporary way, can we refer ourselves to something more than the inalienable right to *privacy,* than individual liberty? It is important to note in passing that today it is the "right to privacy," conceived as the right to free choice and self-determination in personal, sexual, family, health, and other affairs, which appears as the sole guiding principle — on both the cultural and juridical levels — for all the issues we have touched on.

In the third place, the reference to a minimum-universal threshold of human nature as the critical principle constitutes the nodal point also with respect to the much-discussed topic of "human rights" or "fundamental rights." These, beyond the context and historical motivations that accompanied and qualified their onset,[14] today represent the guiding thread of an attempt to construct a common horizon of values in which peoples and cultures can recognize one another in order to enjoy a peaceful coexistence. Now, a similar attempt to identify certain fundamental values and rights to be universally promoted and protected springs from a noble impulse, and is certainly necessary, but, inasmuch as it is the expression and product of a determinate culture, it cannot simply self-confirm and self-justify. This attempt is itself in question, starting precisely with the structure of human nature referred to above. It is therefore necessary, at all cost, to maintain and put to work the distinction between the universality of rights and the universality of the human nature, avoiding the short circuit between the list of fundamental rights and the universal structure of experience. It is necessary that the irreducibility of this structure, continually sought after and recognized by reason in an indomitable attention to experience, brings about a critical vigilance even in facing so-called universal rights. In the contemporary context, the temptation — as we can see from the long list of rights and

14. On this see Luca Antonini, ed., *Il traffico dei diritti insaziabili* (Soveria Mannelli: Rubbettino, 2007).

its constant and purposeful evolution — is to introduce or impose as universal positions those that belong to a determinate setting (if not to restricted circles of cultural elites) and that are promoted by international institutions to "orient" the "development" of the customs of Westerners in their own respective countries. In the absence of critical work, at once philosophical and juridical, universal rights risk becoming instruments of transnational pressure toward a vision of new and greater homogenization, despite the diverse histories and traditions of the peoples.

So let us ask ourselves: where can we look for a significant contribution to the constitution of a space for coexistence and interaction, for respect for difference, and for authentic *interculturality?* The answer seems clear: it cannot come from a residual reason, which takes shelter in the philosophical inconsistency of an accommodating relativism, and which ultimately wishes for the secularization of all identities, carried out by the force of the market and the strategic use of transnational, legal instruments. The contribution can come only from a *reason* that ceaselessly inquires about the originality of the human nature, awaits for its emergence, and exercises from its starting point, from the point of the awareness achieved, a critical vigilance and a continuous reconfiguration of the social space. This is a reason that, in the name of loyalty to experience, refuses to consider cultural identity as "the opaque body of an untranslatable idiom," and is willing to rethink in a non-naïve way (making full use of the lessons of hermeneutics) the challenge of universality, that is, the relationship between singular and universal. It is a reason, therefore, that does not aim for homologization, for uniform thought, but that, on the contrary, takes it upon itself to tackle and move from those ultimate needs and dispositions to which all the different positions and proposals are attempts to answer. This reason tests such positions' and proposals' solidity and aims to build a common horizon that is structurally open, through the necessary negotiations and by virtue of an effective encounter of traditions, heritages, and languages. This encounter, however, does not start from just anywhere: it begins from reason's renewed awareness of its own tradition.

Indeed this reason does not live in abstraction from the world — it is not without either body or history — but belongs to Western identity itself, in its double heritage: Greek and Judeo-Christian. If we consider the inaugural gesture of Socrates — his irreverently questioning his fellow citizens about the consistency of their convictions — it is immediately evident that it is a necessary part of Western identity to question the truth of one's own beliefs, to give an account of them, and to be ready to abandon them in the case that they do not stand up to the test of scrutiny. As Husserl said, philosophical stupor occurs when, for the first time in the history of humanity, the difference is acknowledged between one's own beliefs and the truth, between "world-representation and actual world,"[15] "between a being identical in itself and its multiple subjective modes of apprehension."[16] Western rationality is essentially characterized as a question, as the exercise of critique and self-critique, the search for a truth that is not ownership, but rather an irreducible pole and an endless task. With the advent of Christianity, it did not reach a point of pause, but rather a new foundation and a new revitalization of its original breath. Moreover, Christianity opened an unprecedented horizon of universality that interwove with the Greek *logos*. The concept of "person," the recognition of the person's absolute and irreducible value (founded on creaturely relationship), which Christianity gave to history, opened up a dimension of universality that deactivates the pertinence of certain old and new frontiers, and establishes unconditional respect for singularity. Clearly, the problem is not primarily one of coherence, but whether these elements belong or do not belong to the DNA of a determinate tradition, and whether they can be reclaimed and reactivated.

Being Westerners, we face the unavoidable issues (cultural, legal, political) that the coexistence of diverse cultures presents. If, therefore, we mean to work toward the formation of a space of authentic interaction and hospitality, we must above all rediscover our own "diversity": we must respond to our heritage and the resources it offers, without false eurocentrisms, but also without false obliterations. The problems that pester our present time also carry with them possibilities: the ever-growing co-presence of other peoples, with their respective cultures and religions, within the ever-weaker borders of the Western nation-states is an invitation offered to us by others and by history that compels us to ask ourselves who we are and who we wish to be. Concerning the issue of multiculturalism and its practical failure, much more is at play than a simple alternative between political options and

15. Edmund Husserl, *Die Krisis der europäischen Wissenschaften und die transzendentale Phänomenologie: Eine Einleitung in die phänomenologische Philosophie,* Husserliana 6, ed. Walter Biemel (The Hague: Martinus Nijhoff, 1976), p. 332; translated by David Carr as *The Crisis of European Sciences and Transcendental Phenomenology: An Introduction to Phenomenological Philosophy* (Evanston: Northwestern University Press, 1970), p. 286.

16. Edmund Husserl, *Die Krisis der europäischen Wissenschaften und die transzendentale Phänomenologie: Ergänzungsband; Texte aus dem Nachlass, 1934-1937,* Husserliana 29, ed. Reinhold N. Smid (Dordrecht: Kluwer, 1993), p. 388 (our translation).

normative structures. Moving beyond this model means, more deeply, to become heirs once again, to open ourselves up to the occurrence of a certain experience of human nature and rationality, in its living and historically determinate source. But, in order for this path to be walkable (provided that we recognize its urgency), we need, above all, credible witnesses of its feasibility.

We Need a "Relational Reason" for Different Cultures to Meet and Build a Common World

Pierpaolo Donati

The Challenge of Multiculturalism

How can we approach the growing cultural differences and the diversity found in society as a result of globalization?[1] In other words, how can we treat those people who present relevant cultural differences?

The doctrine of multiculturalism has gained the largest foothold in the West as an answer to these questions, albeit in a variety of forms, simply because it seems to be the most consistent with the liberal premises of Western democracies. This doctrine was, in fact, born to favor respect, tolerance, and the defense of different (minority) cultures. It later morphed into an imaginary collective, under which we would be "all different, all equal." As it turns out, our differences are all placed on the same level and treated under rules which render them *in-different* — that is, it is maintained that the meaning and relevance of those differences make no difference. For instance, any family arrangement in which a child might be raised — the single-parent family, heterosexual parents, homosexual parents, or any other situation — is regarded as functionally equivalent.

This multiculturalism produces a society characterized by the growing pluralization of all cultures. This pluralization is generated not only by migrations of one cultural group into another, but also by the internal dynamics of individual native cultures (national, regional, or local). In particular, mul-

---

1. Though from this point on I will only use "difference" in the text, the reader may assume that what I say about difference applies also to diversity.

ticulturalism erodes the same modern, Western culture that gave rise to it, which loses the rational bases that for many centuries assured it a certain homogeneity. Indeed, multicultural ideology justifies new, so-called post-modern cultures and lifestyles. The multiplication (systematic production) of cultural differences nourishes a social order in which individuals individualize themselves by searching for an identity that refers to particular social circles, and these circles in turn privatize the public sphere.

Our question is therefore as follows: is there a manner of civil coexistence between different cultures that can avoid falling into the ethnic-cultural relativism and political secularism that accompany multiculturalism? The humanity of civilization hangs in the balance.

Since being adopted as official policy in several countries, the ideology of multiculturalism has generated more negative than positive effects (social fragmentation, separateness of minority groups, and cultural relativism in the public sphere).[2] As a political doctrine it seems ever more difficult to put into practice. In this chapter I will discuss the possible alternatives to multiculturalism. Today, in its place, we often speak of *interculturalism,* but this expression too seems more or less vague and uncertain. Indeed, interculturalism is subject to insurmountable deficiencies because it presents an insufficient internal reflectiveness to individual cultures and lacks a relational interface between cultures (i.e., between the subjects that are bearers of culture).

In order to move beyond multiculturalism's shortcomings and the fragilities of interculturalism, a secular approach to the question of coexistence between cultures is needed, namely, one that is capable of restoring life to reason through a new semantics of interhuman difference. A more *relational* reason could best conceive a new societal configuration able to humanize the processes of globalization and the increasing migration of cultures.

The Root Deficit

Multiculturalism is theoretically reductive of encounter and recognition. At the root of its reasoning, multiculturalism expresses the need to find new avenues for the mutual recognition of human dignity by persons who meet each other and perceive the differences that exist between them. In this,

2. For a thorough treatment of this line of inquiry, see Pierpaolo Donati, *Oltre il multiculturalismo: La ragione relazionale per un mondo comune* (Rome: Laterza, 2008).

multiculturalism reflects what is surely a good thing. Its assertion that we must recognize "the value and the dignity of all citizens, independent of their race, ethnicity, language, or religion"[3] recalls us to the Christian view of secularism in the early days of Christianity.[4] This view recognizes the original dignity of every person, prior to and apart from every ethnic and cultural belonging, as well as the fact that the Christian is a citizen like all others. However, even if multiculturalism does provide a motive to rethink the quality and characteristics of the recognition of what is truly human, it does not say sufficiently what that quality and those characteristics are. The multicultural solution is lacking because it does not succeed in filling the gap between citizen and person. To assert that the citizen achieves self-fulfillment in the public sphere by means of the policy of human dignity and the corresponding legal rights (the policy of universalism) while the person achieves self-fulfillment in his or her own cultural community (the policy of difference) leaves empty what exists *between* these two spheres.

Multiculturalism is ambiguous and ambivalent: if on the one hand it underlines the uniqueness of the human person, on the other it renders the person incommunicable from the cultural point of view. Certainly it insists on the *radical otherness* of the "other," urging a better understanding of how recognition between human beings is different from the recognition that a human can give to a nonhuman entity. The point, however, is that multiculturalism promises a recognition that cannot be realized because of its reduced and restricted conception of encounter and recognition. Multicultural recognition, in fact, is conceived as the unilateral act of a collective mentality that attributes an identity on the basis of an autocertification or an identity claim that satisfies neither a veritative criterion[5] nor a criterion of recognition (appreciation). In contrast, social practices show us that recognizing the other (as an individual, but also as of another culture) is a human act if, and only if, it is an act of validation (that sees the truth of the other) inscribed in a circuit of symbolic exchanges (gifts).

Multiculturalism fails to satisfy either of these two requirements. In mul-

---

3. See the website of The Canadian Heritage.

4. Cf. *Letter to Diognetus* (PG 2:1167-86).

5. The adjective "veritative" can be referred to Martin Heidegger's phrase "veritative synthesis," which constitutes the essence of finite knowledge. It is a synthesis because all knowledge is a union of knower and known, and it is veritative because, by reason of this union, the being-to-be-known becomes manifest, i.e., true, simply because it reveals itself as it is. See Heidegger, *Kant and the Problem of Metaphysics,* trans. Richard Taft (Bloomington: Indiana University Press, 1997).

ticulturalism, the one's recognition of the other's identity does not seek out the reasons that legitimate the difference between them, nor does it establish that circuit of reciprocal gifts that is necessary to produce human civilization. To take this step, multiculturalism must adopt the reflectiveness necessary to the processes of recognition.[6] Going beyond the limits of multiculturalism requires the development of a reflexive reasoning that is not the technical or scientific reasoning that we have inherited from modernity. After deifying reason, the Enlightenment ran aground on the shoals of antihumanism, in which reason appears mutilated and twisted. There are two alternatives: either we abandon reason as a veritative criterion (of recognition), or we make an effort to "widen the range of reason."[7] I propose that we follow the second course.

Expanding the Range of Reason with "Relational Reason": An Alternative to Multiculturalism and a Way of Achieving a New "Common World"

What Sort of Reason Should Be Used to Address Differences?

The search for a new rationality appropriate to encounter and recognition between different people and groups requires semantics adequate to understanding and dealing with what constitutes difference. It is a fact that perceived differences are, in general, mixtures of differences in faith and differences in reason, that is, of motives due respectively to faith and to reason, woven together. In ancient societies, which continue to be the benchmark for what is called "classical culture," this interweaving had a solidity, which materialized in a common ethos (and following ethos, in the natural law, and in the doctrine of a common ethic that was eventually dispelled by the modern public ethic, which is no longer based on a shared ethos). Joseph Ratzinger wrote that "the original unified relation between enlightenment and faith . . . was torn apart."[8] However, he also wrote that "the scope of

6. On the paradigms of recognition see Pierpaolo Donati, "Riconoscere la famiglia attraverso il suo valore aggiunto," in *Riconoscere la famiglia: Quale valore aggiunto per la persona e la società?*, ed. Pierpaolo Donati (Cinisello Balsamo: San Paolo, 2007), pp. 25-62.

7. Let me recall that this expression comes from the title of Jacques Maritain's *The Range of Reason* (New York: Charles Scribner's Sons, 1952).

8. Joseph Ratzinger, *Truth and Tolerance: Christian Belief and World Religions,* trans. Henry Taylor (San Francisco: Ignatius Press, 2004), p. 177.

reason must be enlarged once more"[9] and affirmed that "the farewell to truth can never be final."[10] In this expression is contained — in my view — the heart of the issue. Nevertheless it must be noted that we are still very far from having understood what it means. I cannot pause here to discuss whether the laceration was produced (first or second, more or less) by reason or by faith. The question on which I focus my inquiry is this: what is meant by the "relational unity" between faith and reason, and also between religion and culture? Certainly it is a unity in difference. But how do we understand difference?

The Semantics of Difference, Relational Reason, and the Common World

We must develop a new theory of difference (in personal and social identity) that allows us to understand and handle it in a relational way. Since making a distinction is a reflexive operation, we are directed back to the ways in which reflexivity removes and judges differences. I will discuss three fundamental types of reflexivity: dialogical, binary, and relational (triangular).[11]

Dialectic and dialogical semantics conceives of difference as a margin, a distance, or a point of continuous conflict and negotiation that may or may not find an agreement. The cultural encounter between Ego and Alter is represented as a relationship at the border of their respective identities. At this border they meet, discuss, and try to accommodate their differences. Unlike binary semantics in which the border is conceived as a sharp separation offering no possibility of successful communication, the dialectic border is a real space where negotiations can take place between Ego and Alter. What is "in between" the people who meet is a sort of externality for each one with regard to the other. At the point of conflict, Ego and Alter remain estranged. The border is polemogenous by definition (i.e., it is prone to "generate war," or, if not war, at least moral strife), because it is the object of the will to appropriate it by one or the other, the field where one tries to assimilate the other. The border has to do with seeing which of the two can take possession of it, or, alternatively, in what way they can share it or at least turn

---

9. Ratzinger, *Truth and Tolerance*, p. 158.

10. Ratzinger, *Truth and Tolerance*, p. 165.

11. For more details on the different types of reflexivity, see Pierpaolo Donati, *Sociologia della riflessività: Come si entra nel dopo-moderno* (Bologna: il Mulino, 2011).

it into a place of exchanges that are the outputs and inputs of one to the other. Between Ego and Alter there is no real mutual exchange; rather, there is assertion of two identities that stand each facing the other. The two may dialogue, but the agreement they may reach is entirely fleeting (in sociological terms, it is highly contingent, which means that it depends on many variables and is always potentially otherwise, i.e., the existence of the border is possible in many different ways, including its not existing). Here, reciprocity does not require the recognition of a common identity. A clear example of this semantics is given by Jürgen Habermas, according to whom the common border is defined ("constituted") by civic values and a dialogue around them (what he calls "constitutional patriotism").

Binary semantics conceives of difference as discrimination and incommunicability. The border between Ego and Alter is a sharp distinction (division); it is a separation, an irreconcilability, an impossibility of exchanging reciprocal inputs and outputs. This semantics stems from the theory of autopoietic and autoreferential systems of mechanical, functional, and automatic character.[12] Accordingly, culture is a mere by-product of the communication among people, which consists of messages that are disturbances (noise) issuing from the one and affecting the other. There is no possibility for a common world. What is common is simply the problematization of the world — to love one another simply means to recognize that the problems of Ego are also the problems of Alter, and vice versa — and this commonality seeks merely to confront the paradoxes generated by the functional rationality of the system, in which Ego and Alter act without any capacity to influence its operating structures. Society here is a paradox because becoming fellows *(socii)* does not mean sharing something, but, on the contrary, it means drawing binary distinctions that divide some people (the in-group) *from* and *against* other people (the out-group).

Relational semantics understands difference (the distance that separates Ego from Alter) as a social relationship (neither a simple border, nor a slash). The relationship is never just any generic relationship, but is always qualified in some way. It is not a free interaction in the void. Nor is it a mere communication. It emerges from a context, and it has a structure whose shape is based upon the terms of the relationship, and can only come from them. It exists always under determinate conditions. The relationship is constitutive of *Ego's and Alter's identities,* in the sense that the identity of Ego is formed

---

12. Cf. Niklas Luhmann, *Social Systems,* trans. John Bednarz Jr. (Palo Alto: Stanford University Press, 1995).

through the relationship with Alter, and the identity of Alter is formed through the relationship with Ego. The border between them is an area of conflict, struggle, and negotiation, but also of a reciprocal belonging, which is constitutive of them both. The unity of the difference is a relational unity, that is, it is the unity of a real differentiation that exists because of reciprocal reference to a common belonging with respect to which Ego and Alter differentiate their own selves. From here begins the recognition of a *real otherness* (and not — as many scholars claim — the recognition of an Alter-Ego, which is in fact an Alter as imagined, represented, depicted by Ego).

The recognition of authentic otherness does not coincide with total strangeness toward the other, because while relationship bespeaks *distance,* and even separation in some respects, at the same time it bespeaks *sharing.* The sharing is not between two mirror images, but between two distinct, unique entities. These entities, while they maintain their impenetrability without synthesis, reveal themselves by reference to a reality that joins them (their humanity, for example). The otherness is not irreconcilable contradiction, in the degree to which the Other is perceived as another Self and "Oneself (is perceived) as Another" (as Ricoeur says).[13] Yet this other Self is not the same as Oneself *(idem);* rather, it is unique *(ipse).* If Ego and Alter coincided and could be assimilated one with the other *(idem),* the relationship would vanish. If, on the other hand, the relationship were entirely external to Ego and Alter, the result would fall into the two prior cases (semantics I and II). Cultural confrontation must therefore look at the relationship that is constitutive of Ego and Alter, though differently for each. The cultural difference must be seen as the difference between cultures' ways of understanding and configuring the relationship between them, without conceiving this relationship as destined to a dialectical synthesis after the manner of Hegel.

13. Paul Ricoeur, *Oneself as Another,* trans. Kathleen Blamey (Chicago: University of Chicago Press, 1992). According to Ricoeur, selfhood implies otherness to such an extent that selfhood and otherness cannot be separated. The Self implies a relation between the same and the other. This dialectic of the Self and Other contradicts Descartes's *cogito* ("I think, therefore I am"), which posits a subject in the first person (an "I," or an ego) without reference to an Other. The dialectic of Self and Other may lead us to recognize that the Self may refer to itself as not only itself, but as other than itself. This dialectic may be revealed as not only that of Self and not-Self, but as that of oneself as another, oneself and not another, another and not oneself, another as oneself. The dialectic of Self and Other may be dynamically changing.

The Emergence of a Relational Semantics

Western culture has until today used the first two semantics, oscillating be-tween the two. My conviction is that, in the climate of globalization, and in the wake of the flawed experience of multiculturalism, the third semantics is emerging. The third semantics, that of relational difference, interprets and understands cultural differences insofar as they are generated in reference to a "common world" that includes both Ego and Alter. The common world differentiates itself and is regenerated (re-differentiated) through forms of "relational differentiation," that is, of differences that are generated by dif-ferent ways of articulating the founding relationships shared by the people involved in a context (not the functions and roles — in other words, that which is institutionally prescribed as a specialization of actors and performances).[14]

Secularism is the motive that justifies cultural pluralism when it springs from the social relationships among human beings. Properly speaking, the secularity of the state does not consist in the fact that the state authorizes religious freedom, let alone rules based on political principles, like that of the juridical equality of religious denominations (this equality is entirely different from the equality of persons under the law, which is a fundamental principle). The state can be called secular insofar as it limits itself to recog-nizing the original liberty of persons in professing their faith, and insofar as it claims as its own those values and rules that emerge in a shared way from the public debate between religions on the basis of rational argument. To go deeper into this point it is necessary to recall the relational semantics that allows us to see unexplored aspects of human rationality: *relational reason*. What does it consist of?

Relational Reason: Expanding Reason through Social Relationships

Relational rationality is the faculty by which the human person sees the rea-sons (the good motives) inherent to interhuman social *relationships* (not to individuals as individuals, nor to social or cultural systems). Certainly the being-together of different cultures stimulates the deepening of rational (axi-ological) individual choices, within individual reflexivity. But this does not

---

14. On the founding relationship see Pierpaolo Donati, *Sociologia della relazione* (Bo-logna: il Mulino, 2013), p. 124.

suffice to configure the *inter* (what lies in between different cultures) as a social relationship. To turn the *inter* into a common world, the public sphere requires a rationality that takes into account the differentiation between cultures as a *relational differentiation*.[15] In other words, cultural identities are different for the different ways in which they interpret and live their relationships to values that are common to human beings. These "ways" refer to the instrumental and normative dimensions of reason, as well as its concrete aims, while the values refer to the axiological (or teleological) dimensions of reason. The so-called policies of equality of differences, which neutralize relationships or render them indifferent, can only generate new differences, which find no rational solution, but only new forms of dialectic or separation.

The example of marriage speaks very well to this. If marriage is considered from the perspective of equality of individual opportunities, gender identities (male and female) are rendered indifferent because the male-female relationship has no reasons of its own to affirm and foster. It no longer makes sense to speak of male (e.g., paternal) or female (e.g., maternal) symbolic codes, because their relationship has been canceled out. The same goes for the difference between monogamous and polygamous marriage. For those who support policies of equal opportunity (*lib/lab* policies),[16] this difference consists in the two relationships offering different opportunities to the individuals involved — nothing more. Conceiving monogamy and polygamy as alternatives in this way does not touch on the meaning and form of the marital relationship itself. From the relational perspective, on the other hand, only if we recognize the "rights" of differences (of relationships!) can we find human values (and rights).

To make social relationships indifferent, canceling out the discrete reasons that inhere in the identity of each specific kind of relationship, is to annihilate the value of each relationship as a *sui generis* reality. It is to nullify the principle of appreciation that the relationship contains.

Relationship is what — at the same time — joins, differentiates, and diversifies. For example, the conjugal relationship joins a man and a woman in one flesh, but differentiates them in their roles and diversifies them in their

---

15. On the concept of "relational differentiation" see Pierpaolo Donati, *Relational Sociology: A New Paradigm for the Social Sciences* (London: Routledge, 2011).

16. I call *lib/lab* policies those policy measures that are a compromise between liberalism (*lib* side) and socialism (*lab* side), or, in other words, a bargaining between the capitalist market and the state. See Pierpaolo Donati, "Beyond the Market/State Binary Code: The Common Good as a Relational Good," in *Free Markets and the Culture of Common Good,* ed. Martin Schlag and Juan Andrés Mercado (New York: Springer, 2012), pp. 61-81.

identities with respect to the same relationship. The relationship of friendship joins two persons in a circle of symbolic exchanges, differentiates them with respect to that to which they can reciprocally give themselves, and diversifies them with regard to the quality of the friendship. In this way, different relationships are involved.

The reasons inherent to human relationships correspond to the dignity of the human person. They are latent and have morphogenetic potential. For this reason relationships can ground a critique of cultural deviations, whether antihumanism or traditionalist fundamentalism.

To sustain an interculturalism capable of creating consensus on fundamental human values, it is necessary to adopt a relational paradigm that allows us to see and *articulate the reasons* that give shape to the interhuman, to that which is "between" individuals. The field of bioethics in a multicultural society offers many examples of fundamental values emerging in relational contexts, and indeed as the relationships themselves: the right to life, the rights of the human embryo, the right of a child to a family, the right to an education worthy of a human being, the right to a good death, to a healthy environment, and so on — all *relational rights,* because they are rights to relationships (rather than to things or performances). Relationships have their own reasons, which the individuals involved may not be explicitly (linguistically, conversationally) aware of, but which they comprehend according to the type and degree of reflexivity they have; that is, they see the reasons behind the relationships to the extent that they see the human realities implied in nature before they reach the cultural level.

The cultural mediation often talked about can only overcome prejudice and intolerance if people succeed in reasonably bringing values together and giving them relational rationales.

Relational reason validates, rather than hides, differences. Precisely in this way it is capable of moving beyond the ancient configurations of relations between cultures (that is, the segmented differentiation in primitive societies, the stratified differentiation of cultures in premodern societies, and the functional differentiation of early modern societies), which are all forms of differentiation incapable of arriving at shared public reason in a globalized society.

Relational reason gives us an alternative to relational differentiation. Such reason in application signifies the creation of a public sphere that is religiously qualified, in that religions have a role in defining public reason because they orient people toward a reflexive understanding of their own cultural elaborations in their life-worlds.

This reflexive understanding supports and nourishes an expansion of reason. It is a way to go beyond modern Western rationality, which stopped at the distinction between instrumental and substantial reasoning.[17] According to this distinction, the relationship to value (*Wertbeziehung* in Max Weber's theory) is nonrational, because values themselves are nonrational (from the Weberian viewpoint). Relational reason tells us the opposite. It indicates the different ways in which it is possible for Ego to relate to values: it does so, similarly to the way in which it relates to the Other, not on the basis of purely subjective factors (sentiments, moods, emotions, irrational preferences) or acquired habits, but on the basis of reasons that are neither *things* nor rules of exchange, but are goods *(values)* connected to the quality of present and future relationships. These are what I call "relational goods."[18] I propose that we take a new and radical look at the theory of rationality proposed by Max Weber, which profoundly (and negatively) conditioned the social thought of the twentieth century.[19]

Rationality cannot be reduced to the two modalities put forward by Max Weber — that is, means-end, or instrumental, rationality *(Zweckrationalität)* and value- or belief-oriented rationality *(Wertrationalität)*. To reduce human rationality to these two concepts is an operation dense with ambiguity and can be a source of great confusion. *Zweckrationalität* deals with the calculation of means to achieve an end, but ends can also become means, until it is no longer possible to distinguish what is a means and what is an end. The concept is unusable. *Wertrationalität* refers to a value subjectively understood by the social actor, but that value may be a good in itself or merely a personal preference. The reformulation of the Weberian distinction between instrumental and value-oriented rationality undertaken by various authors (e.g., Parsons and Alexander, who translated them respectively as *instrumental* and *normative* rationality) has been unsatisfying and insufficient.

17. Instrumental rationality focuses on the means for achieving certain, given ends. The means are technical instruments by which to pursue these ends, which cannot be discussed or communicated (Weber's polytheism of values). While instrumental rationality seeks convenience, utility, and efficiency, axiological rationality focuses on values, that is, on *ultimate concerns* for the true, the good, and the just.

18. Cf. Pierpaolo Donati and R. Solci, *I beni relazionali: Che cosa sono e quali effetti producono* (Turin: Bollati Boringhieri, 2011).

19. It is well known that Max Weber, notwithstanding his studies of rationality, did not hesitate to assert the absolute impossibility of scientific analysis of values, in this way helping to pave the way for the worst forms of irrationalism and other true monstrosities that afflicted the first half of the last century, and that today deeply wound social thought, modern epistemology, and afflict the life of many populations.

I propose a redefinition of rationality as a faculty of human behavior that has four components or modalities.

(1) *Instrumental rationality* deals with efficiency and involves the means, therefore the adaptive dimension, of thinking and acting (rationality of efficiency). Its analytic counterpart is the economic sphere, and its empirical, macrostructural counterpart is the market.

(2) *Goal-oriented rationality* refers to situated objectives and regards the achievement of defined goals (rationality of efficacy). Its analytic counterpart is the sphere of power, and its empirical, macrostructural counterpart is the political system (the state).

(3) The properly *value-oriented dimension of reason* corresponds to the distinction-guideline that points toward what is good in itself; that is, what is an end and has worth in itself (that which lies at the depths of the actor's *ultimate concerns,* which some call *ultimate values* in the sense of *ultimate realities*). This dimension is the rationality of value as good in itself, of that which has a dignity that is neither instrumental nor goal-oriented (*value rationality* or *axiological rationality,* or *Würderationalität,* or the rationality of dignity). It is important here to understand clearly that, in what I call *value-oriented rationality,* the value is not a situated goal that has a price, but is a "good without price" that no money can buy. Value-oriented rationality is not dependent upon the situation. It is inherent to the dignity of all that deserves respect and recognition, because it is distinctively human (as opposed to the non-human or inhuman). Therefore, this rationality regards in the first place the human person as such (and not because an individual behaves in a particular way). As an analytic counterpart it has the sphere of good in itself or for itself, the symbolic reference — which is nonnegotiable — to that which characterizes the good or a person and distinguishes that person from all the others. The empirical, macrostructural correlate of value-oriented rationality is the religious system, that is, religion understood as a cultural fact distinct from faith (which transcends culture).

(4) The *integrative dimension of reason* integrates among themselves the other dimensions of rationality (instrumental, goal-oriented, and value-oriented) through ethical and moral normativity. It also assures the autonomy of rationality against other kinds of actions and social relationships. This fourth dimension I call *relational rationality (Beziehungsrationalität),* or *nomic rationality* (what is rational in the *nomos*) in the norms of division and distribution, which at the same time divide and

connect the parts in relation. Social relationships have reasons that belong neither to individuals nor to social systems, and which the individuals and systems may not know about and in fact do not possess. As an analytic correlate, this dimension takes the sphere of social bonds; its empirical, macrostructural correlate is civil society inasmuch as it is an associational world.

The four dimensions of reason (instrumental, goal-oriented, value-oriented, and relational) make up a *complex of reason,* or human reason as a complex faculty of which every component is essential for human reason to emerge in its fullness, whether as theoretical or practical. The actions of recognizing, understanding, explaining, and seeking what is rational are all needs of the complex faculty of human reason, as seen from the relational perspective.

From the sociological perspective, reason is a faculty that exists as an emerging social phenomenon. There is no such thing as a purely individual rationality, in the sense of a faculty cut off from social relationships. Reason is a faculty that emerges from the workings of its constitutive elements, each of which has its own characteristics. The faculty which we call "human reason" is generated as an emergent effect of the togetherness, interaction, and interchange between the four fundamental dimensions that comprise it. Encounter and recognition are relational goods[20] not because, as some believe, they carry with them a particular "human warmth," a feeling of good will, or a special *pathos* (elements that in any event have their own weight and importance), but because they realize a relationship upon which depend the goods of those who participate in the relationship. And this dependence is rational, or at least reasonable.

20. Cf. Pierpaolo Donati, *La cittadinanza societaria* (Rome: Laterza, 2000), ch. 2; Pierpaolo Donati, "Different Cultures, Different Citizenships? The Challenge of a Universal Citizenship in a Multicultural Postmodern Society," *Annals of the International Institute of Sociology* 5 (1996): 245-63.

The Link between "Fundamentalism" and "Relativism"

Costantino Esposito

A Theory That Produces a Fact

Multiculturalism is not simply a theory that arises in the attempt to interpret certain facts, but is a theory that aims to produce a fact. This is the case not only within the macrocosm of a multiethnic society, but even and especially within the microcosms of individual mentalities and social practices. Playing a central role in multiculturalism are two additional theories, or phenomena: *fundamentalism* and *relativism,* both of which are characteristic of today's culture. These terms are typically used to denote two opposing fronts in religious, social, philosophical, and cultural contexts; however, on closer inspection they represent two tightly connected positions, related not only as opposites, but also in that they both belong to a common, momentous cultural climate: *nihilism.* If at first it seems that fundamentalism and relativism oppose each other as two alternative concepts, looking at them more carefully, one discovers instead that the one flows into the other — it is precisely in this overflowing of one into the other that we can understand the particular tendency of contemporary nihilism. Nihilism is characterized by both the affirmation of a truth without an "I" *(fundamentalism)* and the affirmation of an "I" without truth *(relativism).*

The Relationship between the Individual and Truth as the Litmus Test of Fundamentalism and Relativism

The two major cultural and philosophical directions that seem to dominate (even if in opposite ways) the entire world today — the East and the West, the Northern and the Southern hemispheres — wind up running a common risk and demarcating a common loss. We see, on the one hand, a process of standardization on the part of the dominant culture in the West, which conceives itself as definitively post-Christian, but at the same time as post-Enlightenment, in the sense that reason is no longer understood or exercised in its structural relationship with truth. Instead, reason is understood as the elaboration of worldviews and techniques aimed at constructing oneself and the world. The individual, for his or her part, comes to be seen essentially as a transient bundle of emotions, feelings, and choices made according to his or her instincts and feelings. As an abstract subject, the individual is isolated and entirely at the mercy of the mechanical action and reaction of his or her own sensory perceptions. This individual exists without a rational, objective criterion that justifies the truth of everything he or she lives or wants to live; or, more precisely, such a criterion exists, but it is entirely external, even completely unrelated to the life of the person, and that criterion is the law promulgated by the power of the state. The law promulgated by the state provides the only embankment against instinct without reason, to which the experience of the "I" is otherwise reduced.

The human being is therefore seen as totally *subjective,* and we could say irrational, while reason is reduced to mere calculation and *objective* measurement, like a function or technique that can and must evaluate without the individual subject's involvement. This applies to the abstract subject of individualistic liberalism, as well as to the "cultural" subject produced by the practices of his or her community. In short, the reduction of both reason and the human being results in a *subject without reason* and *reason without a subject.*

On the other hand, we see (at a bit of a distance from our tradition, to be sure, but in a way that is growing ever closer both as a hypothesis and as a mentality) the Islamic religious culture — the indisputable and unsettling protagonist of the increasingly empty scenario created by Western secularism — according to which the ultimate value of the human person is completely identified with total submission to the absolute will of God. Here the human being, contrary to how he or she appears in the first major cultural direction, seems to be completely bound to the power of truth. But that

45

bond (so conclusive as to assume the character of a strict set of legal precepts) has no reason for existing other than the pure human will to recognize and submit to the equally pure divine will. Consequently, the "I" loses its specific weight, to the extent that absolute faith in the Absolute arrives nearly to the point of dissolving the irreducible value of the human person.

In the first case, which we will call the nihilism of the secularized West, the individual subject appears to be emphasized to the maximum degree but is missing what is in reality his most natural face: the desire for truth and totality. In the second case, which we will call the religious nihilism of fundamentalist leanings, the fideistic affirmation of the truth seems to be entirely missing its subject. This double rift delineates the tragedy of our age — the lack of an objective experience of the self — and at the same time delineates the challenge facing an education that aims to be on par with the humanity, reason, and affection of the self.

The link between relativism and fundamentalism is not limited to the relationship between secularized culture and religious extremism, but can also be found within our Western culture. This becomes clearer when we consider that relativism has become the dominant form of knowledge, even among those who refuse to accept it or who have decided to fight against it. In fact, even those who resist relativism admit the view that the *truth* deals only with the immutable and timeless Absolute, while *history, temporality,* and *contingency* are labeled as simply relative.

Moreover we must not overlook the fact that, even at the theoretical level, relativism tends to be a form of interpretation that is applied to the *whole* of reality, and therefore it represents a position that is literally "absolute" with regard to truth. The most widespread version of such relativism clearly demonstrates its paradoxical elevation to a fundamental principle: on the one hand, it tracks the origin, dynamic, and ultimate significance of individual experiences and of social relationships back to their biological-psychological roots (and therefore is a purely naturalistic relativization of the human); on the other hand, it holds that the meaning and value of everything is only a product of the conditions and organizations communicated at a given time by culture. The entire culture is based on a naturalistic or physical presupposition, and at the same time the only expression and ultimate end of nature is its cultural determination.

Consequently, it appears that a shift has taken place from a conception of culture as the capacity to gather, develop, and transmit the totality of meaning, to a conception under which that totality is merely a product of the culture — indeed, it is simply the culture itself. This totality in its completed form is, directly or indirectly, the "integration of all citizens and the mutual recognition of their subcultural memberships within the framework of a shared political culture."[1] Within this understanding of totality, the different social components make up "subcultural aggregations" that must be led to reciprocal recognition.

According to our hypothesis, multiculturalism — not only as a matter of historical and sociological fact, but as a theory that in some way imposes a fact, or as an imposed common meaning — is based on the link between fundamentalism and relativism. This link plays an essential role in the nihilistic self-understanding of our times. For this reason it may be worthwhile to take another look at the underlying problem of nihilism.

Nihilism: The Problem of the Given

In *The Brothers Karamazov* Dostoyevsky's character Ivan, one of the protagonists of the novel and the perfect literary incarnation of the nihilist, says the following famous words: "If God does not exist, everything is permitted." Seventy years later, Albert Camus commented on this sentence with an observation that has itself become deservedly well-known: "With this 'everything is permitted' the history of contemporary nihilism really begins."[2] Nearly a century later, Michel Foucault, commenting on a passage by Nietzsche, would say: "If interpretation can never be complete, this results from the simple fact that there is nothing to interpret. There is nothing absolutely first to interpret, since, at base, everything is already interpretation, every sign is already in itself not the object that offers itself to interpretation, but interpretation itself."[3]

This excerpt from Foucault (characteristic of French philosophy of the second half of the twentieth century, and lying between a structuralist epistemology and a post-Nietzschean, post-Heideggerian conception of *difference*) is highly indicative of a widespread tendency — *far* beyond the classic contrast between hermeneutic and analytical currents of thought

1. Jürgen Habermas, *Between Naturalism and Religion,* trans. Ciaran Cronin (Cambridge: Polity Press, 2008), p. 270.
2. Albert Camus, *The Rebel: An Essay on Man in Revolt,* trans. Anthony Bower (New York: Vintage, 1991), p. 57.
3. Michel Foucault, "Nietzsche, Marx, Freud," in *Nietzsche,* Cahiers de Royaumont: Philosophie 6 (Paris: Minuit, 1967), p. 189 (our translation).

— to decisively favor an idea of interpretation that absorbs into itself *both* the object of interpretation *and* the individual that interprets it. But in this literally "neutral" structure of interpretation, it is easy to see in advance an inevitable point of arrival: ultimately it is the dominant cultural power who directs the game; or (although this is really the same situation) it is the mechanical apparatus of emotional and irrational impulses — irrational in the sense that they are deprived of critically verified reasons — upon which the cultural power always plays as part of its strategy to produce consensus. In this way, paradoxically, the same *ars interpretandi,* created with the claim of emancipating the individual, ends up subjugating him or her to "public thought," to the "correctness" of the conformism of the day. When this happens it is precisely the irreducible experience of the self that not only is interpreted according to determined cultural parameters (which is only natural), but is itself understood as a mere product of interpretation.

Here a question arises: does nihilism constitute a non-transcendable horizon for our time? If the response is affirmative, this means that multiculturalism is the inevitable destiny of our age, the complete expression of that all-encompassing and self-referential interpretation which ends up reabsorbing both the interpreter and the interpreted.

But if another answer is possible, it could not be simply a strategy of self-regulation from within the phenomenon, nor that of a mere balancing of commands. In other words, all the necessary and unavoidable work of integration and delimitation of unalienable rights and of social obligations, of national identities and of transnational differences will hold up or else crumble only thanks to a new *understanding* of what is "rational"; that is, a new understanding of what enables every culture to make a judgment about the proper form of the human being — within each culture as well as across different cultures. Paradoxically, the challenge is not that of thinking and theorizing about diversity, but rather of grasping and living the unity of human experience, not as an ideological or sociopolitical unity of the various cultures — which would always be in some way artificial — but as an identification of the dynamic proper to reason. For this reason the problem of multiculturalism is born as and remains, in its blueprint and its present structure, a European problem, to the extent to which this rational self-understanding of the human as a place of relationship between different traditions (meeting, but at the same time clashing) has a historical presence in Europe. Naturally we are aware that this idea of Europe is largely overshadowed today, and that the crisis of "European humanity" (as Edmund

Husserl called it in the 1930s), far from being resolved, has become a permanent condition, and is theorized as such. Hence a simple call to return to the Greek, Christian, and Enlightenment roots of Europe cannot resolve the question, nor can putting these roots in a corner according to the vision of secularization and of a postmodern plurality of perspectives. What needs to be proposed anew is the question of Europe as a certain way to experience rationality, and to do so while verifying its possibilities, crises, and resources.

Europe, or Concerning Reason

Jacques Derrida once wrote that "the old name of Europe" now serves only to indicate "what we recall (to ourselves) or what we promise (ourselves)" *(ce que nous [nous] rappelons ou ce que nous [nous] promettons).*[4] And indeed, if we take a look at the perhaps overabundant analyses of the European phenomenon, it seems that the field of philosophical reflection and discussion takes as its poles, on the one hand, the historical and conceptual origin of this phenomenon, and on the other, its purpose, understood as an ideal and as a "program." In the continual oscillation of reminding ourselves and re-promising ourselves, the weaver's shuttle goes back and forth: we experience the persistent impression that going down to the origin, and above all "holding onto" the origin, involves the risk of unraveling the fabric at the top, that is, of unraveling the necessary responses to the contemporary challenges of post-identity relationships (ethnic, economic, and sociopolitical); while, vice versa, the assumption of this duty of response for the future can only occur at the price of fraying the initial matrix of threads.

The issue at stake in our understanding of Europe regards, once again, the nature of "reason," at which we must look anew, challenging the appearance of ingenuity or the verdict of impossibility. If a particular European "reason" exists, it is a reason in the precise sense of a constitution or a curvature, of a style or of a particular form of rationality assumed in that inextricable complex of experiences, intuitions, conflicts, and identities — it is, to use the classic Husserlian expression, "European humanity," which is "our" humanity. And, turning the question upside down, we can ask in what sense this "our" humanity constitutes a particular experience of reason itself

---

4. Jacques Derrida, *The Other Heading: Reflections on Today's Europe,* trans. Pascale-Anne Brault and Michael B. Naas (Bloomington: Indiana University Press, 2002), p. 82.

and can therefore offer a possibility of understanding and of action that is much more than only "ours."

Let us, first of all, propose an explanatory hypothesis: the reason we are speaking about (which each of us probably already knows, not only as an *object* of critical, historical investigation, but also as a *subjective* quality, as the exercise and verification of personal competence) presents itself as the experience of a relationship: an opening of the human individual (an opening that carries the name of "I") in which reality emerges as a given. This opening that establishes the "two" that enter into relationship precedes all the other relationships between the "I" and the world; it comes before every subjectivism or objectivism and sets them up precisely in the structural way in which they relate to one another.

In this conception of reason, Europe would seem to break away with respect to two other geographical-spiritual spheres which it borders. On the one hand, there is Eastern thought, in which reality presents itself in its inconceivable majesty until it eliminates the specific distinction of the "I" (to the extent that the presence of being and the concept of nothing coincide), and from which in some way even European reason derives in the dialectical act of breaking away from it, and which European reason carries within itself as a shadow and abyss. On the other hand, we have that sphere that is "spiritually" even more Western than Western Europe, in which subjectivity becomes the functional and abstract procedure for constructing reality. This sphere is a product and result of European reason, which carries it as a permanent risk. It bears adding that the breakaway also occurs with regard to the sphere in which the reason of the real presents itself in terms that we might call "fundamentalist," in the sense of a rationality that is used without free individuality, and regardless of the absolutely particular experience that is consciousness and its critical competence.

Therefore, the reason of Europe is a faculty of knowing and evaluating, but *at the same time* it is a principle of intelligibility of the world — I would almost say a constituent dimension of reality, or perhaps simply reality's "self-giving" to the subject that receives it. The focal point is the inextricable link between reason as a *faculty* and reason as a *principle* or *sense*.

But to propose the problem of multiculturalism on the level of rationality, as rationality has been experienced — but also, undoubtedly, reduced and betrayed — by the European humanity, is a way of facing our present, not of re-evoking the past. Therefore it does not project a future without history, just as one cannot invoke a history that is not consciousness of the present.

Beyond Multiculturalism

The need to move beyond multiculturalism is expressed by those who consider its disorder unsustainable (as do those who find it still too prominent in a new order), as well as by liberals and radicals, who both propose alternative ways of ordering society.

The first option, the liberal paradigm, is a legal order, that is, a system rebuilt as a procedure of legal integration. It builds on the concept of tolerance, which is reconceived, mediated, and counterbalanced by the guaranteed rights and obligatory duties typical of a public space that hosts diverse individuals and cultures. It is what Jürgen Habermas proposes, for example, identifying in "religious tolerance" the true "pacemaker of cultural rights."

For the religious believer, or for the person with a rich metaphysical background, there is an epistemic preeminence of the Good over the Right. At the base of this assumption, the validity of the ethos that this person embraces depends on the truth of its context, that is, the truth of the image of the world from which the ethos arises. Therefore the different ethical orientations toward life and the competing ways of living are related to claims to the exclusive validity of the images that are at their bases:

> As soon as the idea of the correct life takes its orientation from religious paths to salvation or metaphysical conceptions of the good, a divine perspective (or a "view from nowhere") comes into play from which (or from where) other ways of life appear not just different but *mistaken.* When the alien ethos is not merely a question of relative value but of truth or falsity, the requirement to show each citizen equal respect regardless of her ethical self-understanding or her lifestyle becomes a heavier burden.[5]

Unlike the less-demanding coexistence of different values, the contrast between ethical truths pushes both believers and nonbelievers toward mutual tolerance.

On the side of believers, it leads them to "recognize that they must *reasonably* reckon with the persistence of disagreement in their dealings with adherents of other faiths," and, we might add, with nonbelievers.[6] On the side of "secular consciousness," "the expectation that the disagreement between secular knowledge and religious tradition will persist merits the title 'reasonable' only if religious convictions are accorded an epistemic status as

5. Habermas, *Between Naturalism and Religion,* p. 309.
6. Habermas, *Between Naturalism and Religion,* p. 309.

not simply 'irrational' from the perspective of secular knowledge."[7] Accordingly: "The essential moral content of the constitutional principles is secured through procedures that owe their legitimizing power to the fact that they guarantee impartiality and the equal consideration of the interests of all. They forfeit this power when substantive ethical ideas infiltrate the interpretation and practice of the formal regulations. In this respect the imperative of neutrality can be violated as much by the secular side as by the religious side."[8]

Shared morality, following a principle typical of Kantian ethics, cannot be other than a formalist morality, that is, one in which value is constituted precisely by unshackling duty from the "material" goals of the individuals, from the groups to which one belongs, from cultural identities, and from specific ways of life. Public morality, in other words, does not consist in upholding common and rationally justified values, but in the fact that the form of their proposal and their shared-ness bears no truth claims, a fact that would transform multicultural coexistence *ipso facto* into a claim of mono-culturalism. Certainly Habermas helps us to understand with dispassionate clarity (which did not fail to arouse irritation on the part of cultural radicals) that even secularism can breach this ethic of the cultural form, and that therefore the inveterate and often instrumental identification of secularism with neutrality toward the principles and practices of identity is no longer valid.

Here it is interesting to note a certain strange asymmetry: on the one hand, both the religious and the secular are exposed to the temptation to violate the formal neutrality of constitutional democracy — the only shared horizon, according to Habermas, in a multicultural society. But on the other hand, at the moment in which reasons must be given for affirming certain values as common and public — that is, at the moment in which we ask ourselves what true affirmation or negation is — secularism discovers a substantial lack of such reasons, apart from the reason that all theories are admissible, except those that claim to be true. So, paradoxically, if secularism wants to exhibit the principles of its own neutrality, it is obliged to listen (or at least not to exclude a priori) those experiences of identity in which values are actively exercised. This would not only involve permitting a polytheism of values within the neutral field of the formal constitution, but also permitting the fact that the constitution itself is presented as a public bond not in

7. Habermas, *Between Naturalism and Religion,* pp. 309-10.
8. Habermas, *Between Naturalism and Religion,* pp. 265-66.

the name of every single virtual possibility, but in the name of real and determinate experiences, like religious ones.

The second option — the radical paradigm — is that of a further, permanent deconstruction of the system of traditions of identity in these traditions' positive encounters and clashes, and that of the acceleration of the process of decay and contamination present within each culture. With regard to this we can think of the most extreme developments of so-called "postcolonial thought" (we can think, for example, of an author like Homi Bhabha).[9] The goal here is to "escape from the *impasse* of a debate that, even in its multiple variants, always reproduces the same existential vision of the so-called ethnic identity — what the multiculturalists would like to preserve and the assimilationist liberal paradigm would like to standardize into a sort of peaceful cultural homogeneity."[10]

Because this radical paradigm starts from the momentous fact that the individual and his or her identity — considering both at all levels — are on the way toward ultimate fragmentation, and that we are completely losing the very idea of a possible unity between them, the only thing that remains is a dynamic that is literally amorphous and directionless:

> Set against the crystallization and the reification of the identities that are part of the Western discourse on multiculturalism are the so-called *hybrid* or *meticciati* narratives. These narratives try to show that every process of the formation of identity is a dynamic process, a process of constant negotiation between self and others, whereas the contrasting representation of these processes as crystallized within determinate boundaries (those of the culture of a group or individual) is determined by power dynamics, by material needs, and by historical situations.[11]

The consequence is that we can only think of identity — we can only think of the *self* — as a "narrative, material, and asymmetrical construction":

> Identities, including religious ones, are not substances, are not things that are possessed or entities by which we are possessed. Rather they are *routines,* shared practices, a mobile and asymmetrical background that serves

9. See Homi Bhabha, *The Location of Culture* (New York: Routledge Classics, 2004).

10. Maria Laura Lanzillo, "Strategie multiculturali: Aporie e contraddizioni di un'ideologia," *Post Filosofie* 2 (2006): 169 (our translation). For a brief overview, see Francesco Fistetti, *Multiculturalismo: Una mappa tra filosofia e scienze sociali* (Turin: UTET Università, 2008).

11. Lanzillo, "Strategie," 169.

as a reference for the actions of subjects involved in symbolic exchanges. Nonetheless, many practices are unfavorable to "internal deconstructions" promoted by subaltern subjects, the weakest, within them. What is at stake . . . is the elimination of the asymmetries between initial positions, asymmetries that exist both *between* communities as well as *within* communities without recourse to the use of force.[12]

This makes evident what is truly at stake in multiculturalist theories, which end up taking a step beyond the concept of relativized "cultural identity" to arrive at the idea that it is literally impossible to maintain every identity, and more radically, every subjectivity, in any form of verified stability, since any permanence would result from the imposition of one identity on another, or of one factor on another within the same identity. Being in some way "racist" therefore would not consist only in the exclusion of one identity in favor of another, but also in the very affirmation of an identity as the net worth of reasons and practices taken to be true and stable. Thus different cultures no longer even express a point-of-view critique of the world, because the only law of the *self* is the loss and self-criticism of the *self*. One might say it is a true heterogenesis of ends arising from multiculturalist ideology, ranging from the defense of differences to the removal of asymmetries (and not only those between weak and strong, but between identity and the individual, between the individual and what he or she belongs to, and between narrative and the truth of what is narrated).

A contradictory and aporetic outcome exists in this second option as well: it consists in the fact that postmulticulturalism, through its radical criticism of any claim of a stable and normative cultural identity, reaches the extreme opposite that reached by the liberal interpretation, which it considers to be its adversary. In both cases, though they begin from entirely different premises, any claim of truth coming from the belonging to an identity as such is progressively erased. And so a shift occurs from requesting that one give reasons for holding one's position in the face of the reasons underlying different positions, to calling into question even the assumption that one could give true and stable reasons for positions that express the identities of personal subjects and social subjectivities.

What is missing in both of these interpretations is the irreducible status of the human person, sometimes identified at the base of his or her right to

12. Barbara Henry, "Conflitti identitari e laicità: Una premessa al dibattito sul multiculturalismo," *Post Filosofie* 2 (2006): 180 (our translation).

possess and manage a certain quantity of goods (beginning with the "good" that he or she is), and sometimes identified at the base of his or her right to dispose of his or her own identity in an absolutely subjective way. And so, on both sides the same prohibition is imposed on the ability to make a claim, or even raise a question, of truth in the experience of persons and cultures: in the first, liberal case, for fear that such claims lead to intolerance, and in the second, radical case because of the conclusion that an objectivity and a truth of human experience is constitutively impossible — or is at least out-and-out nonsense. Multiculturalism, which seemed to be formally guaranteed by the neutrality of legislation, ends up imploding, paradoxically affirming the anthropological image of radical liberalism in which every individual is the result of her ability and possessions, before which — that is, before that which she *wants* to be or that which the political-economic-formative society *allows* her to be — she is effectively nothing. The multicultural individual in this way risks being as *abstract* as the liberal individual.

Perhaps it is possible to think of a *third option* to overcome the impasse of multiculturalism. In this case we would begin not with the question, what rights do we have? but from the question, what do we need? To answer this question would naturally require a different and broader conception of what constitutes a "need," a requirement that complies with, but at the same time surpasses, those twentieth-century theories in which needs were literally annihilated: I am thinking of the Marxist analysis, at the socioeconomic level, which was first opposed and then paradoxically made true in the identification of market forces as the ultimate horizon for the creation and satisfaction of needs; but I am also thinking, at the individual level, of the psychoanalytical structuring of need centered on repression.

Characteristic of this third idea is the fact that the need of the "I," the people, and the community cannot be reduced. Nor can the dynamic of need be halted before being recognized as the *need for truth*. The need for truth is not a "spiritual" need that attaches to "material" needs, but rather the engine and the inner tendency of every other need. Let us think of the recent words of Pope Benedict XVI:

> Our faith is decisively opposed to the attitude of resignation that considers man incapable of truth — as if this were more than he could cope with. This attitude of resignation with regard to truth, I am convinced, lies at the heart of the crisis of the West, the crisis of Europe. If truth does not exist for man, then neither can he ultimately distinguish between good and evil. And then the great and wonderful discoveries of science become

double-edged: they can open up significant possibilities for good, for the benefit of mankind, but also, as we see only too clearly, they can pose a terrible threat, involving the destruction of man and the world. We need truth. Yet admittedly, in the light of our history we are fearful that faith in the truth might entail intolerance. If we are gripped by this fear, which is historically well grounded, then it is time to look towards Jesus as we see him in the shrine at Mariazell. We see him here in two images: as the child in his Mother's arms, and above the high altar of the Basilica as the Crucified. These two images in the Basilica tell us this: truth prevails not through external force, but it is humble and it yields itself to man only via the inner force of its veracity. . . . It is never our property, never our product, just as love can never be produced, but only received and handed on as a gift. We need this inner force of truth.[13]

This concept — which, unlike the others, is indeed truly "radical" — of need as the desire for truth, that is to say, the recognition that within each necessity or problem exists an irreducible demand for perfection, happiness, beauty, goodness, and justice, allows us to understand *all* that is at stake in the neediness of humankind. Liberalism, like multiculturalism, will have to deal with the fact that the origin of this need is never completely explained by a greater or lesser competitiveness, or by a more or less developed social redistribution. The achievement of perfect conditions, at the beginning just as at the end of the social-relations dynamic, would never alone impede the continuing emergence of this need in the deepest — I would almost say in the most "metaphysical," that is, in the most concrete — sense. Nor would the most perfect realization of conditions of justice or social compensation ever really satisfy this need. It inhabits the consciousness, and even more, the existence, of each person, and it is found at the base of every culture and every social relationship — and this precisely because it is *not* a man-made construct, nor a product of culture, but is, on the contrary, the original and permanent desire that alone permits the existence of culture and experience at the level of human expectation. The truth that humanity needs comes not at the risk of intolerance, but may actually be the thing that will finally allow for understanding and reasoned critique between cultures, and will provide to laws a shared justification.

13. Benedict XVI, homily on the occasion of the 850th anniversary of the foundation of the shrine of Mariazell (Basilica of Mariazell, Mariazell, Austria, September 8, 2007).

Retrieval of Otherness in a Technological Culture

Antonio López

It has become a platitude to describe modern liberal culture as a technological culture and to analyze how its unifying power imposes itself all around the globe. Technological culture, in fact, determines the way peoples and societies order daily life and conceive their roles in history. It is less obvious to determine what is specific about technological culture and why a civilization of technical unity merits the name "culture." Technology has become the matrix, so to say, within which cultures exist and meet each other. The present essay has this limited aim: to explore the meaning of technology and to indicate why, by blocking wonder, the technological mindset is unable to perceive the other as other and, therefore, makes us homeless. The essay begins by posing the question on technology in a non-technological way. This will clear the way for a reflection on the nature of technology with its unique inversion of thinking and making. The last two parts of the essay deal with that type of knowing and acting informed by wonder that technology seeks to preclude.

The Labor of Asking

To speak about technology is a rather challenging task because, as Heidegger says, "technology is not equivalent to the essence of technology."[1] We need

---

1. Martin Heidegger, "The Question concerning Technology," in *Basic Writings,* ed. David Farrell Krell (New York: HarperCollins, 1993), pp. 311-41, at 311. While the terms will become clear in this chapter, it is perhaps useful to indicate at the outset that by "technol-

to avoid the impatient and technological question, *what do we do with or in this technological world of ours?* Alternatively, engaging the question, *what is technology?* prevents us from quickly arriving at an inadequate answer to the first question. Such an inadequate answer would prompt us to take an active role in the world and to do so in such a way that our engagement with the world would remain within the parameters of a certain conception of power: a capacity to make that has in itself its own origin and *telos*. To ask after the essence of technology requires that one be truly open to an answer that departs from the common way of seeing the world; because technology has become the metaphysics of our time, honestly asking this question invites a wholesale reconception of reality, thus of oneself.

However, even having identified the correct question, when thinking about technology it is stunningly easy to miss the target. For example, we could consider technology instrumentally and thus conceive of it as a means to an end. Elucidating the essence of technology indeed requires considering the nature of tools. Yet if we regard technology as merely the sum of tools whose quality and reliability evolve with time, we still mistakenly locate the essence of technology in "making" and consequently disregard the epistemological paradigm that this making presupposes and enhances.[2] We could also approach technology from the moral perspective. Undoubtedly, we must ask whether technology and its consequences are good or evil. Yet to deem a given instrument (e.g., an airplane, cell phone, or atomic bomb) good, that is, useful, requires us to resolve technology's inherent and insuppressible ambiguity in one way or the other, that is, to demonize it or to divinize it.

Paradoxically, the same utilitarian measure that would resolve the moral ambiguity tends both to create the tool and to ask the question regarding its goodness and the rightness of its use.[3] Technology may also be approached

---

ogy," as distinct from the "essence of technology," is meant the various manifestations of that essence: the material innovations, new possibilities they create, and effects on human life that both tools and their suggestion of potential bring to bear. "Technological" refers to the mode of operation centered on human "making" understood primarily as the manipulation of singular beings, perceived as infinitely malleable, for the betterment of the human condition.

2. This is the weakness of the otherwise remarkable book of Lewis Mumford, *Technics and Civilization* (Chicago: University of Chicago Press, 2010). Among many others, Joseph Weizenbaum has written very lucidly about the meaning of tools and the relationship between science and technology. See his *Computer Power and Human Reason: From Judgment to Calculation* (New York: Penguin, 1984).

3. George Grant, "Thinking about Technology," *Communio* 28.3 (Fall 2001): 294.

sociologically. Works like those of Jacques Ellul, Neil Postman, and others are extremely instructive. However, limiting the study of technology to the exploration of the extent to which it has changed our society bars entrance into its essence.[4] Effects point in the direction of the cause but do not necessarily tell us what the cause is. Finally, we could also approach technology from its integral relation with modern science. Discussing the circularity between science and technology helps us see the peculiar restlessness that characterizes the development of both science and technology. Yet, it still does not disclose why they came together in modernity or what their ever-intensifying reciprocity entails for each of them.

The Canadian philosopher George Grant (1918-1988) points us in the right direction when he indicates that "technology is the metaphysics of our age. . . . It is the way being appears to us."[5] Being interviewed by Gad Horowitz, Grant specified some of technology's fundamental traits:

> [A technological society] is a society in which people think of the world around them as mere indifferent stuff which they are absolutely free to control any way they want through technology. I don't think of the technological society as something outside us, you know, like just a bunch of machines. It is . . . the basic way Western men experience their own existence in the world. Out of it come large organizations, bureaucracy, machines, and the belief that all problems can be solved scientifically, in an immediate quantifiable way. The technological society is one in which men are bent on dominating and controlling human and non-human nature.[6]

If we want to approach the essence of technology, therefore, it is crucial to see that technology has moral, sociological, practical, and scientific implications precisely because it represents a novel and peculiar relation between thinking and making. Thinking is no longer understood as the contemplative "letting be" of what is, which, in wonder, affirms what is in its inexhaustible wholeness. Rather, thinking becomes the non-contemplative

---

4. See Neil Postman's *The Disappearance of Childhood* (New York: Vintage, 1994); Neil Postman, *Technopoly: The Surrender of Culture to Technology* (New York: Vintage, 1993). See also Nicholas Carr, *The Shallows: What the Internet is Doing to Our Brains* (New York: W. W. Norton, 2010).

5. George Grant, "Technology and Man," in *Collected Works of George Grant,* vol. 3, *1960-1969,* ed. Arthur Davis and Henry Roper (Toronto: University of Toronto Press, 2005), pp. 595-602, at 596.

6. Grant, "Technology and Man," p. 595.

and impatient perception of the whole as fragmented and thus docilely at the disposal of human will. Technology is the horizon within which our practical operations and indeed every thought take place.[7] After our presentation of the way technology informs thinking and making, we shall deal with that type of knowing and acting informed by wonder that technology precludes.

Technology Reconsidered

A Qualitative Change

Is there anything essentially new about technology, or should we simply surrender to the fact that we continually get better at "making" *(techne)*? The fact that, for example, electricity serves us much better than fire, and e-mail better than conventional means of communication fettered by paper and slow delivery time — does not this indicate that we have gotten better at what we have always tried to do, namely, to make this world a more habitable place by relieving the burdens of common life and dominating threats to our existence? If we bring to mind negative instances of technology (atomic bomb, genetic manipulation), is it enough to contend that the ambiguity of technology is sequestered in bad tools (atomic bomb) or in the immoral use of something that is objectively good (nuclear energy, scientific research on life), and hence to presume that time and experience will be able to correct and improve these technological instantiations? Or does not this ambiguity, instead, reveal something fundamental about the nature of technology?

Among many authors who have spent time dealing with the difficult question regarding the nature of technology, Hans Jonas contends that "if we roughly describe technology as comprising the use of artificial implements for the business of life," there is a *qualitative* difference between post-Scientific Revolution "technological" making and the making that preceded it. Before becoming "an enterprise and process," Jonas tells us, technology was "a possession and a state," and its users were content with "a stable equilibrium of ends and means." There was also a characteristic slowness to

---

7. George Grant, "Technique(s) and the Good," in *Collected Works of George Grant,* vol. 4, *1970-1988,* ed. Arthur Davis and Henry Roper (Toronto: University of Toronto Press, 2009), pp. 118-43, at 129.

man's creation of tools, since once tools achieved their ends there was no hankering to "improve" and do more. Techniques and goals remained un-varied for centuries, and there was no anxiety to let others know what one was doing. In contrast to these features, modern technology knows no "equi-librium or saturation point in the process of fitting means to ends."[8] There is even a fluidity of ends themselves: technology not only offers better means for the same ends, but constantly proposes different and attainable ends. In fact, the relation between means and ends has become circular: technology offers new ends to anyone because it makes them possible; and it offers them at full speed.

The ever-intensifying reciprocity between the ends and the means to reach them reveals a fundamental trait of technology: progress. Progress, which is not simply a synonym of change, is built upon the conviction that what comes afterwards (the utterly indispensable upgrade) is far superior to what came earlier. Left to itself, progress always leads to a higher, not lower, state. Contemporary technological progress is thus inherently restless: there is always something new and better to find. Even when the ecological crisis seems to jeopardize the naïve idea of eternal progress (since, after all, re-sources appear to be limited), the human being labors to create synthetic products to replace what Mother Nature is no longer able to provide. We cannot simply accept, then, that the transition from, for example, man's walking, riding a horse, driving a car, to his flying an airplane represents uninterrupted progress.

Besides clarifying the difference between contemporary technology and the earlier production and use of tools, Jonas's elucidation of technology is also helpful in another regard: by destroying the balance between means and ends, the notion of progress reveals that technology is the fruit of a change in the perception of both the nature of beings and of human cogni-tion. Continuous innovation of the kind brought about by scientific-technological progress is qualitatively different than the old manner of mak-ing in which means were fitted to ends. To grasp technology's essence, says Jonas, we must be aware that technology presupposes a new ontological and epistemological worldview.[9] This newness also comes to light if we remem-ber that, as Grant indicates, the very term "technology" is a neologism that,

8. Hans Jonas, "Toward a Philosophy of Technology," in *Philosophy of Technology: The Technological Condition; An Anthology,* ed. Robert C. Scharff and Val Dusek (Malden, MA: Blackwell Publishing, 2003), pp. 191-204, at 192.

9. Jonas, "Toward a Philosophy of Technology," pp. 194.

rather than meaning " 'systematic speeches [*logos*] about the arts [*techne*],' " indicates "those forms of making that are capable of being penetrated at their very heart by the discoveries of modern science."[10]

The Movement towards Modern Technology

It is hard to pinpoint when the nature *(physis)* of the singular being began to be understood not as an ontological principle of life, rest, and movement, but as a phenomenon deprived of interiority whose movement is governed by ever-simpler physical laws.[11] This ontological paradigm shift was ushered in by certain technological developments. Francis Bacon (1561-1626) indicates that printing, gunpowder, and the nautical needle "have changed the face and status of the world of men, first in learning, next in warfare, and finally in navigation."[12] Looking backwards from the present time on technology's development, Lewis Mumford enjoys the distance necessary to indicate other, more fundamental "inventions" that changed man's perception of himself, the world, and God. The first is the clock, an informational tool designed to operate indefinitely and to generate knowledge actively. Although it was first used in monasteries to coordinate the monks' prayer life, by 1370 — when the first modern clock was designed — it had become clear that the clock "dissociated time from human events and helped create the belief in an independent world of mathematically measurable sequences: the special world of science."[13] The perception of place as empty "space"

10. George Grant, "Knowing and Making," in *Collected Works,* 4:269-79, at 273-74. In "Knowing and Making," Grant says that "technology" refers to the dependency of science upon art and of art upon science. Science has priority in this relationship, to the extent that "fine arts" and "liberal arts" have become synonymous with "entertainment" and spurious activity.

11. The difficulty of pinpointing when the change occurred comes from the fact that thought about technological development precedes its actualization. Therefore, it may seem out of place to take concrete inventions as the starting point for our reflection on technology. Nevertheless, since tools educate people in the worldview that generated them and, at the same time, clarify the presuppositions of technology, it is easier to begin with what is more readily at hand. Later, we shall revisit the epistemology these inventions entail. A good philosophical account of twelfth-century changes in the conception of nature is found in Marie-Dominique Chenu, *Nature, Man, and Society in the Twelfth Century: Essays on New Theological Perspectives in the Latin West,* ed. and trans. Jerome Taylor and Lester K. Little (Toronto: University of Toronto Press, 1997).

12. Quoted in Scharff and Dusek, eds., *Philosophy of Technology,* p. 27.

13. Mumford, *Technics and Civilization,* p. 15.

where things are, so Mumford contends, was triggered by the invention of perspective in painting and the use of the invisible lines of latitude and longitude by cartographers (for example, Andrea Banco's *mapa mundi*, 1436). These two inventions — time and space as distinct from human events — fostered the abstraction that contemporary science needed in order to complete the principle most fascinating at the time: the set of laws enabling the determination of movement, itself no longer understood as change (of which rest is a kind) but exclusively as locomotion. Whereas the understanding of time brought by the clock severed time's intrinsic relation with eternity and the person's organic relation with reality (eating, for instance, is now tied to a schedule and not so much to a biological need), the understanding of space brought man to perceive the scriptural threefold cosmology of heaven, earth, and hell as simply a product of Christian imagination.[14] "The categories of time and space," Mumford writes, "once practically dissociated, had become united: and the abstractions of measured time and measured space undermined the earlier conceptions of infinity and eternity."[15]

We will revisit the significance of severing time from eternity and earth from heaven in the following discussion of the theological difference undergirding modern technology. For now we need to see that this epistemological worldview informed the ontological paradigm shift carried forward by Newtonian physics, according to which "nature appeared simple, almost crude, running its show with a few kinds of basic entities and forces by a few universal laws."[16] This account of the physical world (where *physis* no longer means nature or being) opened the way to today's dominant philosophical system, fathered by Auguste Comte (1798-1857): positivism.[17] In line with Ockham's account of singular beings, Comte's philosophical system conveyed a perception of finitude in terms of opaque givenness that was more readily subsumable under the laws of (even sociological) physics.[18]

14. Simon Oliver, *Philosophy, God, and Motion* (London: Routledge, 2005).

15. Mumford, *Technics and Civilization*, p. 22. See also Michael J. Buckley, *Denying and Disclosing God: The Ambiguous Progress of Modern Atheism* (New Haven, CT: Yale University Press, 2004).

16. Jonas, "Toward a Philosophy of Technology," p. 195.

17. See Auguste Comte, *Introduction to Positive Philosophy*, ed. and trans. Frederick Ferré (Indianapolis: Hackett, 1988), pp. 1-33. See also Henri de Lubac's critique of positivism in his *The Drama of Atheist Humanism*, trans. Edith M. Riley, Anne E. Nash, and Mark Sebanc (San Francisco: Ignatius Press, 1995).

18. "The fundamental character of the positive philosophy is to consider all phenomena as subject to invariable natural laws. The exact discovery of these laws and their reduction to the least possible number constitute the goal of all our efforts; for we regard the search

ANTONIO LÓPEZ

A further ontological shift occurred as the monotony of Newton's scientific worldview, according to Jonas, was shattered by continuous scientific "progress." Correlative to scientific and technological advances since the nineteenth century, "the very essence of matter has turned from a blunt, irreducible ultimate to an always reopened challenge for further penetration."[19] To obtain this end science requires the support of ever more sophisticated technological means, which, in turn, exacerbate scientific restlessness. To appreciate the profundity of this latter ontological shift, it is important to recall the metaphysical and theological understanding of the ancient and medieval world. For the ancients the question regarding the "whatness" of singular beings and their truth was answered both ontologically and epistemologically. Singular beings exist because they have been invited to be, that is, to participate in God's being. Whereas, as Aquinas says, God's *esse* is complete, simple, and subsistent, finite *esse* is complete and simple, but not subsistent.[20] Since God does not use anything to bring the world into existence, his creation is an absolute affirmation of himself that fructifies in another ontologically different from him.[21] The radical contingency of singular beings that creation *ex nihilo* discloses prevents us from regarding creation, like Heidegger does, as a sort of production. God does not produce the world; he communicates his own *esse* as non-subsistent and thereby distinguishes himself from it so that the finite singular being may be itself. The exchange of this creative ontology for the implicit denial of ontology assumed by the Newtonian and nineteenth-century perspectives underlies a corresponding and more definitive epistemological shift.[22]

From Being to Technology: An Epistemological Paradigm

How can we describe the epistemological paradigm that prompts technological discoveries? Fundamentally, it is manifested as modernity's reversal

---

after what are called causes, whether first or final, as absolutely inaccessible and unmeaning." Comte, *Introduction to Positive Philosophy*, p. 10.

19. Jonas, "Toward a Philosophy of Technology," p. 195.

20. Thomas Aquinas, *De potentia Dei* 1.1.c.

21. Ferdinand Ulrich, *Der Mensch als Anfang: Zur philosophischen Anthropologie der Kindheit* (Einsiedeln: Johannes Verlag, 1970).

22. Whereas we see in this section a budding epistemological worldview manifested as a new ontology, in the following section we shall see the further loss of ontology manifested as a dominating epistemology that drives technology's endless search for knowledge.

64

of the relationship between thinking and making. In the ancient-medieval worldview described above, the radical contingency that *ex nihilo* requires does not permit irrational randomness (a-logos) because, as Aquinas says, the gift of creation reflects God's being.[23] Singular beings are true because they participate in the divine logos. The human being, made in the image of God, is allowed to participate in God's vision: he has been given the possibility of participating in the logos and, hence, not only to speak, but also to see in a limited way the relation between the logos of each singular being and the divine logos. Correspondingly, the Judeo-Christian tradition attributes to human "work" a dignity unknown to the Greek world ("My Father is working still," John 5:17). Man is asked to subdue and have dominion over the earth, that is, not to subjugate it, but to put it in relation with its Creator so that all created beings may attain the divine goal: that they worship the Creator and let his glory shine through them. On this worldview, *techne* is at the service of art and contemplation; thinking informs making.

Ratzinger cogently indicates that modernity changed this perception of thinking and making. Truth lost its ontological dimension and became the product of human making: *verum quia factum,* truth is what we have made ourselves, says Vico (1668-1744).[24] What prompted Vico to propose this change, whose philosophical presuppositions are elucidated by Descartes (1596-1650), Kant (1724-1804), and others, was the conviction that if scientific knowledge depends on the knowledge of causes, only what man makes is comprehensible to him. This understanding of causality, which presumes a reduction of the fourfold causality to efficient causality as well as a nominalistic epistemology, prompted the belief that only demonstrable knowledge is able to offer the desired degree of certainty. Mathematics and history were the predominant sciences in this regard. Yet, as Ratzinger also indicates, history soon proved itself to consist of simple facts in need of interpretation, rendering historical accounts inadequate as causal explanations. The separation of logos from being that undergirds this conception of history led, as we know, to historical relativism. Vico's dictum was carried forward by Marx: "So far philosophers have contemplated the world; now they must set about changing it." In Ratzinger's words: *verum quia faciendum,* truth is

23. This is the Thomistic doctrine of the divine ideas. The divine idea is the way in which God understands himself as capable of being imitated by a creature. Thomas Aquinas, *Summa theologiae (= ST)* 1.15.1.3; 1.15.1.2; *De ver.* 3.2. Exemplar causality needs to be considered together with the fact that God is a triune being. *ST* 1.44.3; 1.45.7.

24. Joseph Ratzinger, *Introduction to Christianity,* trans. J. R. Foster (San Francisco: Ignatius Press, 2004), pp. 57-69.

feasibility.[25] Because in this second development the fact alone is no longer reliable, only the scientific method, by combining mathematics and facts in repeated experiments — or, as Robert Spaemann would say, "homogenized experience" — yields the certain knowledge man desires.[26] In modernity's worldview, *art* has become subservient to *techne;* making informs knowing. As the Nobel Prize-winning physicist Richard Feynman (1918-1988), noted for his work on quantum electrodynamics, states: "What I cannot create I cannot understand."[27]

For our purpose it is crucial to realize that technology's pervasive claim to neutrality is a paradigmatic expression of this understanding of truth *(verum quia faciendum),* of a scientific epistemology effectively replacing ontology. In fact, as Grant has argued numerous times, the claim that, on the one hand, technological tools are neutral, that is, that they do not set their use in a predetermined direction, and that, on the other hand, singular beings are neutral, that is, that they are mainly facts upon which we may conduct experiments at will for the sake of humanity's good, is an alluring — but deceptive — expression of man's capacity to make reality. It is a claim that presupposes a radical revision of the nature of the whole. Singular beings, in this view, are no longer "wholes" but "heaps" of fragments that can be put together or disassociated at will. The claim that, for example, computers simply process information, far from being innocent, rests on the presumption that reality is a quantifiable collection of fragments that can be divided into simple units and reorganized for ulterior (and far more effective) purposes. If, instead, singular beings are wholes rather than heaps, we have to "obey" their nature, and scientific progress meets its insurmountable limit. In contrast, "neutral" tools and reality present no "limits" to scientific

25. Ratzinger, *Introduction to Christianity,* p. 35.

26. "By 'experience,' [experimental science] means planned and homogenized experience, i.e., experiment. The experiment is the domestication of experience. It is that sort of experience in which the experiencing subject remains at all times the 'master of the situation,' because he is the one who fixed the conditions of the experiment and formulated the questions, which allow only one of two possible answers: either 'yes' or 'no.' The way experiments are set up therefore makes certain experiences impossible. Whoever wanted to assure himself that he can trust his friend by performing an experiment would precisely fail to have an experience of friendship. If we wished to summarize the program of the modern enlightenment in a succinct formula, we could say that it homogenizes experience." Robert Spaemann, "Ende der Modernität?" in *Philosophische Essays* (Stuttgart: Reclam, 1994), pp. 232-60, at 240-41; unpublished English translation by David C. Schindler, p. 6.

27. Quoted in Stephen W. Hawking, *The Universe in a Nutshell* (London: Bantam, 2001), p. 83.

research. Being neutral, singular beings are infinitely malleable, and there is no answer whatsoever to the question regarding the right use of technology or how far technological research may be brought.[28]

It is also essential to grasp that in the relationship between thinking and making that sees singular beings as heaps and not wholes, contemplation is abandoned. Hannah Arendt, in fact, contends that the reversal that took place starting in the seventeenth century "concerned only the relationship between thinking and doing, whereas contemplation, in the original sense of beholding the truth, was altogether eliminated." Even more clearly, she says that the "reversal concerned only thinking, which from then on was the handmaiden of doing. . . . Contemplation itself became altogether meaningless."[29] We can press this very insightful point a bit further and indicate that even today, contemplation, for those who still hold to it, tends to be conceived as being at the service of man's making. It is not by chance that much of contemporary theology is, in one way or another, pastoral theology. Much of contemporary theology has become the provider of resources to be put at the service of transforming a world that long ago rejected Christian civilization. Presuming arrogantly to have seen and grasped the truth of dogma, we often believe that what is left for us to do is to change history and culture by convincing others of what we think ourselves to possess. Technology's epistemology reveals that man knows (and is interested in knowing) only what he can make. The will and capacity to make has become the form of knowledge.[30]

Technology's Ambiguity

To consider thinking as a form of making reveals that technology is a species of power and as such possesses an inherent ambiguity. The scientific and technological perception of nature as an unending challenge for penetration,

---

28. The coalescence of technology and science prevents setting any limit to biotechnological research. Grant cogently contends that the absolute conquest of nature (and human nature) requires nature's changeability. Nature's unchangeability presupposes an unchangeable good, which is an ontological presupposition that sets a limit to indefinite progress. See George Grant, "Man-Made Man," in *Collected Works,* 3:255-70, at 262-63.

29. Hannah Arendt, *The Human Condition,* 2nd ed. (Chicago: University of Chicago Press, 1998), pp. 291-92.

30. Think, for example, of the role ascribed to experiment in the scientific dynamic of knowing.

casting it therefore in terms of infinite potentiality, now also means that nature is seen as a bottomless resource. Nature, as Heidegger argued, is perceived in terms of energy that stands in reserve, waiting for man's manipulation. The new epistemological paradigm proper to technology challenges nature to reveal itself as energy in reserve to be used (that is, dominated) by the human being. "What the river [Rhine] is now, namely, a water-power supplier, derives from the essence of the power station."[31] Heidegger's reflection could prompt us to think that Bacon's third aphorism identifying knowledge with power has struck home again.[32] In a sense it is true: to perceive nature in terms of "energy" that can be controlled (as it was when man captured electricity) presupposes perceiving knowledge as power. Technology's thinking, then, is at the service of man's mastery of nature. Technology helps us shape what earlier seemed untamable necessity: both subhuman nature and, with the help of biotechnology, our own nature. Thanks to technology, thinking has come to mean mainly "summoning." Reason summons nature and asks it to open itself up and give what it conceals so that the human being can bring a greater good out of it. This summoning belongs to any exercise of reason and to every segment of reality: from the physical sciences to the bureaucratic and capitalist institutions that govern our country. Large organizations and bureaucracies of any sort — whose size and existence are made possible and enhanced only by technology — summon the person, seeing him only as a number, never as a person, and forcing him to obey their laws for the sake of a well-ordered and prosperous society. In this regard, it is difficult not to concur with Grant, for whom technology's thinking is a non-contemplative perception of the whole in terms of will.

Heidegger, however, has seen more deeply than Bacon. The identification of knowledge with power at the root of modern technology is far more than human mastery of an unruly, endlessly rich nature. The essence of technology is radically ambiguous. Unfolding nature to release its stored potentialities is both a human activity and something that man himself responds to: as Heidegger says, "Modern technology . . . is thus no mere human doing."[33] To perceive the role nature itself plays in the essence of technology, it is helpful to refer to Jacques Ellul's description of technology's autonomy

31. Heidegger, "Question concerning Technology," p. 321.

32. "Human knowledge and human power come to the same thing, because ignorance of cause frustrates effect. For Nature is conquered only by obedience; and that which in thought is a cause, is like a rule in practice." Francis Bacon, *The New Organon,* ed. Lisa Jardine and Michael Silverthorne (Cambridge: Cambridge University Press, 2000), p. 33.

33. Heidegger, "Question concerning Technology," p. 324.

(while keeping in mind that he has an instrumental understanding of technology). By "autonomy" we should not imagine self-governing machines whose purpose is to annihilate and replace the human race — as many science-fiction movies and novels would have us believe. By "autonomy" Ellul meant negatively that technique is not limited by anything external to itself. Positively, we can say that technology imposes itself upon the human being. As J. Robert Oppenheimer declared: "When you see something that is technically sweet, you go ahead and do it and you argue about what to do about it only after you have had your technical success. That is the way it was with the atomic bomb."[34] The purported possibilities offered by technological tools end up imposing themselves on the "users" and forcing their implementation. This "being summoned" by what stands in reserve indicates that technology is not simply about imposing a human measure on nature. Rather, it also signals the fact that, through technology, what gives itself to be seen imposes itself on man.

Heidegger's understanding of the relationship between thinking and making at the heart of technology contends that the human being is called to participate in the event of revelation that, according to him, all thinking is.[35] Yet, he says, at the same time the essence of technology harbors an ambiguity within itself, a risk; namely, that of blocking the view of the event of revelation. Technology "radically endangers the relation to the essence of truth" since truth, according to Heidegger, is *a-letheia,* that is, unconcealedness.[36] To him, the positive side of technology consists in the fact that the reciprocal summoning of nature upon man to order nature and of man upon nature to provide him with the reserved energies it conceals indicates more deeply the granting that lets the human being fulfill his destiny of safekeeping being. In its goodness, technology foretells the event that gives and which, in its giving, reveals the reciprocal relation of what calls upon and what is called for. The negative side of technology's essence is that it prevents

---

34. Quoted in Richard Polenberg, ed., *In the Matter of J. Robert Oppenheimer: The Security Clearance Hearing* (Ithaca, NY: Cornell University Press, 2002), pp. 46-47.

35. Heidegger refers to the essence of technology with the term *Gestell,* which is normally translated as "enframing" or, more faithfully to the original German word, "challenging." His understanding of "revelation," however, should not be confused with the Christian concept of revelation or contemplation mentioned earlier. For Heidegger's understanding of revelation see his account of Plato's doctrine of truth in *Pathmarks,* ed. William McNeill (Cambridge: Cambridge University Press, 1998), pp. 155-82; see also his *The Principle of Reason,* trans. Reginald Lilly (Bloomington: Indiana University Press, 1996).

36. Heidegger, "Question concerning Technology," p. 338.

the real thinking of being as such. Heidegger claims that technology's ambiguity cannot be resolved, just as the history of philosophy is a manifestation of being both revealing and concealing itself. What is dangerous is the "destining of revealing," and it has already struck man. Yet the essence of technology needs to be endured, because, as he says quoting Hölderlin: "But where danger is, grows / The saving power also. . . ."[37] Heidegger indicates that, given that the essence of technology is not technological, "essential reflection upon technology and decisive confrontation with it must happen in a realm that is, on the one hand, akin to the essence of technology and, on the other, fundamentally different from it."[38] For Heidegger, the realm in which the granting needs to be perceived is art (no surprise that his last essays dealt with the question of poetry).

Instead of approaching the questions about the whole from the realm of art, since art could also be reduced to a form of making (human creativity), we would like to return to the type of contemplation of being that initiated man's engagement with the world (as *techne* and *poiesis*) and which the essence of technology makes impossible: wonder. "Perhaps," says Grant, "we are lacking the recognition that our response to the whole should not most deeply be that of doing, nor even that of terror and anguish, but that of wondering or marveling at what is, being amazed or astonished by it."[39] We wonder not so much before Heidegger's granting but before being's gift. Wonder as response will also help us grasp technology's ambiguity ontologically and not ethically. Thus, on the one hand, the fact that technological making has brought out "good" things and has improved human existence indicates the inextricable coextensiveness of the transcendentals. On the other hand, the danger of technology is real in that it entails a rejection of being and a systematic flight from the present to an empty future that promises to remain utterly docile to man's manipulation. Flight from the present, which normally takes the banal form of systematic distraction, is a rejection of the gift that the present is. Heidegger's understanding of the "reciprocal summoning" on nature and man by technology's essence rightly signals that the singular being (understood in the Aristotelian-Thomistic tradition, not *Dasein*) flourishes in and through the human being. Man's relation with the singular contributes to the flourishing of created realities. Yet, instead of thinking of this relation-

37. Heidegger, "Question concerning Technology," p. 333.
38. Heidegger, "Question concerning Technology," p. 340.
39. George Grant, "In Defense of North America," *Technology and Empire: Perspectives on North America* (Toronto: House of Anansi, 1969), pp. 15-40, at 35.

ship in terms of *Ereignis* (event of appropriation) or summoning as Heidegger does, it seems truer to approach it from the perception of being that wonder suggests and which modern technology makes impossible: gift (not given-ness). The reciprocity of making and thinking — that is, of how thinking gives form to making, and how human making affects our perception of thinking — should be elucidated in terms of "gift" rather than of "claiming" and "summoning." To approach thinking and making in light of wonder and gift, we need to consider one fundamental assumption responsible for the techno-logically understood relationship between thinking and making.

A Theological Difference

George Grant's profound (and still not well-known) philosophical work contributes significantly to reflection on the essence of technology by signaling the inseparable relationship between technology and Christian religion, particularly in its Calvinist expression. To him, both Ellul's and Max Weber's otherwise remarkable accounts of technological and American society miss the decisive connection between technological society and Christian religion. While this assertion may seem awkward at first, it is fundamental to see that the peculiar relationship between thinking and making proper to technology is primordially dependent on the understanding of God (and consequently of man) that it presupposes. Indeed, as Schelling was fond of repeating, our conception of God gives form to whatever we are thinking.

Trying to preserve God's glory, Calvin offers a perception of God as *radically other* from fallen creation. The human being is born with a naturally implanted knowledge of God and with a capacity to see his glory in creation.[40] Yet because of the fall, this knowledge is to no avail. Now, God can only be known through faith in Christ as he is revealed in Scripture, and faith alone will enable man to again see creation as a sign of God's glory.[41] With this account, Calvin precludes any analogical understanding of being, thus creation can no longer be discovered as a rational expression of the divine logos. Reason, according to Calvin, is not to digress by dwelling on God's essence; the human being, rather, has the duty to worship God. Additionally,

40. "On each of his works his glory is engraved in characters so bright, so distinct, and so illustrious, that none, however dull and illiterate, can plead ignorance as their excuse." John Calvin, *Institutes of the Christian Religion,* 1.5.1, trans. Henry Beveridge (Grand Rapids: Eerdmans, 1997), p. 51.

41. Calvin, *Institutes of the Christian Religion,* pp. 65ff.

Calvin's theory of double predestination attests to the fact that he conceives of God in terms of absolute, unquestionable will that freely determines what is. Ironically, even though original sin obliterates God's image in man, if God is mainly perceived as an absolute, sovereign will (although a loving and merciful one), the human being will conceive of himself accordingly. It is not by chance that contemporary American liberalism considers freedom to be the essence of the human being.

Grant rightly signals Calvin's idea of God as the dominant one, because it is in North America, the most technological society to date, that the nuptials of Calvin's Protestantism and the new sciences acquire their archetypal form. In his famous essay *In Defense of North America,* Grant indicates that Calvinism and the modern sciences came together for both a negative and a positive reason — in fact, in Europe, Protestant theologians were the first ones to espouse Bacon's understanding of science. The negative reason is that, for different purposes, both scientists and Protestant theologians wanted to get rid of medieval metaphysics. The scientists thought that hylemorphic metaphysics (in both its Thomistic and far more popular nominalistic expressions) prevents man from observing and understanding the world as it is. The Protestants wanted to free man from an excessive reliance on human reason and to ease his abandonment to divine revelation. Rather than through nature, God is to be known through faith in Jesus Christ. In this sense, Grant contends that, despite claims to the contrary, Calvinist theology contributed to freeing man from contemplation.[42] Thus, modern science directed itself toward the world, and Calvinism toward God, yet both upheld the separation of the two.

To show the positive reason why Protestantism was open to the empiricism and utilitarianism that gave rise to modern technology, Grant refers to Troeltsch's reflection. He claims that "Calvinism, with its abolition of the absolute goodness and rationality of the Divine nature, with its disintegration of the Divine activity into mere separate will-acts, connected by no inner necessity and no metaphysical unity of substance, essentially tends to the emphasizing of the individual and empirical, the renunciation of the conceptions of absolute causality and unity, the practically free and utilitarian individual judgment of all things."[43] If, according to Calvin's theology,

---

42. Grant, "In Defense of North America," pp. 19 and 35.

43. Ernst Troeltsch, *Protestantism and Progress: A Historical Study of the Relation of Protestantism to the Modern World,* trans. W. Montgomery (Boston: Beacon Press, 1958), pp. 162-63.

the world no longer speaks of God in a way that human reason can understand, if Christian sacraments do not change human nature but are only at the service of the believer's faith, and if the Church is reduced to a congregation that knows no liturgy, God's salvific will can only be perceived in action, not in contemplation. Successful, ever-fruitful action is the only place where the human being can perceive whether he is pleasing to God or not. Grant states that "those uncontemplative, and unflinching wills, without which technological society cannot exist, were shaped from the crucible of pioneering Protestant liberalism."[44] It is thus not surprising to see that, although American Puritanism emphasizes inwardness and the presence of the infinite, paradoxically, it ends up producing a society with no interiority and little awareness of God. Puritans who wanted to reform the world for the sake of the Kingdom of God found an ally in liberalism since it also wanted to reform the world, although simply for the sake of man.

This desire to reform the world, coupled with the understanding of God as radically other and omnipotent will, opens to a type of thinking that almost inevitably ends up embracing the form of making proper to the essence of technology. In fact, scientific-technological knowledge is true knowledge because it is able to change the world.[45]

Severing the intrinsic relation between God and the world modifies the scope of scientific, technological operations in at least two respects. First, modern science's conquest of nature's necessity not only represents the extension of the realm of freedom,[46] but also attempts to overcome sacrifice and suffering. The restless nature of technological and scientific progress is a refusal to sacrifice and to suffer. By this I do not mean to disregard the amount of effort we put into bettering our living conditions. I simply wish to indicate that science and technology's lack of restraint, for example, in the manipulation of human life, reveals an attempt to master life without regard to its gift-nature. While trying to tame suffering, technology inflicts on human beings something far deeper than physical suffering: the systematic oblivion of the fact that we are not our own, as Grant contended, that is, that we belong to God.[47] Of course, we cannot actually avoid suffering

44. Grant, "In Defense of North America," p. 25.

45. George Grant, "The Uses of Freedom," in *Collected Works of George Grant*, vol. 2, *1951-1959*, ed. Arthur Davis (Toronto: University of Toronto Press, 2002), pp. 190-203, at 193-95. Grant also shows that the idea of "changing the world" is both altruistic and, more often than not, hedonistic.

46. Grant, "Man-Made Man," in *Collected Works*, 3:258.

47. George Grant, "Conversation: Intellectual Background," in *George Grant in Process,*

and sacrifice, but we can postpone them or dilute responsibility for them, for example, among different medical and financial institutions. This rejection of suffering and sacrifice, which manifests the expansion of human freedom over nature, is directly related to technology's epistemological paradigm in that it preempts real thinking. In fact, there is no thinking without the sacrifice of embracing the truth for what it is and the suffering that this embrace may cause in the human being — here, as Grant frequently notes, the figures of Socrates and, more radically, Jesus Christ come together.

The second change, which can only be mentioned here, is that, as Grant lucidly explains, the theology undergirding technology severs the link between eternity and time, and hence conceives of time as history, "which is consciously and voluntarily made by the human being."[48] Determining time by the succession of human actions, the man who judges his value primarily by his fruitful actions is born "to make history." Disengaged from eternity, time is deprived of the past, and the present is perceived only as the beginning of an ever-open future docile to the manipulation of human will. As history, time forces us to move forward. The transformation of time into history reveals that the epistemological pattern of technology flattens the previously transcendent horizon of time (as, for example, elucidated by Plato and Augustine) into an infinite succession of discrete moments. Instead of living the relation of belonging with the eternal God, historical time reinforces the fact that the pursuit of wisdom and contemplation has been transformed into the acquisition and manipulation of data whose noble purpose is that of making our life a little more human.

If we wish to synthesize what we have seen so far about the essence of technology, we could say that it is a perception of the whole (of the world, oneself, God, and the relation that binds them) that irretrievably shatters it into simple, self-referential parts whose arbitrary unity is temporarily pieced together by means of a self-affirming will. As the epitome of modernity, technology's epistemological paradigm transforms human action (and rea-

---

ed. Larry Schmidt (Toronto: House of Anansi, 1978), p. 63. This fundamental insight for Grant echoes Calvin's remarks: "But if we are not our own, but the Lord's, it is plain both what error is to be shunned, and to what end the actions of our lives ought to be directed. We are not our own; therefore, neither is our own reason or will to rule our acts and counsels. . . . We are not our own; therefore, as far as possible let us forget ourselves and the things that are ours. On the other hand, we are God's; let us, therefore, live and die to him (Rom. 14:8). We are God's; therefore, let his wisdom and will preside over all our actions. We are God's; to him, then, as the only legitimate end, let every part of our life be directed." Calvin, *Institutes of the Christian Religion*, 2.7.1, trans. Beveridge, p. 7.

48. Grant, *Philosophy in the Mass Age*, in *Collected Works*, 2:310-407, at 322.

son) into the sheer exercise of control and power. Consequently, technology makes it impossible for us to perceive being's otherness and relate to it adequately. Furthermore, casting us into the arms of historicism, technology a priori evacuates the singular's constitutive relationship with the infinite and with others. Technology thus understood preempts accounting for the real novelty towards which the experience of wonder discretely beckons.

Wonder and the Retrieval of Knowing

"Wonder," says Plato, "is the feeling *(pathos)* of a philosopher, and philosophy begins *(archē)* in wonder."[49] As is known, Heidegger indicates that the Greeks did not understand *archē* chronologically, as if it were a starting point that could be left behind.[50] Rather, they perceived *archē* as a permanent and ruling source. How Heidegger understands the meaning of source does not concern us here.[51] Our concern now is to see how thinking and making are perceived in light of the *permanent source* of philosophy (wonder) and hence to discover the perception of the whole and the singular being that they entail when so illuminated.

It is easy to miss the fact that, as a *pathos,* wonder entails man's concrete and lived bodiliness. Through this embodiment, wonder introduces us to the perception of the distinctive unity of the whole (of oneself, the world, and God).[52] We should not think that bodiliness is just the means through which

---

49. Plato, *Thaetetus* 155d.

50. Heidegger writes that "wonder as *pathos,* is the *archē* of philosophy. We must understand the Greek word *archē* in its full sense. It names that whence something goes out. But this 'from whence' is not left behind in the going out; the *archē* rather becomes what the verb *archein* says: that which rules. The pathos of wonder thus does not simply stand at the beginning of philosophy as, for example, the washing of hands precedes the surgeon's operation. Wonder supports and rules philosophy through and through." Martin Heidegger, *What Is That — Philosophy?* trans. Eva T. H. Brann (Annapolis, MD: St. John's College, 1991), p. 32. See also Heidegger, "On the Essence and Concept of φύσις in Aristotle's *Physics* B, I," in *Pathmarks,* pp. 183-230.

51. For Heidegger's idea of "principle" see both Reiner Schürmann, *Heidegger on Being and Acting: From Principles to Anarchy* (Bloomington: Indiana University Press, 1990); and Kenneth L. Schmitz, "From Anarchy to Principles: Deconstruction and the Resources of Christian Philosophy," in *The Texture of Being: Essays in First Philosophy* (Washington, DC: Catholic University of America Press, 2007), pp. 37-53.

52. See Adrian Walker, "On 'Rephilosophizing' Theology," *Communio* 31 (Spring 2004): 143-68.

we acquire data or come to be seen and embraced. Rather, because the soul informs the body, the very corporeality of the person is a mode of being that, on the one hand, reminds the human being of the "giftness" of all that is (himself, first and foremost) and, on the other hand, renders the question of God's existence inevitable. As John Paul II's immensely rich reflection on the sacramentality of the body elucidates, the body, with its inescapable, intrinsic reference to another and its witness to the ontological difference between our essence and our existence, reminds us constantly of our having been made (and our continuously *being* made) by another.[53] The body permanently roots us in the original experience of our own filiality. Man's original solitude, discovered through his body, reveals to him that God is his only adequate partner, and, being called to communion, he also discovers relation with others as constitutive of his own being. These others are in the first instance his parents (and, through them, the divine source to which they also owe gratitude for their very existence), and in the second all the others with whom he is given to live. Through his lived bodiliness, which testifies to the truth of the ancients' creative ontology, the person perceives that the unity that constitutes every singular being has the form of, and, in fact, *is* a gift.[54]

If we ponder a bit more what wonder discloses, we see that the perception of oneself and every other being (human and subhuman) as gift comes not as a conquest but as a permanent surprise. "Surprise," rather than simply being the happening of what is totally unexpected, represents the coming together of newness and memory. In other terms, we are surprised because we perceive that the originality of a finite being (newness) is always already coming from the same source as we are (memory).

Surprise indicates further that knowing takes the form of "excess" and "fruition." By the excessive nature of knowing I mean that, since the singular reveals itself as a gift — thus pointing back to a giver intending a recipient — knowing takes place inside a prior being known. The "excess" in this case regards the fact that knowledge of oneself takes place only through another. This "other," however, is both the other concrete singular (let it be either the world or a human person) and the primordial source that is the origin of both oneself and the other singular. Thus, within this being known, knowl-

53. For the relation between the ontological difference and the sexual difference see Angelo Scola, *The Nuptial Mystery,* trans. Michelle K. Borras (Grand Rapids: Eerdmans, 2005).

54. John Paul II, *Man and Woman He Created Them: A Theology of the Body* (Boston: Pauline Books and Media, 2006); Carl Anderson and José Granados, *Called to Love: Approaching John Paul II's Theology of the Body* (New York: Doubleday, 2009).

edge — and the thinking that is fitting to it — regards the perception that beings simply exist and that they exist as other from oneself, the beholder. The "to be" *(esse)* of the singular is its wealth, and not simply, as Kant contended, an *addendum* to the concept. *Esse* is the perfection of all perfections, as Aquinas elucidated. The existence *(esse)* of the singular being causes wonder because its *esse* is not reducible to its essence, and its essence, while limiting the *esse* of the singular being, exists because it always already participates in the mysterious fullness of *esse commune* — which we could describe with Aquinas as "simple, complete, but not subsistent."[55] It is this gratuitous, asymmetrical reciprocity of *esse* and essence that grounds the inexhaustible wholeness of the singular. Beings, however, are not really seen until we perceive that the dual unity of *esse* and essence is kept open because of *esse commune*'s participation in the divine *esse*. The "excess" proper to knowing, therefore, is not quantitative in nature — although fruitfulness is indeed a sign of being's wealth. Rather, "excess" regards the distinctive, inexhaustible singularity of each finite being in its relation with the divine source that takes place through *esse commune*. Through this relation the singular knows and is known in its constitutively exceeding itself. Singular being is an inexhaustible whole because of its constitutive dual unity of *esse* and essence, which comes permanently as gift from its source.

Besides illuminating excess, wonder allows us to see that true knowledge also takes the form of fruition, that is, of selfless enjoyment of the richness of being for its own sake. We wonder not only because the other and we ourselves *are,* but also because we take delight in the miracle of the other's being. That singular beings are, simply are — rather than not being at all, or than being just an extension of ourselves or of God — causes sheer gladness. As Aquinas said, "Omnia admirabilia sunt delectabilia."[56] The other elicits delight because it is a whole, and its wholeness, because of its constitutive relation with the source, is inexhaustible. The other's inexhaustibility is thus a participation in the goodness and truth of the divine source. Delight therefore is the inseparable "taste" of the perception of the intrinsic goodness and truth of what is. Apart from the relationship with the original, permanent source — no matter how unknown the source is — the singular would neither exist nor cause delight because it would not be perceived in its ultimate positivity. However, because of its relation with the source, we can say negatively that the singular other, as a whole, cannot be exhausted

55. Aquinas, *De potentia Dei* 1.1.
56. Aquinas, *ST* 1-2.32.8.

by our intellectual or affective grasp of it. Positively, we can say that it is a bottomless richness that causes delight. The "neutrality" with which technological reason perceives the singular (even if it is considered a resource) sees potentialities that tend to send the gaze back to the self and thus block knowing altogether. In contrast, if we listen to a cello virtuoso playing a sonata, we see that he reaches a level of unity with and "mastery" of what is given to him (the musical instrument, score, sound, time and silence, his body, the audience, the joy and suffering of playing, and the mystery of which the music speaks) that technology precludes. In fact, when the artist focuses simply on technical brilliance, his performance becomes flat.

The coalescence of excess and fruition in the surprise proper to wonder indicates not only the inseparability of knowing and loving (affection), but also, more importantly, that it is not possible to grasp the wholeness of the singular other unless we "let the singular be." If the singular were at our disposal, it would not cause delight. It would only entertain us until we became satiated. Wonder invites us to look at the singular other in its otherness with reverence. In fact, at first, we do not even think about what to do with what we behold. Perceiving the inexhaustible wholeness of the other (a person, starry night, flower, etc.), we do not feel the need to grasp; rather, we delight in the singular other and let it be. Why the act of thinking has everything to do with this "letting be" deserves a closer look.

To be authentic, letting be requires that the beholder allow himself to be given back to himself. To wonder, in fact, not only invites recognition of the otherness of the singular; it also invites us to become aware of our own giftness. In this regard, the singular other "gives us back" to ourselves. The return to ourselves, with the delighted acknowledgment of the giftness of the other and ourselves, occurs both as questioning and as not grasping (for ourselves or for the other singular). This return expresses itself as questioning because wonder seeks to know more fully what gives itself to be seen. Our wonder is also an indication that we do not know and that we will not be able to exhaust the richness of the singular.[57] The wonderer is he who accepts having been put on the way to his own origin by being's call, who is fundamentally poor, and who acknowledges that this poverty is his wisdom. As Socrates confessed in the *Apology:*

57. As Pieper indicates, Hegel interprets this negative aspect of wondering differently: philosophy must begin with confusion and depends on maintaining it; one must doubt everything, give up all of one's preconceptions, in order to regain it all again through the creation of a concept. Josef Pieper, *Leisure, the Basis of Culture,* trans. Gerald Malsbary (South Bend, IN: St. Augustine's Press, 1998), p. 104.

But the truth is, O men of Athens, that God only is wise; and in this oracle he means to say that the wisdom of men is little or nothing; he is not speaking of Socrates, he is only using my name as an illustration, as if he said, He, O men, is the wisest, who, like Socrates, knows that his wisdom is in truth worth nothing. And so I go my way, obedient to the god, and make inquisition into the wisdom of anyone, whether citizen or stranger, who appears to be wise. . . . And I have a witness of the truth of what I say; my poverty is a sufficient witness.[58]

If the wonderer were to grasp, thinking that he knew, he would bring upon himself Midas's malediction: whatever he grasped would become a mirror of his own self-imposed ideal. The singular would become an extension of the beholder, and it would lose its own logos. The only thing left for the wonderer "to do," as in the passage from Marx cited earlier, would be to turn the singular toward his predetermined purposes. While to let be entails not grasping, it is not, however, "to abandon" or "to let go." To let be is to acknowledge the singular's otherness and its relation with the source that continuously makes the singular be. There is no fruition or wonder if the third, that is, the source that unifies the singular and the beholder while preserving each one's irreducible wholeness, is not also acknowledged.

It is important that we perceive the integrity of the form of thinking that the original experience of wonder requires. The encounter between the beholder and the singular other is always already taking place. It is not up to the former to decide when or whether it is to happen. In this encounter, the other's allowing its wholeness to be perceived as such indicates that, in a mysterious way, the other finds its fullness in the beholder. This, of course, is true ultimately because the beholder, through his knowing, participates in God's vision; he sees in his being seen, as we said earlier. Just as the subhuman flourishes in the human consciousness, so the person unfolds himself more fully through human others and ultimately in God. The perception of the singular as a whole is simultaneous with its "being let be." Yet this letting be is not the fruit of the beholder's decision. It is rather a response to the beauty of the singular whole that interiorly draws the beholder to let the singular whole be, that is, to affirm its relation with the ultimate source in the acknowledgement of its giftness. In this regard, just as going up a mountain offers the climber new vistas of the same landscape, so wonder allows the beholder — not without sacrifices — to become reacquainted ever anew with the wholeness of the

---

58. Plato, *Apology* 23a-b, 31c.

singular other. The questions that the philosopher asks in wonder are answered not through the domination of the known. True answers are rather a reacquaintance with the inexhaustible wholeness of the singular (like seeing it for the first time). Thinking, therefore, rather than being another form of making as happens in technology, is this contemplative letting be that affirms the singular in its inexhaustible wholeness; that is, in its intrinsic, dynamic relation with the source of both the singular and the beholder.

We need to make explicit another element implied in the foregoing elucidation of wonder. As a form of contemplation, wonder is not a static endeavor — not simply because searching for the truth of the singular frequently brings us to a different place from that in which the question first emerged, but because we are enticed out of ourselves to pursue what remains greater than ourselves. Knowing, in this regard, does not take place without suffering because it asks us to grow in a truth of which we are not the origin, and hence it requires leaving open the possibility of real, radical change. When the beholder contemplates he temporarily rests in the singular being (this is why wonder causes delight), yet this rest is not stillness but a new way of dwelling in being that sends the beholder both back to himself and further ahead toward the source of the singular other. The time that it takes to discover and let the other be reveals the unity that binds the beholder with the being that is thought. Time and finite being shed light reciprocally when the relation with the eternal source is not severed. Inexhaustibility, in this regard, is not endlessness or universal progress but relation with the source. "Progress" in this sense will never go so far that we will no longer know where we are headed, as Goethe said.[59]

The unity between the wonderer and the singular being is dynamic in yet another respect that restores the non-technological relation between thinking and making. The contemplation of the singular in its intrinsic relation to the source and to others reveals its finitude not only as an inexhaustible wholeness, but also as a call for its own completion. In other terms, its form, without being undetermined, waits to be unfolded by man's engagement with it. Human making, then, emerges organically from the unity between the beholder, the singular, and the source of both, a unity that we are given to live through the experience of wonder. Rather than considering a single instance of "making," to understand what the thinking informed by wonder reveals of the nature of making it will be more fruitful to look at

---

59. "The furthest one can go is to reach a point at which one no longer knows where one is headed." Quoted in Spaemann, *Philosophische Essays,* p. 237 (our translation).

"work." Work, in fact, as a wider instance of man's engagement with the world, discloses more clearly what takes place in man's making.

Work and the Overcoming of Homelessness

Given the fragmentation of the world we live in, if we wish to perceive the nature of work, it is crucial first to retrieve an adequate sense of "home." It is rather difficult today to understand what a home or monastery — for my purpose "home" will designate both — is, since technology, in fact, leaves us homeless. Pushing the human being always to do more and better, to try different things, and to master nature, the technological mindset and the tools that it creates project the human being ahead in the future, preventing him from living the present. Tragically, since the future is not yet and the past is no longer, by preventing him from dwelling in the present, technology places the human being nowhere. Because he is nowhere, technology cannot but consider the human person abstractly, that is, as an individual to whose nature relations, space, and time remain extrinsic. Defined, as is today most common, by his freedom, this individual is a holder of rights who determines himself in action. Yet, taking him as an individual, technological thinking quantifies the subject. It abandons man to laws and policies that accentuate his homelessness. Because of this quantification of the person (think of the salary as remuneration for work — it is just a number), the promise of social life collapses into a sequence of individual encounters that not only leave him radically isolated but, more intensively, degrade his relationships with others to exercises of power and instinctivity.

Because the technological mindset has rendered us homeless, the rediscovery of the home is fundamental for the recovery of wonder and hence for the affirmation of the meaning of work as such. Obviously, by home, I do not have in mind a neutral, anonymous space in which to carry out various functions. Rather, the home is the place that divine love generates by allowing people to participate and dwell in it. In this sense, the home, with the shared life it entails, is not only the place into which the person is born but also the place that continuously helps him rediscover his own constitutive childlikeness. This character, which is true of the paternal home in which he is born and grows up, is also the case for the home within which he lives his adult life. The home reminds the family or the community that adult life, in the vocational forms of both marriage (home) and consecration to the living God (monastery), is not the creation of the human person. Both the celibate and the (sexually differentiated) couple choose and have been chosen for a particular state of life. Thanks to the home, both marriage and celibacy can be acknowledged as two different forms of sonship, for the home is the continuous, living reminder of our being begotten, of the giftness of life, and of the task of existing. At home, a person's vocation happens permanently, and thanks to this he is brought ever more deeply into being. As concrete, lived bodiliness, wonder remains in time if the beholder does not move away from his home, that is, if he dwells in the place given to him in which his permanent sonship is called to become fruitful. Conversely, without the knowing proper to wonder — that is, the kind that lets the other be by acknowledging its inexhaustible wholeness and specific relation to the divine mystery — the home becomes simply a stopping place that speaks more of what the person has accomplished and what lies ahead in the future than of the gift (of love and being) that makes him be. The reciprocity between the home and wonder is asymmetrical: First, it is the dwelling place that makes possible and allows the recovery and deepening of wonder. Then, within the context that divine love generates, wonder enables the human person not to reduce the other to a means for a further end, which would destroy the home and its ability to nurture wonder.

The home is indispensable not only for the recovery of the attitude of wonder but also because, as the place that allows for filiation to be lived, it clarifies the scope and nature of human work. Technological thinking makes us believe that what happens at home and what we make at work are two separate things. Instead, given that they are both expressions of love, what happens at home flows into what we make at work, and what we make at work enlarges and deepens the concrete form of love we are given to live at home. Just as the child reminds the parents of their love's fruitfulness and gives this love a radically new depth, so work signifies the fruit of the love we are given to live and, by transfiguring reality, enlarges the love we enjoy. Here again, there is an asymmetrical reciprocity between the home and work, giving the home a certain priority since each person's place in being has a grounding dimension that work does not have. The home enables the "worker" to remember that, although his task contributes to his fulfillment, it does not begin with him and does not have him as its goal. In other terms, the task is at the service of something greater than himself, namely, the divine love that gave him a home in the first place.

Away from a position of wonder conceived as lived bodiliness within a dwelling place, work tends to be reduced to technological making, that is, to a type of production in which the person is never taken fully into account.

However, through wonder thus understood, work recuperates the integrity of the person. In this regard, work is not simply an expression of the individual's mastery over nature, that is, a demonstration of the extent of his power, but an expression of the entire person, in both his utter poverty and wealth of being. If, as we saw, wonder allows us to perceive the singular being for what it is — not a heap of data to be manipulated or processed, but a whole that cannot be severed from its relation with the source and that seeks its fulfillment in another — then work entails carrying out in the world the transfiguration of reality, that is, allowing what exists to find its partial fulfillment in its relation with the divine source.

The dynamic aspect of wonder indicated earlier reveals something fundamental about the nature of work. As the experience of wonder witnesses, the singular being is given to itself in order to be and yet, at the same time — since it is not complete in itself — reaches its fulfillment only in relation with others. Contributing to this relation, the change that human work is called to effect in the world is a participation in a deeper change that was neither begun nor will be completed by man alone. That beings are, that they exist in a communion of beings, and that each one of them can neither become itself nor bear fruit without the others means that human work is a participation in a far deeper working. He who wonders and is aware of his poverty knows that the logos of singular beings is a participation in the divine logos, that is, in God's design. Wonder enables us to see that the world follows a hidden harmony, a design in which the human being is called to participate. In this regard, the human being, called to make — through the infinite variety of human making, from curing cancer to washing dishes — participates in the fulfillment of the design that he is not able to master. What is untrue in technological making is not human beings' need to engage with the world, to collaborate in the revelation of what the world is; rather, it is obliviousness to the truth that human making reveals a light that is not man's own but the divine mystery's, and that what man "produces" reflects his finite glory only inasmuch as it reflects the mystery's glory. Away from wonder and oblivious of God, technological making, under the guise of novelty, increases boredom and homelessness.

In wonder before the singular being, work reveals itself as the expression of the person's relationship with the divine mystery. Properly speaking, the person works by giving form to everything (himself, those who live with him, his specific work) while being mindful of the belonging of everything to God. He does collaborate in the transfiguration of reality (land, nature, and history) according to a plan that is suggested to him through the singular itself but that is not his (it is God's). Only by participation in God's love and its logos (design), which nourishes and educates the human person within a dwelling place, can man actually work (otherwise, he simply produces), aware that his work (from the most banal to the most sublime) is always a tiny step inside the divine mystery that calls man to collaborate in the construction of the cosmos.

Being in the world, the human person is surprised by the singular otherness of beings and is given to enjoy and contemplate this otherness, that is, to let it be. At the same time, being in the world, man discovers the call to collaborate in the betterment of the world, to work, that is, to let it shine with the light that comes from the source of all that is. Through the experience of wonder, we are given to perceive that working and thinking, rather than being manifestations of making, as technological development contends, are coincident with prayer. Thinking and making participate in and seek a unity that finds its ultimate form in prayer, the human act which receives from God and entrusts all things to God. In fact, only prayer unites what seems to be fragmented with the giving source, who alone can affirm fully the positivity of all that has been invited to be. Prayer unites because, as the truth of thought, it affirms the singularity of what exists in its belonging to the mysterious source. Prayer also unites because the transfiguration of the world, rather than an affirmation of ourselves, is the act of entrusting the world with ourselves to the one who calls what is not into being. Thinking about technology's essence invites us therefore to move beyond this essence into the recollection of the depth of being as gift that calls man to pray, that is, to let be and to possess and transfigure by offering.

PART II

ORDERING SOCIAL LIFE

Human Rights and Cultural Plurality: A Possible Path

Marta Cartabia

Multiculturalism and the Universality of Human Rights

Important transformations are taking place in the area of the protection of human rights. The first originated from the system of the European Convention on Human Rights and, more precisely, from the jurisprudence of the Strasbourg Court, which for years has been growing in authority, influencing the jurisdictional and constitutional interpretations of the rights of many national authorities.[1] The second has to do with the expansion of the protection of fundamental rights by the European Union (EU) in areas that are intertwined with powers reserved to the States.[2] The third transformation is connected to the widespread tendency among judicial authorities, both within and outside Italy, to use cases, materials, and jurisdictional decisions coming from foreign systems to find solutions to new and difficult cases in

1. At the apex of this evolution are the 2007 decisions 348 and 349 of the Italian Constitutional Court, which recognized in the European Convention a constitutional cover, elevating the Convention to the rank of a standard imposed on constitutionally legitimate judgments. All the decisions of the Italian Constitutional Court are available at http://www .cortecostituzionale.it/actionRicercaMassima.do.

2. For a thorough treatment of this point, see Marta Cartabia, "L'ora dei diritti nell'Unione europea," in *I diritti in azione,* ed. Marta Cartabia (Bologna: il Mulino, 2007), pp. 14ff. The tendencies I point out have been confirmed by recent decisions of the Court of Justice of the European Union. See, for example, Case C-267/06, Tadao Maruko v Versorgungsanstalt der deutschen Bühnen [2008], E.C.R. I-1757, which recognizes the right of homosexual couples civilly registered according to German law to transfer pension rights, and which will take the place of the powers of individual states in family matters.

the area of fundamental rights, especially when these cases involve issues that are ethically controversial. In short, if, until the end of the last century, the territory of fundamental rights was jealously guarded by national constitutions — so much so that we spoke of "constitutional patriotism" with regard to fundamental constitutional values (Jürgen Habermas) — today the transformations just mentioned (and others which could be included as well) denote an irresistible diffusion of fundamental rights beyond the boundaries of individual countries. This is one of the most distinguishing features of contemporary constitutionalism.[3]

This phenomenon is not new. After the Second World War, an entire political season was marked by the multiplication of international tools concerning human rights, starting with the United Nations' Universal Declaration of Human Rights in 1948.[4] From that point forward, "the march has gone on. . . . It proceeds slowly from the recognition of the rights of the citizen of a single state, to the recognition of the rights of the citizen of the world, the first to proclaim which was the Universal Declaration of Human Rights; from the internal law of the individual states, through the law between states, to cosmopolitical law."[5]

Still, in recent years fundamental rights have been exposed to new, and in part contradictory, challenges. On the one hand, there is a strong acceleration toward the universalization of fundamental rights. Never so much as today have human rights been the principal point of reference for international political agendas. On the other hand, paradoxically, never so much as today has the very idea of human rights been so radically called into question by postmodern and relativist critiques. The advancement of human rights has grown up with a doubt about their universality — a doubt that strikes them at the root, calling into question the idea that they can be objectively defined, universally applied, and philosophically justified.

For observers of the second postwar period, there were no doubts about the foundations of universal human rights: the "attempts at international declaration and organization of human rights are based on a general conception of life and the world that, faced with the many denials of recent times, brought to the fore the Christian and European idea of the human being as reason and freedom, as inescapable purpose — with respect to which every

3. Already baptized "neoconstitutionalism" by some philosophical schools. In the Italian canon an example can be found in Tecla Mazzarese, ed., *Neocostituzionalismo e tutela (sovra)nazionale dei diritti fondamentali* (Turin: Giappichelli, 2002).

4. Antonio Cassese, *I diritti umani oggi* (Rome: Laterza, 2005), p. 15.

5. Norberto Bobbio, *L'età dei diritti* (Turin: Einaudi, 1992), p. xii (our translation).

social order has a purely instrumental nature — as fundamental value and foundational principle of every social and historical life."[6] On the contrary, already by the end of the twentieth century, multiculturalist critiques had insinuated a radical doubt about the very possibility of recognizing human rights,[7] asserting, among other claims, that they mask with apparent universality a cultural vision that is both partial and typical of the West. Relativism's goal is ultimately Western imperialism, which, in the part relevant to the present essay, under the seductive guise of human rights would frustrate every cultural expression that is not recognized by the culture developed on the two sides of the Atlantic.

Upon close inspection, the multiculturalist critique of human rights finds its footing in certain tendencies which are growing within the most prestigious international institutions for protecting human rights. As Mary Ann Glendon points out,[8] starting in the 1990s the fundamental rights institutions under the United Nations betrayed, in many cases, the inclusive spirit of the Universal Declaration[9] and since then have been occupied by lobbying groups which have begun to promote a vision of partial human rights, the expression of a hyper-libertarian culture centered upon an isolated individual who is abstracted from society — an individual who is, in turn, centered upon him- or herself and entirely self-determined. The first victim of this tendency was the dignity-centered conception of rights,[10] which refers not to the abstract individual, but to the person who springs from a *we,* to the person as a rational being, to the person in all his or her concreteness and historicity. And Europe, with its courts and agencies of rights, seems inexplicably to be a particularly fertile ground for sowing this hyper-libertarian,

---

6. Giuseppe Capograssi, *Opere,* vol. 5 (Milan: Giuffré, 1959), p. 8 (our translation). The same clarity emerges in the preparatory works for the Italian Constitution, specifically in discussions concerning the future Art. 2 on the priority of human rights over the state and any other source of power as the only guarantee of their inviolability.

7. On this point see the debate between Jürgen Habermas and Charles Taylor, *Multiculturalismo: Lotte per il riconoscimento* (Milan: Feltrinelli, 2002).

8. Mary Ann Glendon, "La visione dignitaria dei diritti sotto assalto," in *Il traffico dei diritti insaziabili,* ed. Luca Antonini (Soveria Mannelli: Rubbettino, 2007).

9. On the origins, cultural climate, and dynamics that led to the approval of the Universal Declaration of Human Rights see the wonderful book by Mary Ann Glendon, *A World Made New: Eleanor Roosevelt and the Universal Declaration of Human Rights* (New York: Random House, 2001).

10. Mary Ann Glendon, *Tradizioni in subbuglio,* ed. Paolo G. Carozza and Marta Cartabia (Soveria Mannelli: Rubbettino, 2007), pp. 90ff; originally published as *Traditions in Turmoil* (Ann Arbor: Sapientia, 2006).

hyper-individualist vision, becoming in turn a promoter of it. In the words of Chabod,

> Contemporary human rights culture is not fueled only by Christian inspiration. It also derives from the project of the absolute autonomy of the human individual created by modernity and giving rise to hedonistic individualism. The current convergence on fundamental rights feeds on this antagonistic dualism. The anthropological Christian matrix — even if secularized — which strongly inspired the official documents of half of the twentieth century, tends to leave room for another reading — a reading that, in the name of freedom, absolutely raises up the ego of the human being, reduced to the capacity to enjoy material goods, with no check on this enjoyment save social utility.[11]

The contemporary era is marked, therefore, by contradictory forces, which create strong tensions in the area of human rights: the universality of rights at once appears as an insuppressible need and as the target of a strong attack, fueled by the tendency to absolutize individual liberty understood as autonomy and self-determination — a vision in which many cultures do not recognize themselves.

Fundamental Rights through the Dignity of Every Human Person and Historical-Cultural Diversity

At the root of these contradictory forces is the ambivalent nature of fundamental rights, placed at the crossroads between universality and history: "In considering human rights we can observe persistent ambiguity and contradiction. On the one hand they are perceived as absolute, as insuppressible needs, as self-evident values beneath every sky and in every age. But, on the other, we cannot deny the realization that they are historically contingent. They have a history, their own evolution, and, in a certain sense, they mutate."[12]

In fundamental rights there is an aspiration to universality that justifies the need to overcome the confines of a single legal system; but there is also

---

11. J. L. Chabod, "L'Unione europea e i diritti dell'uomo," *La società* (2001): 40 (our translation).

12. Francesco Viola, *Diritti dell'uomo, diritto naturale, etica contemporanea* (Turin: Giappichelli, 1989), p. 157 (our translation).

a historical element in them, which reflects the tradition and deepest aware-ness of each people, of which constitutions are a primary expression. Rooted in the value of human dignity, the idea of fundamental rights necessarily contains a universal dimension. Rooted in the religious, moral, linguistic, and political specifics of each people, the concrete application of these rights is an expression of both particularity and pluralism.[13] This tension was well known to the drafters of the Universal Declaration of Human Rights, who worked not a little to find ways to reconcile different views. The agreement that was unexpectedly reached concerning the text of the Universal Decla-ration did not, however, resolve the problem once and for all. The task of safeguarding the universality of the rights of the person without sacrificing the cultural distinctiveness of each people and tradition always falls to the interpreter, or more precisely, the interpreters, as they face the demands of reality.

A Possible Path

Are we obliged to surrender to relativistic resignation, renouncing the in-heritance of universal rights left to us by the history of the second half of the twentieth century? It is history itself, more than any cultural option, which answers this temptation with an unequivocal "no." The construction of a European *jus commune* of rights or of a European constitutional patrimony, the development of human rights' international role, and the migration of constitutional concepts from one country to the next and one continent to the next all speak of an insuppressible push toward recognizing an inheri-tance belonging to every human being and traceable anywhere, even if tak-ing different expressions or forms. What avenues are there, then, to resetting this tension between the universality and historicity of human rights? Which rights are universal, and how can we trace a line between these and the contingent, culturally characterized expressions of them?

For example, all the democratic systems guarantee freedom of expres-sion. Nevertheless, even in the Western world, there are multifarious differ-ences in the protection offered to this freedom. The American concept, for example, is characterized by the absence of limitations, while the European one continues to evolve in the direction of "protected" forms, introducing

13. Paolo G. Carozza, "Uses and Misuses of Comparative Law in International Human Rights," *Notre Dame Law Review* 73.5 (1998): 1235.

substantial limitations on the right to free speech (e.g., introducing crimes of opinion, as in the areas of hate speech and homophobia). In these different versions of free thought, which protective components are universal, and which are culturally conditioned by the bearers of history and by the specific problems of a determinate society?

These problems' obvious severity eliminates any temptation to attempt an exhaustive response. It is possible, however, to sketch out some avenues for reflection, and to point to some that hold particular promise. I would like to start from a passage that seems to me particularly illuminating:

> Is the claim that every human person is the subject of unalienable rights a view particular to the West, or does it lead to the expression, in a way and a language inevitably determinate and singular, of *something* universally recognizable as valid (or more valid) by human "reason" in every culture?
>
> That is, beyond the different historically bound persons, is there a *threshold,* a *style,* a *common nucleus* that characterizes the human as such (as we would say in our philosophical terminology), capable of multiple iterations, ever open and indefinite? If we stay loyal to experience, shouldn't we perhaps speak about an occurrence of the human that, beyond all incommunicability, allows different historically bound instantiations of human nature and their respective totalities of meanings to meet and communicate?
>
> Does not precisely this event arise from encounter and contrast with the other, with the other's difference and the other's universe of meanings?[14]

These few lines provide some ideas, some words, if you like, that outline a potential route to travel: a universal elementary experience and the encounter with the other as the possibility for an occurrence of the human.

A Universal Elementary Experience

When we wonder about issues like the death penalty; about widespread practices in cultures past and present like human sacrifice, cannibalism,

---

14. Carmine Di Martino, "La convivenza tra culture," in Cartabia, *I diritti in azione,* p. 495 (our translation).

slavery, or racial segregation; about persistent discrimination, direct or indirect, based on gender; when, in a word, we tap the fundamental issues of human rights, the relativist argument gives way to the need to recognize and reaffirm a common heritage of every human being. No supporter of multiculturalism would maintain that cultural diversity justifies cannibalism, human sacrifice, genital mutilation, and other practices that are clearly detrimental to human dignity. Even the currents of thought most sensitive to the demands of multiculturalism and to the value of the various cultures do not hesitate to recognize the common inheritance of each human person. In this regard Charles Taylor emblematically says that "the liberalism of equal dignity seems to have to assume that there are some universal, difference-blind principles. Even though we may not have defined them yet, the project of defining them remains alive and essential."[15] When it comes to human rights, the existence of an intangible nucleus of rights belonging to every person seems beyond doubt. The contents of these rights, however, remain an open question. If the examples mentioned above denote that a universal heritage exists, they also suggest that this heritage involves an elementary threshold of human experience. The search for universal values must be launched at a minimalist and essential level; it must involve elementary aspects of human experience. The more we distance ourselves from this minimal and elementary level, the more we get into cultural specificities.

If we can agree on the existence of a universal, elementary threshold belonging to the experience of every human person, certain consequences for the legal world become inevitable. There are many of these, but here I will highlight two.

First, we must look with a critical eye upon the impressive expansion of the catalog of human rights, at times written in charters, but more frequently laid out by courts and tribunals. Never prior to the last several years has there been such an expansion of fundamental rights without precedents. Every desire, every human aspiration rendered abstractly realizable by the evolution of science and technology, is claimed in the language of fundamental rights, lengthening the catalog to the point of exaggeration. Rights charters have multiplied and their contents have expanded; the jurisprudence of courts, both national and European, further enriches the list.

---

15. Charles Taylor, "The Politics of Recognition," in *Multiculturalism: Examining the Politics of Recognition,* ed. Amy Gutmann (Princeton, NJ: Princeton University Press, 1994), pp. 43-44.

If in past decades the most fertile ground for the growth of new rights was socioeconomic, "new fundamental rights" today spring from the stem of *privacy,* or the right to respect for private life, understood as a right to self-determination.

A highly sophisticated and refined development of the catalog of rights constitutes an enrichment in many ways, but in others it amplifies the tension between the universal and historical-cultural dimensions of rights discussed above. If we do not want to undermine the very concept of human rights, we must oppose this inclination toward rights inflation, reserving the category of universal human rights for only what belongs to the elementary experience of every human person.

Second, the criterion of elementary experience could help distinguish the roles played by national, supranational, and international institutions in the protection of fundamental rights. The distinction between the universal-elementary and the historical-cultural aspects of rights could usefully contribute to maintaining balanced relationships within multilevel systems of rights protection, such as that in Europe.

The broader the level at which rights are protected, the more restricted and essential the spread of recognized rights should be, leaving to lower levels of governance the role of attuning the spectrum of rights in a way that reflects cultural particularities. Speaking specifically of the EU, we have already noted the marked tendency toward centralization of fundamental rights protection, occurring since the approval of the EU *Charter of Fundamental Rights* and its expansion. If we wish to avoid a degrading cultural homogenization, or worse, a cultural colonization through leanings that dominate in a determinate, historical moment within European institutions, we must keep the common, constitutional rights heritage of Europe within a minimal threshold. A useful aid in regulating the relationships between different institutional levels, as has been suggested,[16] could be offered by the principle of subsidiarity. Still, doctrines like the margin of appreciation, the principle of proportionality, or, under the EU, the doctrine of incorporation must be accurately preserved in the jurisprudence of European courts as indispensable mediators between universal and particular, integration and differentiation, harmonization and diversity.

16. Paolo G. Carozza, "La sussidiarietà come principio strutturale dei diritti umani nel diritto internazionale," in *Europa e costituzione,* ed. Pietro G. Grasso (Naples: Edizioni Scientifiche Italiane, 2005), pp. 129ff.

The Encounter with the Other

At this point we can go one step further by asking how we can identify the elementary, universal threshold. What method may be used?

Defining the contents of that intangible and unchanging nucleus of universal values is a difficulty limiting universal rights theories: we can affirm the existence of such contents but cannot specify them in a satisfying and enduring way. Even in the case of the supra- and international efforts to enshrine rights in writing, the resultant texts remain inevitably vague and indeterminate, left at an intermediate stage that subjects the contents of individual rights to future interpretation.

The difficulty of grasping the content of universal elementary experience is perhaps due to a methodological issue: we would like to define human rights once and for all, in the abstract, moving from a method of logical deduction — as if given the idea of human nature or of the person we could consequently derive universal rights. But it seems to me that this method must be overturned.

The universal human heritage is less a table of values and more an experience that emerges from within the living history of peoples. This heritage cannot be grasped without an individual who is the heir to it: it does not exist without *l'homme situé*, as G. Burdeau would say, without the person who lives at a given latitude, in a certain historical age, in a determinate social, political, and cultural context. It is from observing persons and peoples in action and in their interrelation that the heritage typical of the human can emerge.

Still more, this heritage that is elementary, human experience reveals itself in the encounter between different cultures because it does not belong to an abstract world that disregards the cultural forms, historically and positively determinate, in which people live out their existence.[17] Observing the various historically determinate expressions of fundamental rights and the interaction between these expressions makes it possible to recognize the universal meaning they carry. In this light, today's contemporary societies, inhabited by diverse and fairly heterogeneous groups, become the most fertile ground for the emergence of what is common. History shows us that this is precisely the dynamic that led to the most unexpected result of the twen-

17. On the inseparable nexus between universal and particular, see the astute observations of Francesco Botturi, "Declino del minimo comun denominatore," *Oasis* 5 (2007): 16-19.

tieth century: brought together by Eleanor Roosevelt's wise and passionate reception at the time of the drafting of the Universal Declaration, five representatives from the most distant and rival cultures were in a short time able to overcome all obstacles and recognize a heritage of rights common to all humanity.

It was not the synthesis of texts but the meeting between people that brought about the emergence of the common heritage of rights now delivered to history. To understand this dynamic, Martha Nussbaum's theory of specific citizenship and cosmopolitan citizenship, reworked from classical origins, can be of use: "Each of us is a member of 'two communities: one that is truly great and truly common . . . in which we look neither to this corner nor to that, but measure the boundaries of our nation by the sun; the other, the one to which we have been assigned by birth.' "[18] One enters into life with a culture, just as one learns how to communicate through a native language, and it is only in belonging to a given and particular culture that one can aspire to cosmopolitan citizenship. Similarly to how we attain cosmopolitan citizenship, we achieve universal human rights not by disregarding or abstracting from the different historical and cultural experiences, but by remaining profoundly immanent to them.

But in what way can the encounter and confrontation between cultures make "what is truly important and truly common" — in our terms, unalienable human rights — emerge? Here I would like to highlight a particularly delicate point.

In the legal world, what most resembles the encounter with the other is comparison. This encounter emerges in a particular way when legal cases are compared with one another, for in each case a cross section of the living and historical problems of persons and peoples is presented. But those familiar with comparison are well aware that the combination of different experiences may result, on the one hand, in a sterile juxtaposition without actual encounter. On the other hand, comparison may result in the simple migration of ideas, easily conducting the import-export of fundamental rights such that the list of rights is excessively expanded without the comparison having facilitated recognition of what is truly common. Nevertheless, comparison can also foster a reflective and critical examination of traditions. The encounter between experiences can allow us to distinguish what is particularistic from what is a value for all, what is arbitrarily unjustified

18. Martha Nussbaum, *Cultivating Humanity: A Classical Defense of Reform in Liberal Education* (Cambridge, MA: Harvard University Press, 2003).

from what could be justified through reasoned argument. Martha Nussbaum provides us with another relevant idea in her re-proposal of the Socratic method as a way of connecting different traditions with cosmopolitan citizenship.

Socratic self-examination is an "appeal to reason [that] frequently does not require us to take a stand outside the culture from which we begin,"[19] but rather recalls the duty of reason to "take a hard look at local conventions and assumptions, in the light of more general human needs and aspirations."[20]

All of these considerations present the encounter between different cultural experiences as the place where an elementary experience common to all humanity and recognizable to human reason emerges. What route does this encounter suggest for the legal world, particularly regarding its engagement with the fundamental rights concerns discussed above?

Here I will limit myself to only a few considerations regarding dialogue between courts, because it seems to me that, like it or not, the emphasis on fundamental rights is leading to the development of a *Richterstaat,* and the most relevant tensions come out between universal human rights and fundamental rights as a historical-cultural expression of a given tradition.

The value of the encounter between different historical experiences that emerges in legal cases and decisions is not so much that of the circulation of cultural models — the purpose of which is fusion and cross-pollination between different legal traditions — but rather the birth of new legal breeds, originating, to use the famous expression of Gadamer, from the fusion of cultural horizons. Regarding human rights, such legal creativity appears impracticable because it would lead to the compilation of long and broad lists of rights, in which every cultural particularity would have to be included, with contradictory results. This would miss the goal of letting universal and common rights emerge. Thus, the purpose of legal comparison with regard to human rights is neither the fusion of legal traditions nor the expansion of the catalog of rights.

The purpose of the comparison and observation of other experiences is not to measure a consensus. Particularly delicate in this regard is the practice of applying foreign legal precedent to cases that have no clear solution within a given legal order. In many cases, foreign jurisprudence is cited in the attempt to highlight a consensus being reached in various parts of the world. The simple fact of evoking a widespread consensus seems to corroborate the

19. Nussbaum, *Cultivating Humanity,* p. 63.
20. Nussbaum, *Cultivating Humanity,* p. 58.

legitimacy of a certain choice. If such consensus were the purpose of referring to foreign experiences, it would be necessary to apply basic democratic rules to jurisdictional dialogue, and to measure consensus according to the principle of majority — all this assuming that these procedures are adequate for jurisdictional activity, which, to the contrary, is by nature characterized by a *countermajoritarian* logic in the area of rights.

Comparison as the point of encounter between diverse cultural experiences has an undeniable, intrinsic value for enlarging the cognitive horizon and putting the judge and the interpreter in a better position to adequately understand the problem he or she is called upon to answer. Comparison would lose all of its meaning if it became the vehicle for mechanical imitation or blind importation of the leading cultural models. If this were the case, comparison would become the most powerful, and at the same time seductive, tool of that imperialist drift undertaken in the name of human rights. On the other hand, if comparison of legal experiences does not devolve into imitation of solutions, but rather penetrates to the level of the *rationes decidendi,* it can become a formidable resource for enriching the reasons that sustain one or the other of the possible solutions.

In other words, as has been effectively suggested,[21] it is one thing to compare the facts in evidence, referring to comparative law only to bring in uncritical solutions or to avoid confirming a decision that has already been made based on other considerations. It is another thing to perform a cognitive comparison. Understood as the place of encounter with other experiences, comparison has the undeniable capacity to enlarge reason, deepening and amplifying the understanding of diverse traditions, and letting both the common elements and the contingent particularities emerge. It does not look first and foremost at the solutions, but at the arguments. Comparison should never become a shortcut for legal reasoning, nor a channel for strict importation of solutions, but rather an opportunity for the enrichment of arguments and reasons, leading to the embrace — or the refutation — of legal responses tried in other parts of the world.

What is at stake is not of little value. If the global, legal dialogue that is developing around human rights is understood as a rhetorical tool for importing decisions made elsewhere, it opens the door to cultural uniformity, which puts both individual traditions and universal principles at the mercy

21. Andrea Lollini, "La circolazione degli argomenti: metodo comparato e parametri interpretativi extra-sistemici nella giurisprudenza costituzionale sudafricana," *Diritto Pubblico Comparato ed Europeo* 1 (2007): 485.

of the dominant culture. On the other hand, if legal dialogue taps the deepest level of the arguments, undertakes a careful analysis of the single human event that gave rise to the legal case, and gives sufficient attention to the historical context in which it occurs, this dialogue can become a useful tool for the expansion of reasons and motivations, capable of distinguishing the responses tied to and conditioned by context from those that can be usefully generalized because they contribute to the flourishing of human dignity.

Multiculturalism and Ethically Controversial Questions: What Form Should Regulation Take?

Lorenza Violini

From Pluralism to Multiculturalism

In order for lawyers to reflect on multiculturalism, two issues need to be addressed. The first issue is a methodological one: how does one construct a rule capable of regulating societies that have lost the unitary foundation offered by religion and shared culture? The second issue regards substance: what concrete solutions must these rules contain to favor the *reductio ad unum* of such societies?

As a premise, it is worth noting that the modern, national states were created precisely for the purpose of reuniting legal-political societies that had lost the cultural and religious unity that, until that moment, had been granted by Christianity. It is not within the scope of this paper to go into further depth on this point. I wish here only to recall the many studies that have brought into focus the influence of secularization on modern constitutional systems,[1] particularly its shaping decision-making processes in a liberal-democratic way. The constitutions in force today — which represent the last stage of the process of obtaining political unity — are a factor in the growth of that same unity. They define not only procedures, but above all fundamental rights, whose valuable contents are removed from the volatility of political processes and the threat of the so-called "tyranny of the majority."

---

1. Ernst-Wolfgang Böckenförde, "Die Entstehung des Staates als Vorgang der Säkularisation," in *Recht, Staat, Freiheit: Studien zur Rechtsphilosophie, Staatstheorie, und Verfassungsgeschichte* (Frankfurt: Suhrkamp, 1991), pp. 92ff.

The constitutions also refer in different ways to meta-legal origins,[2] and although these are never clearly identified, their fundamental structure has remained intact despite significant assaults coming from radical culture since the 1970s. Fundamental values are also preserved in the laws on divorce and abortion; although these are the offspring of liberal thought, they aim, at least formally, to save even the values they contradict (human life and the family), constructing the two institutions as exceptions that are extremely qualified in their use.

Now the situation seems to have changed: rather than increasing unity, liberal culture and secular relativism's need to obtain ever more permissive laws inevitably corrodes the common cultural foundation — not to mention the essence of law itself. To that end, they refer to the phenomenon of multiculturalism, exaggerating its features and calling into question not only values, but also the traditional ways of exercising power. These are considered obsolete in that they are no longer able to respond to a diversity that is shifting from pluralism to multiculturalism.[3]

The exaggeration of multiculturalism for liberal ends means that, despite the fact that all democratic systems are pressured to find common values and shared decision-making procedures in order to deal with issues relevant to coexistence (which involve multiple positions that, coexisting, by definition cannot be unanimously shared),[4] many of these values and procedures are labeled as "ethically" controversial. This suggests that dissent alone is enough to render as a form of violence against freedom — in particular the

2. To verify this assertion, it is enough to think of the preambles to constitutions, with their open references to God and religion, which, in some cases, assume a foundational status in the constitutional order (this occurs, for example, in the Irish constitution). Other constitutions recognize the value of religious associations as an element that contributes to the pursuit of the common good, as does, for example, the constitution of Baden-Württemberg, *(Ihre Bedeutung für die Bewahrung und Festigung der religiosen und sittlichen Grundlagen des menschlichen Leben wird anerkannt).* For more on this, see Joseph H. H. Weiler, *Un'Europa Cristiana: Un saggio esplorativo* (Milan: Rizzoli, 2003).

3. For a timely distinction between pluralism and multiculturalism, see F. Viola, "La democrazia deliberativa tra costituzionalismo e multiculturalismo," *Ragion Pratica* 1 (2003): 33-72. Criticizing the "multiculturalist" model and its alter ego, the "integrationist" model, see Carmine Di Martino, "La convivenza tra culture," in *I diritti in azione,* ed. Marta Cartabia (Bologna: il Mulino, 2007), p. 491.

4. "A legal order can be more or less tolerant, but cannot be the mirror of pure tolerance, because in that case it would have no ordering function and, ultimately, would prescribe nothing." Donato Carusi, "La (imminente?) legge italiana sulla procreazione assistita: Considerazioni nella prospettiva della 'bioetica laica,' " *Politica del Diritto* 2 (2003): 287-310 (our translation).

individual's freedom of conscience and action — those laws that protect indefeasible values with criminal sanctions.[5] There is evidence to support the suspicion that this is a way to surreptitiously assert a liberal ethic, and not to affirm the value of tolerance: under a contemporary reading of the secular and radical culture, so-called multiculturalism — which is a factual reality — tends to become prescriptive for the ordering of the entire system, and to dictate to the law the conditions for its legitimization. It no longer matters that the law has been generated according to democratic processes and constitutional values; it is necessary that laws adhere to the most rigorous ethical neutrality,[6] that they do not trample a single cultural or religious current in society. In order to do this, a law must never take a position: it must be constructed in such a way as to leave the maximum possible space for freedom, and it must avoid expressing certainties and values in order to leave everyone free to fill the "gap in the laws" with their own certainties, their own values and preferences.[7] In this way, a true contradiction in terms is established: the laws created to regulate precisely those issues that are most important for humankind and civil coexistence (life, death, scientific research, health, sickness, etc.) only achieve their goal when they no longer regulate anything, when — instead of providing guidelines — they limit themselves to codifying the infinite exceptions based on individual, even ethical, preferences.

5. See Sergio Bartole's comment on the decision of the Italian Constitutional Court that partially decriminalized abortion (Corte costitutionale, sentenza no. 27/1975): "Value judgments are more or less implicit in a brief decision on abortion." Bartole, "Scelte di valore più o meno implicite in una laconica sentenza sull'aborto," *Giurisprudenza Costituzionale* 2-3 (1975): 2099ff (our translation).

6. The presumed "neutrality" of the law is the inescapable consequence of the principle of the secularism of the state. Many authors have taken issue with this approach. Among them see Giovanni Grottanelli, *Note introduttive di diritto costituzionale* (Turin: Giappichelli, 2004), p. 128. For a fuller treatment see also Karl-Heinz Ladeur and Ino Augsberg, "Der Mythos vom neutralen Staat," *JuristenZeitung* 62.1 (2007): 12-18.

7. For example, a volume commenting on Law 40 of 2004 on assisted fertility contains essays from which "emerges the conviction that any law dealing with ethically controversial topics, especially those in which medical science and clinical practice can offer much guidance, should be inspired by a healthy self-restraint, keeping far from useless ideological-cultural proclamations. In sectors like this, the abstract and absolute impositions of the law not only crush with unconscious cruelty the sentiments, hopes, and life projects of many individuals, but also risk provoking ethical rebellions insensitive to medical and scientific certainties." Alfonso Celotto and Nicolò Zanon, *La procreazione medicalmente assistita: Al margine di una legge controversa* (Milan: FrancoAngeli, 2004), back cover (our translation).

True multiculturalism, however, does not coincide with its reductive liberal version: it is a real issue that calls into question the existing order not merely to demolish it, but rather in an attempt to make clear those fundamental, universal points without which an orderly civil coexistence, based on norms everyone recognizes as binding, is unthinkable.[8] Understood in this way — and given that even at the base of liberal culture there is a continuous pull to identify a shared vision of the common good — multiculturalism cannot be confused with the attempt to progressively loosen the ties that are a necessary part of belonging to a determined social context, or with destroying the values of that social context.[9] We now turn our attention to this idea, in order to determine its foundations in the new social context.

Regulatory Solutions for Ethical Controversies: In Pursuit of Shared Rational Motivations

Considering what we have just said, we must ask ourselves if the existence of a law that has been approved by a democratically elected body and takes a definite position on controversial issues is compatible with the democratic and pluralistic character of a state. A negative response to this question dominated the debate surrounding the referendum on Italian Law 40 of 2004, which regulated medically assisted procreation and banned the use of embryos for scientific purposes. Among the arguments levied against the law, one of the most evocative claimed that since there is a multitude of scientific and moral ideas about the nature of an embryo and the other issues covered by the law, the most appropriate choice would have been to not introduce any prohibitions, but to leave the field totally open to personal choice. From a viewpoint that hopes to optimize the consequences of laws, a "nonauthoritarian" law would increase user choice, allowing the greatest number of

---

8. See Javier Prades, "Il dibattito sulla multiculturalità: Una società postindustriale e globalizzata," *Atlantide* 2 (2007): 17.

9. With regard to this it has been said that "no matter how liberal, no legal order succeeds in being neutral with respect to the varying conceptions of the common good present in a society." Giuliano Amato, "Libertà: Involucro del tornaconto o della responsabilità individuale?" *Political del diritto* (1990): 47 (our translation). Further, "constitutionally recognized rights to liberty have at their base a value to protect (life, freedom from physical coercion, freedom to associate), not a generic freedom to act." Augusto Barbera, "Il cammino alla laicità," in *Laicità è diritto,* ed. Stefano Canestrari (Bologna: Bononia University Press, 2007), pp. 33ff (our translation).

people to go forward without being contradicted or inhibited by public authorities. If such a nonauthoritarian view prevailed, there would be, at least concerning the exercise of personal freedom, a strong imbalance between laws that prohibit and laws that permit, such that the latter would be favored.

We can reflect more deeply on this theme by looking at a particular aspect of the law cited above, starting with the prohibition of artificial insemination by donor sperm, and moving on to the principle that inspires it: the right to life of an embryo. Considering the former, the objection mentioned above consists in the assertion that, if the law permitted artificial insemination with donor sperm without forcing anyone to use the procedure, it would permit those who wanted a child with a genetic background at least partly similar to their own to obtain one. On the other hand, prohibiting such a practice would increase the number of citizens who would have to sacrifice their ethical vision in order to obey the law. In short, an ethically definite law would contradict the plurality of ethical visions present in civil society.

Seen in this way, the issue risks leading to abhorrent consequences: what would be the difference between ethical choices not to be imposed and the more ordinary value judgments that every state, no matter how secular and multiculturalist, is called upon to make every time it decides to regulate (e.g., by imposing penal sanctions on certain actions, or creating fiscal rules for some groups of citizens while not for others)? When it comes to these matters, no one questions the state's ability to favor some and restrict others as long as these actions reflect the will of the majority, and as long as the goal is not to obtain an internal, ethical conformism,[10] but only certain ways of acting.

If we focus on lawmaking and its foundations, it is not hard to see that many factors are at play behind legislative choices: ethical, ideological, and cultural motivations are mixed with practical concerns attuned to the social relevance of the behavior addressed by a rule. If a certain behavior has consequences that are considered socially undesirable, it will be forbidden; therefore, the criteria that motivate the legislative choice are practical and rational by nature, and can be shared even by those with a different vision of the moral value of the choice itself. The invocation of the religious argument ("it's against my religion!") to avoid the application of the law could

---

10. On the other hand, for a discussion of "moral adhesion to constitutional values," see Gustavo Zagrebelsky, *Il futuro della costituzione* (Turin: Einaudi, 1996).

be either the extreme assertion of one's own liberty of conscience, or an interesting strategy for obtaining benefits; the line between the two is subtle and primarily depends on the importance of the protected good. Furthermore, it is essential to have a rational and political assessment of the request made, of possible alternative forms of the rule by which to avoid injuring personal convictions, of the rule itself for which an exception is requested (if dealing with an obligation or a prohibition), and of the consequences all of these would have for the collective. A choice could be adopted only in extreme cases and in defense of fundamental goods, and never in the case of any purportedly controversial imposition.

In the case of artificial insemination, a typical example of this kind of issue,[11] the choice to ban it may have been determined in part by moral and principled judgments. However, considerations about the necessity of protecting a natural genetic relationship between parents and offspring were certainly relevant as well. So we can conclude that the motives behind the ban were not (or at least, not only) based on the presumed immorality of the practice, but were also based on foreseeable, socially undesirable consequences, the arguments against which require at least a degree of effort (as well as the capacity to convince the majority of the Italian Parliament). A similar argument can be made concerning the recent political pushes to introduce legislation on euthanasia: even people who do not share the idea of the sanctity of life can share in the idea that life itself cannot be regulated like just another legal good (life being not only a good or a right, but the a priori that allows for the possession of every other good and the exercise of every other right).[12] We could also agree that opposing the legal permission of regulated death procedures is justified by the fear that, once introduced into law, they could have deleterious effects on a sociocultural orientation that respects life.[13] And there are many other examples that tend to show that prohibitions (inherent to any legal system, and touching upon moral issues that are roundly discussed) do not contain the germs of totalitarianism just because the multitude of religious views present in civil society has taken away a *general* consensus. On the contrary, each prohibition

---

11. See Stefano Canestrari, "La legge 19 febbraio 2004, n. 40: procreazione e punizione," *Bioetica* 12.3 (2004): 421-35.

12. Adriano Pessina, *Eutanasia: Della morte e di altre cose* (Siena: Cantagalli, 2007), p. 30.

13. The link between individual behavior and (inescapably) the social relevance of the same is brought to light in Romano Guardini, "Il diritto alla vita prima della nascita," in *Scritti* (Brescia: Morcelliana, 1972), p. 390.

must be evaluated in light of the motivations that sustain it, and assessed against the internal coherence of the whole legal system. Only when a prohibition is contrary to this system is it possible to eliminate it on grounds of unconstitutionality.

If it is true that "the function of the law consists in its ability to reconcile freedom and rules so that the exercise of freedom does not lead to chaotic consequences in community life, without suppressing its fertile roots,"[14] then through democratic processes, choices are made that crystallize the distinction between the positives of exercising human freedom and the negatives that produce chaotic consequences for community life. All of this must be achieved without transforming the ordinary limitations to freedom — those necessary acts in a modern constitutional order, which must take into consideration the different ideas present within it — into "ethically sensitive issues."

A Common, but Not Minimum, Standard

Taking a look at the ground we have covered so far, we can say that, in a multicultural and multiethnic society in which the common base that would enable shared choices seems to have been dissolved, it is clearly an inadequate solution to merely invoke the exercise of freedom as an alternative to the obligatory nature of legislative enactments. It is precisely in the presence of radically different views about the proper bases for community life that it becomes fundamental to recover rational elements of dialogue and argument, as well as the capacity to make laws that are instruments of cohesion with respect to the values to be shared. With this in mind, it becomes clear that freedom for freedom's sake cannot be the decisive criterion in legislative choices, but rather freedom directed toward the pursuit of determined principles and values, some of which must be understood as inalienable in order for the socio-legal order not to lose its internal coherence. One example, in addition to those offered above, is the case of legal sanctions recently introduced in Italy for practitioners of female genital mutilation.[15] Here it is clear

14. Augusto Cerri, "Diritto e scienza: Indifferenza, interferenza, protezione, promozione, limitazione," in *Studi parlamentari e di politica costituzionale* (2003): 7ff (our translation).

15. Law 9 gennaio 2006, no. 7, "Disposizioni concernenti la prevenzione e il divieto delle pratiche di mutilazione genitale femminile," G.U. Serie Generale, no. 14 del 18 gennaio 2006, with particular reference to Art. 6, which incorporates Art. 583 of the Penal Code. On

that what is at issue is not the excessive defense of liberty, but rather a legislative calculation that considers such mutilation an objective affront to a woman's dignity, even when she consents to submit to the practice. An improper use of freedom at the expense of dignity, that is, an extreme exaggeration of the individual will at the expense of objectively conceived values that the established order guarantees through democratic legitimacy, shows itself therefore unable to comprehend the very essence of the order created by this legitimate rule.

Choices similar to the female mutilation ban unanimously passed by the Italian Parliament can participate in this ultimate nature of rules, which are to value dignity before liberty. Italian law achieved such participation when it explicitly identified the beginning of human life with the moment of fertilization, wherever it occurs. The choice is a radical one and — obviously — justified. However, to orient the search for its justifications we may refer to the ongoing legal doctrine debate surrounding the meaning and extent of human dignity. There is a widespread belief that the moment at which the protection of human dignity should begin is not a choice that should be left to science as such, or to law as such.[16] This may appear paradoxical without the added hypothesis that, therefore, the choice depends on a given fact, natural and incontrovertible, to which first law and then science must bend. It is the subtle divide that separates the juridical from the prelegal, and that leads us to identify an elementary experience that we all have when, encountering another, we cannot help but recognize a dignity equal to our own, else we risk debasing our own dignity. One can assume that this is what our Italian constitution suggests when it asserts the "recognition" of fundamental rights, and what the German constitution means by its radical formulation concerning the protection of human dignity — a formulation that at the time of the Constituent Assembly was called by T. Heuss "the uninterpreted thesis."[17] Upon this background are grafted the most radical visions and safeguards of human dignity. The philosophical base is entirely Kantian: man is an end unto himself, a being for himself *(Dasein um seiner selbst willen),* and

---

this topic see Giuseppe Cassano and Francesco Patruno, "Mutilazioni genitali femminili," *Famiglia e Diritto* 2 (2007): 179.

16. Jutta Limbach, "Mensch ohne Makel," *Frankfurter Allgemeine Zeitung* 47, February 25, 2002, p. 51.

17. For the debates that unfolded in preparation for the Parlamentarisches Rat and surrounding the work of the German Constituent Assembly, see Fiammetta Berardo, " 'La dignità umana è intangibile': Il dibattito costituente sull'art. 1 del Grundgesetz," *Quaderni Costituzionali* 26.2 (2006): 387-400.

it follows that he can never be reduced to a means for obtaining other ends, no matter how noble. So radical is the nonreduction of the human being to an instrument that it supports an analogous radicalism in the extent of the protection of dignity: wherever he or she may be on the planet, the human person has the right to be protected inasmuch as he or she possesses a unique and inimitable dignity. The temporal extent is set up in a way analogous to the spatial extent — it must reach the point of no return, the point at which there is no reasonable doubt as to its material existence. Therefore, to say that protection of human dignity is owed to embryos is not a sort of ontological fundamentalism for culturally homogeneous societies. The key issue is the nonreduction of the protection of human dignity according to all its legal content, which reconceives the entire formation process of the human being. In short, the protection of human dignity as a fundamental norm can encompass the full protection of embryos, and not on religious or ethical grounds but on the basis of rational justifications.

Against this absolute ban on the violation of human dignity are a variety of positions that instead aim to lessen its significance.[18] United in their tendency to call into question the absolute nature of the protection of human dignity, they remain deeply different among themselves in their articulations of the temporal extent of that protection.

How can we choose between such divergent approaches? Would it not be more in keeping with a multicultural society to prohibit any rules that do not suffer exceptions? This question was posed in an evocative way by Niklas Luhmann during a conference, using a hypothetical: an atomic time bomb was triggered in an undisclosed location by a terrorist who has been captured and is being held as a prisoner. At the conference Luhmann asked if, under these circumstances, it is acceptable to torture the prisoner. The question was posed in such a way as to render the affirmative response inevitable, and to show that the existence of inviolable rights is irrational. Indeed, it would have been unreasonable to reject a cost-benefit analysis of the possibility to save many (innocent) people, in order to protect one (guilty) individual.

As a counter-reading to the relativism that underlies this cost-benefit idea,[19] it was proposed that we consider human dignity along the same lines

18. For a reconstruction of the German doctrinal debate, see Josef Isensee, "Menschenwürde: Die säkulare Gesellschaft auf der Suche nach dem Absoluten," *Archiv des Öffentlichen Rechts* 131 (2006): 175-218.

19. See Ralf Poscher, "Die Würde des Menschen ist unantastbar," *JuristenZeitung* 59 (2004): 756.

as a taboo, which can be neither relativized nor diluted.[20] It can, however (as anthropological studies show), be violated, and such violation can then be followed up with corresponding reparations by the culpable party. We must understand "the rule that does not suffer exceptions" in an analogous way: although it cannot be diluted, it is nevertheless reasonable because, in the face of the theoretical need for its violation, there is no (practical) request to introduce foreseen exceptions to the rule. However, there is an assumption of moral and legal responsibility by the person who, aware that he or she is formally violating the rule and is therefore subject to the sanction, nevertheless follows the moral obligation to violate it.

The intrinsic reasonableness of absolute values enshrined in rules without foreseen exceptions is therefore maintained, as is the coherence between law and morality, each in its proper place and not violated in its ultimate substance. The law conserves its foundation and integrity, while morality, founded on personal conscience and the individual assumption of responsibility, remains protected. Moreover, the existence of an objective sanction, together with the subjective risk of incurring it, ensures both that the occasional violations necessary to exceptional circumstances do not degenerate into a generalized weakening of the value that the rule guarantees and the sanction protects.

In concrete terms, if the torture of a single person really were the only way to save the population from certain catastrophe, the act could be carried out by a single actor whose action, however, is not "allowed" by the rule, and remains subject to scrutiny based on whether or not the state of emergency or state of necessity effectively exists. With no risk of punishment, and therefore with an a priori guarantee of immunity, the risk that degeneration will devalue the principles in play (in this case that of human dignity) ends up outweighing the benefit obtained by loosening the unconditional prohibition. Even the most accurate formulation never succeeds in truly neutralizing the risk of extensive interpretations.

If the situation really is as we have said, there appears to be no contrast between the existence of prohibitions that cannot be derogated and circumstances in which the lawmaker is called to make choices on a rational basis. Therefore, such prohibitions can belong to a legal system — no matter how multicultural — without undermining its coherence. The democratic method

---

20. Representative of the relativist position is Matthias Herdegen's commentary on Art. 1 of the *Grundgesetz;* see Theodor Maunz and Günter Dürig, *Grundgesetz: Kommentar* (Munich: Beck, 2006).

and, at the level of content, the protection of human dignity, are the two pillars that, now more than ever, must be preserved in order to face the difficult situation of postmodern society and the innumerable religious and cultural differences that it hosts.

Conclusion

To make an initial conclusion, we should first acknowledge the fact that the contemporary moment is characterized by two elements in apparently irreducible opposition: that of an epic clash between radically divergent visions,[21] and that of a lively call for dialogue across different cultures.[22] The contrasts are clearly evident regarding regulation of the treatment of human life according to the nature of the human embryo, the management of end-of-life choices, the health and well-being of the population, the concept of the person, and the configuration of the family. The debates center on the great themes of Western philosophy: being and becoming, reason and its struggle for universality, the destiny of humanity, and, therefore, the relationship between the person and both the present and the future.[23]

Law, as a human science, cannot refuse to acknowledge this climate and participate in it, turning back to reflect upon the original impulses that inspired it, on its ontology that is often overlooked but inevitably present. Now is the time to take on the task of making this ontology explicit, asking with seriousness what a human person is, and whether it is possible to protect human dignity while still giving due recognition to human liberty. The arguments outlined above intend to shed light on how the unconditional de-

21. For all see Leon Kass, "Science, Religion, and the Human Future," *Commentary* (2007): 36-48.

22. See Jürgen Habermas and Joseph Ratzinger, *Ragione e fede in dialogo* (Venice: Marsilio, 2005); René Girard and Gianni Vattimo, *Verità o fede debole? Dialogo su Cristianesimo e relativismo* (Pisa: Transeuropa, 2006); and G. Rusconi and A. Scola, *Prove di dialogo, tra fede e ragione* (Bologna: il Mulino, 2006), pp. 369ff.

23. Ronald Dworkin, likewise starting from a debatable position, arrives at the point that "we must hope to find sufficient shared fundamental convictions on equality and individual liberty to establish genuine conversations, and hope that our opinions, which we may also change during the course of those conversations, are contagious. . . . It is not a prospect for tomorrow or the next day, but it is everything we have . . . , it offers an important advantage in the long run: we have the truth on our side." "Cosa sono I diritti umani?" *Ragion pratica* 2 (2007): 480 (our translation).

fense of human dignity by the legal system best expresses the irreducibility of the human person. Human dignity is not just one of many constitutional values to be weighed, but is the very scale in the hand of justice, or, as Gaetano Silvestri recently wrote, "[Justice] is not the effect of balancing, but is the scale itself."[24]

24. Gaetano Silvestri, "Considerazioni sul valore costituzionale della dignità della persona," speech given at the trilateral conference of constitutional courts of Italy, Portugal, and Spain, October 1, 2007, http://archivio.rivistaaic.it/dottrina/libertadiritti/silvestri.html (our translation).

The Abraham Model of Multicultural Integration: *Ger* and *Toshav*

Joseph H. H. Weiler

Of all the narratives in Genesis, chapter 23 seems of minor consequence, almost a breathing space between the fear and trembling of the binding of Isaac that immediately precedes it and the dramatic saga of Isaac, Rebekah, and their progeny that follows. After all, what happens in this chapter? Our matriarch Sarah dies and Abraham makes arrangements for her burial.

And yet it is often in these interstitial passages that the biblical narrative touches upon the most profound issues of the human condition. This would seem to be the case here. In a mere three hundred words,[1] we have a profound evocation of one the most vexed issues to challenge our societies, which has never been more pertinent than in our present circumstance. Let us refresh our memory using the King James Version, which of all English translations best conveys the majestic cadence and archaic gravitas of the original Hebrew, if not always, as we shall see, its actual, literal meaning:

> And Sarah was an hundred and seven and twenty years old: these were the years of the life of Sarah. And Sarah died in Kirjatharba; the same is Hebron in the land of Canaan: and Abraham came to mourn for Sarah, and to weep for her. And Abraham stood up from before his dead, and spake unto the sons of Heth, saying, I am a stranger and a sojourner with you: give me a possession of a buryingplace with you, that I may bury my dead out of my sight. And the children of Heth answered Abraham, saying unto

1. That is, three hundred words in the original Hebrew.

him, Hear us, my lord: thou art a mighty prince among us: in the choice of our sepulchres bury thy dead; none of us shall withhold from thee his sepulchre, but that thou mayest bury thy dead. And Abraham stood up, and bowed himself to the people of the land, even to the children of Heth. And he communed with them, saying, If it be your mind that I should bury my dead out of my sight; hear me, and entreat for me to Ephron the son of Zohar, that he may give me the cave of Machpelah, which he hath, which is in the end of his field; for as much money as it is worth he shall give it me for a possession of a burying place amongst you. And Ephron dwelt among the children of Heth: and Ephron the Hittite answered Abraham in the audience of the children of Heth, even of all that went in at the gate of his city, saying, Nay, my lord, hear me: the field give I thee, and the cave that is therein, I give it thee; in the presence of the sons of my people give I it thee: bury thy dead. And Abraham bowed down himself before the people of the land. And he spake unto Ephron in the audience of the people of the land, saying, But if thou wilt give it, I pray thee, hear me: I will give thee money for the field; take it of me, and I will bury my dead there. And Ephron answered Abraham, saying unto him, My lord, hearken unto me: the land is worth four hundred shekels of silver; what is that betwixt me and thee? bury therefore thy dead. And Abraham hearkened unto Ephron; and Abraham weighed to Ephron the silver, which he had named in the audience of the sons of Heth, four hundred shekels of silver, current money with the merchant. And the field of Ephron which was in Machpelah, which was before Mamre, the field, and the cave which was therein, and all the trees that were in the field, that were in all the borders round about, were made sure unto Abraham for a possession in the presence of the children of Heth, before all that went in at the gate of his city. And after this, Abraham buried Sarah his wife in the cave of the field of Machpelah before Mamre: the same is Hebron in the land of Canaan. And the field, and the cave that is therein, were made sure unto Abraham for a possession of a burying place by the sons of Heth. (Gen. 23:1-20)

I invite the reader to take note of three puzzles in the text, the first lexical and the other two pertaining to narrative.

I am a stranger and a sojourner with you: give me a possession of a burying place with you, that I may bury my dead out of my sight.

I am a "stranger" and a "sojourner" is the King James translation of the Hebrew *ger* and *toshav*. The English Standard Version inverts this order: "I am a sojourner and foreigner." The New King James Version prefers "I am a foreigner and a visitor among you." Meanwhile the New International Version opts for "I am an alien and a stranger among you." None in my view get it quite right.

Translations into other languages do not escape the difficulty with these two words. Thus the Reina-Valera Antigua renders *peregrino y advenedizo,* but its 1995 version chooses *extranjero y forastero.* The Nueva Versión Internacional makes life easy for itself by taking liberty with the text and opting for *Entre ustedes yo soy un extranjero,* as does La Bible du Semeur: *Je ne suis qu'un étranger chez vous.* The Portuguese O Livro is no better: *Como sou estrangeiro aqui nesta terra.* Luther chose *Ich bin ein Fremder und Einwohner bei euch,* but the Elberfelder prefers *Ein Fremder und Beisasse bin ich bei euch.* La Nuova Diodati translates *io sono straniero e avventizio fra voi.* The Vulgate renders *advena sum et peregrinus apud vos,* and the Nova Vulgata *Advena sum et inquilinus apud vos.* The Louis Segond renders *Je suis étranger et habitant parmi vous.*

The difficulty is understandable: the word *ger* in the original Hebrew has shifted its meaning over the centuries, meaning one thing in biblical Hebrew, another in the exilic period, and yet another in today's vernacular. But there is a deeper source of the translators' difficulties: it is simply not clear what our patriarch Abraham had in mind when he said *ger* and *toshav* am I among you; there is a tension between the two terms. *Ger* in its biblical context connotes both the alien and the weak. This is apparent in the Decalogue's Sabbath commandment where the *ger* at the gate is the last and lowest — after the servants and the beasts — for whom the day of rest is mandated. Other famous passages are in Exodus 22:21, "And a *ger* shalt thou not wrong, neither shalt thou oppress him; for ye were *gerim* in the land of Egypt"; Exodus 23:9, "And a *ger* shalt thou not oppress; for ye know the heart of a *ger,* seeing ye were *gerim* in the land of Egypt"; Leviticus 19:33-34, "And if a *ger* sojourn with thee in your land, ye shall not do him wrong. The *ger* that lives with you shall be unto you as the homeborn among you."

It seems clear from these contexts that the principal quality of the *ger* is that he or she is an alien, a stranger, and not an integral part of the dominant culture. But now the difficulty: it also seems a quality of the *ger,* the alien, the stranger, that he is in fact living within a dominant culture — he is not a person of passage. And yet that is exactly the meaning of the second word that Abraham uses: *toshav.* Here the Louis Segond *habitant* or Luther's *Einwohner* seem to capture best the original Hebrew. But if the very word *ger* already captures the situation of the stranger who resides permanently with the dominant culture, what is Abraham trying to convey to his interlocutors with the addition of the word *toshav*?[2]

The narrative also has its difficulties. Consider first the following:

> And the children of Heth answered Abraham, saying unto him, Hear us, my lord: thou art a mighty prince among us: in the choice of our sepulchres bury thy dead; none of us shall withhold from thee his sepulchre, but that thou mayest bury thy dead. And Abraham stood up, and bowed himself to the people of the land, even to the children of Heth. And he communed with them, saying, If it be your mind that I should bury my dead out of my sight; hear me, and intreat for me to Ephron the son of Zohar, that he may give me the cave of Machpelah, which he hath, which is in the end of his field; for as much money as it is worth he shall give it me for a possession of a burying place amongst you.

Why does Abraham turn down their generous offer? Consider further:

> And Ephron dwelt among the children of Heth: and Ephron the Hittite answered Abraham in the audience of the children of Heth, even of all that went in at the gate of his city, saying, Nay, my lord, hear me: the field give I thee, and the cave that is therein, I give it thee; in the presence of the sons of my people give I it thee: bury thy dead. And Abraham bowed down himself before the people of the land. And he spake unto Ephron in the audience of the people of the land, saying, But if thou wilt give it, I pray thee, hear me: I will give thee money for the field; take it of me, and I will bury my dead there. And Ephron answered Abraham, saying unto him, My lord, hearken unto me: the land is worth four hundred shekels of silver; what is that betwixt me and thee? Bury therefore thy dead. And Abraham hearkened unto Ephron; and Abraham weighed to Ephron the silver, which he had named in the audience of the sons of Heth, four hundred shekels of silver, current money with the merchant. And the field of Ephron which was in Machpelah, which was before Mamre, the field, and the cave which was therein, and all the trees that were in the field, that were in all the borders round about, were made sure unto Abraham for a

---

2. It is true that the word *ger* alone would seem to capture the dual nature of the situation, but this does not excuse the sloppiness of those translations that simply render *ger* and *toshav* as "stranger," since that single word does not itself capture the duality.

possession in the presence of the children of Heth, before all that went in at the gate of his city.

Again, why does Abraham turn down this second generous offer? Commentators over the ages have addressed these questions. Three themes dominate the commentary. The first is one of human dignity: Who wants acts of charity? Abraham is meticulously polite, almost obsequious, but insists as a matter of dignity that he pay for the asset. The second is one of legal efficiency: What if later relations sour and the donor repents his gift? Will a land transaction for which there was no consideration stand up to such a subsequent challenge? What about his descendants and the descendants of the donors — will the transaction survive the original parties? Better, it is argued, to commercialize the transaction and solemnize it with all due process so as to guarantee as far as possible its irreversibility and legal finality. The third theme is anthropological: the initial offer of the children of Heth and then of Ephron was just *pro forma,* a cultural custom whereby the good is offered as a gift with the expectation that the offer will be rejected and then the real negotiation begin. There is support for this in the fact that both the children of Heth and Ephron make the same gesture.

All these lines of interpretation are plausible. We should remember that with a text such as the Bible, it is rare that one interpretation is exclusive and equally rare that multiple interpretations are mutually exclusive.

One weakness of the interpretations offered above is the fact that they do not do justice to Abraham's opening gambit: *ger* and *toshav* am I among you: stranger and habitant am I among you. It is this very line that captures one of the deep meanings that this narrative conveys, a meaning that makes this narrative ever relevant.

It seems to me that both in his opening words and in his comportment in the subsequent negotiations, Abraham is trying to convey a complex message as to his situation. Textually, what is critical is that Abraham does not simply say, "Give me a possession of a burying place with you, that I may bury my dead out of my sight." He does not say, "*I am Abraham;* give me a possession of a burying place with you, that I may bury my dead out of my sight. He says instead: "*I am a stranger and a sojourner with you:* give me a possession of a burying place with you, that I may bury my dead out of my sight." He is not of passage; he is not a *Gastarbeiter.* I am a habitant, he claims, a *toshav* — I am here to stay; please accept me as such. And yet at the very same time he says: I am a *ger.* An alien. I am different, and I want to maintain my difference. I am of you, I want to be of you, but at the same time

I want to maintain my difference. It is a radical position — for it envisages a redefinition of the social and the political by which, to use the Bible's own terms, the *ger* can be a *toshav*.

The children of Heth respond to the Abrahamic challenge:

> Hear us, my lord: thou art a mighty prince among us: in the choice of our sepulchres bury thy dead; none of us shall withhold from thee his sepulchre, but that thou mayest bury thy dead.

They clearly do not grasp the situation correctly. Their response is a generous act of charity, but it would situate Abraham as a tourist, a person of passage who is in need of a burial place and is offered such a burial place but, notably, in the sepulcher of someone else: "None of us shall withhold from thee *his* sepulchre." A person of passage would neither need, nor wish to have, a permanent sepulcher. But for someone who is there to stay, having one's own sepulcher is exactly one of the hallmarks of permanence and integration. Moreover, the gesture of the children of Heth is not one that would have been extended towards an equal. Such an offer would not have been made in the normal course of business among themselves. Not only in a temporal sense but also in a hierarchical sense, acceptance would have become a sign of inequality, inferiority. Thus Abraham rejects the kind offer.

And Ephron?

> Nay, my lord, hear me: the field give I thee, and the cave that is therein, I give it thee; in the presence of the sons of my people give I it thee: bury thy dead.

Abraham in this case will have his own sepulcher and more: both the field and the cave. It is somewhat difficult to explain his rejection this time by the "legal certainty" theory. Ephron's offer is, after all, both public and formal: "In the presence of the sons of my people give I it thee." It is not simply the dignity of not wishing charity that prompts Abraham's rejection. Ephron's gesture is of the kind that one makes to a son, to a family member. It is an invitation to Abraham to join that clan; to become one of them. Accepting the gift would not only indebt him to Ephron in a material sense. It would symbolize forsaking his independent identity.

Both in its lexical dimension and its key narrative moments, the story represents the timeless challenge of social mobility, identity and integration. Abraham is not simply a *ger*, a stranger — he *wants* to maintain that separate identity. At the same time he does not merely or only want to be a stranger.

117

He wants to become a *toshav,* a resident, a permanent part of the community.

It is always dangerous to read the biblical tales normatively. Their timelessness rests in the fact that they are an invitation to reflect and ask questions rather than a source of definitive answers. And yet, one can speak of the "Abraham model" of immigration — a model that has frequently been used by his nomadic descendants, the Jews, in their long exilic experience. Jews, when allowed to, have often tried to prove what may at first be considered impossible: the ability to be model citizens in their new communities while maintaining their distinct identity. The history of the Jews in modern, postemancipation Europe has typically followed Abraham's model: Jews have embraced their new national identities — in Germany, France, Italy, and the UK — and have thrown themselves into all aspects of their new polities (often being resented just for that). They have harbored a dual aspiration for their children: to be fully French, German, or Italian and yet to maintain their distinct Jewishness — burying their dead in their own sepulchers. World War I is a high point of this model: consider its complexity, glory, and disappointments, reflected in the oeuvre of Joseph Roth, notably *The Radetzky March.* Abraham's is still, in my view, the most attractive model for Europe's current multicultural challenge.

PART III

THE RECOGNITION OF GOD
AS THE ULTIMATE GROUND

Church, Modernity, and Multiculturalism: An Extemporaneous Reflection

Francisco Javier Martínez Fernández

In this brief essay I would like to propose the following idea (albeit in a simplified and therefore necessarily inadequate way): a Church that understands itself and reality through the prevailing categories of secular modernity (whether in their postmodern or Enlightenment form, or merely constituted as reactions to either of these) is doomed to disappear.[1] Or at any rate, it will undergo such a metamorphosis that its continuity with "historical" Christianity would be broken (indeed, it has in part already been broken). By "historical" Christianity I mean the sacred Tradition that originated with the incarnation of the Word, as recounted by the New Testament and Church Fathers, and which is also found in the living magisterium of the Church. Moreover, a Church that uses secular categories is incapable of having a productive and sincere encounter with people of other religious and cultural traditions. To the extent that it adapts itself to the categories of secular mo-

---

1. The brevity of this essay does not allow me to refer to the sources of my thought. They are so numerous that I do not consider these ideas to be mine in any "intellectual property" sense. I would like to be able to say that they simply belong to the Christian tradition that they hope to serve, without in any sense owning this tradition. In any case, I would like above all to recognize my enormous debt to the work of Henri de Lubac and Hans Urs von Balthasar. More specifically, on the topic of the relationship between Christianity and the tradition of modernity, or other traditions, I am indebted to the thought of Alasdair MacIntyre and the theology of Stanley Hauerwas and John Milbank. For some of the thoughts expressed here I am also particularly indebted to Gavin D'Costa's work *The Meeting of Religions and the Trinity* (Maryknoll, NY: Orbis Books, 2000) and to various works by D. Stephen Long and William T. Cavanaugh.

dernity, it takes on the precise role that modernity assigns to it; insofar as it embraces this role, the Church can only dissolve, or else be an instrument of violence and division. In order to meet every man and every woman in a way that allows all of us — Christians and non-Christians — to grow in our common humanity, the Church must free itself from the categories of modernity and recover its identity from within its own particular Tradition.

The Church and Culture

The Church is influenced by the culture in which it lives. This assertion does not imply any dualism, as though the Church were a pure "being" in and of itself, more or less contaminated by history and culture conceived as elements external to it.[2] The Church only exists in concrete cultural forms, on which the encounter with Christ — which from the beginning has always occurred in a concrete cultural form — has had varying degrees of impact. This encounter can be the determining factor of the human experience, or it can remain merely a partial or marginal aspect thereof. The task of Christian education consists entirely in helping people pass from the latter condition to the former. For people in the latter situation, the categories determining Christian life continue to be those of the surrounding culture. And those categories will influence and weigh on the thought of individuals and peoples depending on how decisive the encounter with the Risen and Living Christ, Center and Lord of the cosmos and of history, has been in determining their self-awareness and awareness of reality.

The Church has always lived with this tension. Christ's disciples were Jews, more or less influenced by Hellenistic culture, and they expressed their experience within that context. But for centuries afterward, the Church had to deal with the serious issues that arose from its spreading within the Hellenistic world, and, from very early on, even to the towns located on the outskirts or beyond the borders of that world. This situation has been repeated every time the Church has come into contact with other cultures over the course of history. In each of these encounters, the tension between cultural categories and the encounter with Christ has manifested itself in a unique and unrepeatable way that can only be understood empirically.

---

2. This dualism is often found in rather inappropriate expressions, such as "dialogue between faith and culture" (as if faith could exist at all outside of a historical and contingent cultural expression), or in the confused discussion on the "inculturation" of faith.

Modernity and Postmodernity: Two Variations

How is this tension expressed in our time? Today, as a result of the wide-spread dissemination of the Enlightenment, the dominant culture (of the West, at least) has two basic variations: the modern, which is increasingly just official rhetoric, but which does continue to have a certain amount of influence (and for this reason continues to be invoked in certain contexts); and the postmodern, which is, on the one hand, the rejection of Enlightenment modernity — or the disenchantment resulting from its unfulfilled promises — and, on the other hand, the intensification thereof. The true culture of our countries tends to be an amalgam of heterogeneous elements of these two variations, mixed together in varying proportions, depending on the case. And if it is true, as MacIntyre and others have convincingly argued, that the Enlightenment inevitably leads to nihilism, then it is also true that often the reaction against the vertigo brought on by the nihilist deconstruction of all desire for moral or intellectual coherence is nothing more than a return to the Enlightenment. This creates a strange, vicious cycle, making it very difficult to escape the complicated place in which we find ourselves, or even to imagine a true alternative.

The greatest difference between modernity and postmodernity as they concern Christianity is that the residually Christian environment in which Kant and Hegel lived allowed them to continue thinking that Christianity was the highest possible form of humanity, and that its "essence" could still be — and perhaps had to be — saved for modern man. Modern man, how-ever, because he was able to behave ethically by simply following the dictates of "pure reason," lacked any "supernatural" attachments. He could also re-interpret Christian dogma symbolically. But for the postmodern man, Christianity — if he thinks about it at all — is nothing more than one supermarket product (and not even necessarily from the religious supermarket) among many, no more or less interesting than all the others.

Leaving the distinction between modern and postmodern cultures aside — though I do not claim that it is unimportant — the view of Christianity is fundamentally the same in both variations of secular culture: Christianity is a subset of the "religion" category, and this fact clearly sets it apart from other spheres of human activity such as rational knowledge, work and art, the economy, ethics, and politics. Because it is "religion," it is assigned cer-tain characteristics so that it will fit into the term's preexisting, modern defi-nition: religion is, above all, a set of beliefs that are not rationally verifiable, and are therefore designated "religious sentiment" and assigned to the irrational realm of preference. They must remain tokens of a past culture fit only for a museum, or they must be contained within the private sphere. Because these beliefs are irrational and rigidly separated from the other spheres of human activity, they may not be guidelines for anything "real" that has social significance or value — whether politics, economics, or family life. In general, these beliefs are depicted in fixed ritual expressions established by tradition and are often used as the foundation for specific ethical codes. An ethical code will be "tolerated" as long as its members live it as a free, private choice: that is, as long as it is not imposed by any person or institution, and as long as it cannot interfere with other beliefs and other ethical systems. If religion and the ethical code derived from it sought to emerge from the strictly private realm or the realm of folklore, they would become sources of violence. The mission and duty of preventing this violence falls to the state, the supreme protector and guarantor of individual liberties and the common good.

With regard to religious beliefs themselves, there are two possibilities: either they are granted no value (beyond that of a nice museum piece), or, if they are granted some value, it is only as a pretext for or symbolic expression of something else, generally of some "ethical principles" that would be just as accessible to those who do not hold such beliefs. In this way, for example, Christian dogma, beginning with faith in the Holy Trinity and in Jesus Christ as the Incarnate Son of God, must be pushed aside as a contingent human construction. In order to fit into this framework, the New Testament must be reinterpreted in an attempt to explain how "the Christ of faith" came about from something that, in reality, did not originally contain such a concept. Of course, Jesus' resurrection and his virgin birth are either kept quiet, or the question of their truth is camouflaged by clever or not-so-clever wordplay. Curiously, and as others have noted, the "historical Jesus" that we are offered in exchange is usually entirely anachronistic and not at all "historical," and his existence seems to be determined by categories that, under rigorous scrutiny, turn out to be decidedly modern.

For Christians, therefore, accepting the theological premises of the Enlightenment means renouncing a strong Christology and ecclesiology, and usually a strong theology as well. It means, moreover, subordinating theology to ethics, and more specifically, to the ethical ideas specific to secular modernity. God's existence can be acknowledged or denied, but when it is acknowledged, this God is certainly not the God of the religious traditions descended from Abraham, and of course is not the God of the Christian experience. Rather, this God is either the "watchmaker" god of modern deism, which is an idea so intellectually weak (e.g., with regard to the problems of evil and suffering) that it inevitably cancels itself out, or a more or less disguised version of cosmic pantheism, or even of that ancient polytheism that predated the emergence of Greek philosophy and Jewish monotheism (and that, e.g., attributes special "positive energy" to places and things).

As a result, in the dominant secular culture (naturally much less of a single entity than the term would imply), the Church does not have a space that can be recognized as deriving from its own Tradition. Secular modernity has room for only two absolutes (two religious elements, we might say, in the specifically modern sense of the word "religion"), both of which it created and are therefore largely considered legitimate even without justification: the individual, made up of his or her rights and freedoms, and the various forms of the state-market duality. These various forms have been the subject of the bloodiest and most abject struggles and wars in history, but the state and the market cooperate ever more closely to define and regulate individuals' rights and freedoms. Everything that is not part of these two entities must be either reduced to them or integrated within them. In every culture and religion, "tolerance" — a key concept for modern society — has an insurmountable limit: it must adopt as its starting point the coordinates established by secular society. Take, for example, so-called civil society, which, because of the extraordinary complexity of contemporary life and its security needs, is ever more thoroughly absorbed into the institutional state. The same thing occurs with so-called intermediate institutions; not by accident does the very term "intermediate" define the relationship of these institutions with the two modern absolutes, the individual and the state.

Given the assumptions of secular, modern society, the Church is left with two fundamental possibilities, which are not mutually exclusive, and which can be combined in different ways and to varying degrees. Either the Church accepts its role as a cultural leftover from the past, or it must dissolve into the surrounding society. The former means transforming into an optional collection of individuals who share certain beliefs, rites, moral rules, and tastes concerning one aspect of life that remains separate from the other aspects and is called "religious." The latter road leads before long to the disappearance of any identifiable Christian social reality, or at least of any Christian reality that can be identified with its own Tradition.

Toward a Solution

Let's suppose that some people are aware of these dangers — the two possibilities I just described — and wish to address them. This is not uncommon. Nevertheless, unless they have experienced something different, and are therefore able to make a lucid intellectual judgment about the root of the conflict between the Church and modernity, their proposed "recovery" will fail to escape the parameters of modernity and will remain merely superficial. This is because their response will be made according to those same parameters, meaning that, on the one hand, the Church will continue to see its own faith as a closed system of abstract truths that only pertain to one particular aspect of life (that which is understood as "religious" or "supernatural"). On the other hand, in its temporal development, the Church will increasingly adopt organizational structures that are based upon the two forms of modern secular power: that of the state, and that of business.

The temptation is more common and insidious than it might seem to be. The problem is not that the Church understands itself as a state or as a political party. These options are ruled out a priori, although both have occurred over the course of history and do still continue to occur today, if only residually. With regard to this pole of the state-market duality, it would be easiest for the Church to seek to position itself in the shadow of some ideology or party within the array of possibilities in contemporary politics, or to position itself as just another lobby within this array. In this way it would seek to secure for itself some share of secular and worldly power, or at least the protection of or some influence over this power. Spain's experience with this was disastrous, and I am not convinced that we have learned our lesson. The tendency to identify with the market pole is, however, altogether more evident: here, the Church or the various ecclesial bodies move toward understanding themselves as businesses that develop or produce certain wares (religious, moral, cultural, or educational) required and demanded by society. The state itself may also tend to see the Church this way.

The danger lies above all in accepting a way of relating to reality that ends up generating within the Church, almost unconsciously, a particular way of understanding itself. In its well-intentioned effort to gain "relevance" in the modern world, the Church in reality runs the risk (both in its relationship to the world and in its internal life) of increasingly taking on the ways of operating and organizing, the methods and procedures, and the deep underlying logic that characterize the market and the state in present-day society. This underlying logic is instrumental logic: it is a bureaucratic logic that replaces goodwill toward others with compliance with formal, established requirements. It is a manipulative logic that asserts self-interest as the supreme criterion of the rationality of human relationships. In this view, the "other" can only be seen as an adversary, an object to be conquered — even if this conquest is simply intellectual or moral (which can be the most disgraceful) — and therefore as a potential subject, voter, or client. And to make him one of these, he is seen as a target for advertising.[3] To resort to this instrumental logic — which is at the heart of modern anthropology, and which derives from the idea of the "self" and the "freedom of the self" as absolutes — is to go against the logic that derives from the event of Christ. The turn to instrumental logic leads to the inevitable rejection of the Christian faith, as well as the (justifiable) critique of a religion so conceived. There are many signs that this logic is more or less infiltrating the Church, and this infiltration can be seen in the institutional structures of both the apostolic ministry and the so-called charisms. An obvious sign of this infiltration can be observed when concern for securing a space in the public life of secular society takes precedence over the concern for understanding what it is to be Christian and to live better as Christians, with eyes fixed on Christ and on the sacred Tradition. This kind of reaction "against" the disappearance of the Church into the ideologies of modernity is as troubling as the disappearance itself: in reality, it is just another form, perhaps the most subtle, of that disappearance.

It would be interesting to demonstrate how certain developments in Christian theology over the course of modernity, in particular those dealing with the understanding of the "mystery of the supernatural" and its implications for the Church's relationship with the world, have affected the issues we are discussing. It would also be interesting to see how certain communal categories of the Tradition recovered for the Church by the Second Vatican Council, like that of the "People of God" and particularly that of the "Body of Christ," have failed to become a part of the common experience and vocabulary of the Christian population, and to try to understand why this is

---

3. A relatively impartial observer could not help but note that this description of instrumental logic corresponds quite closely to an attitude frequently held by Muslims toward Europe, or toward non-Muslims in general. And the observer would also note that, while the policies of secularism would not tolerate, or would harshly criticize, the smallest indication of this kind of attitude in Christians, their benevolence toward the same logic in Islam is almost without limits. Aside from fear and cowardice, which undoubtedly play a role here, this policy bias clearly makes evident the awareness that Christianity has a capacity to accept rational criticism that Islam lacks.

so. But that is not possible here. What I feel is most important to underline here is simply that instrumental logic, which is inseparable from modern anthropology, inevitably transforms every person and every social reality into a source of violence. Above all I would like to stress that the Church itself would risk becoming such a source, or would simply be one, if it fully assumed the categories of modernity, because in these categories there are no "neighbors," but only competitors for territory or market share. Competitors or slaves.

In the mythology of modernity, the dubious distinction of being a cause of violence and division is primarily attributed to religions. The essentially violent nature of religion is an indisputable dogma of faith for the common man of today. The reason regularly put forth to justify this position (aside from certain references to ancient or recent history) is that the assertion of an Absolute (God), of nonnegotiable moral principles, or of practices that derive from belief in God necessarily leads to violence. Surely there is no social reality or human being that is not exposed to violence, is not itself a cause of violence, or that does not allow itself to be swept away by violence. Without a doubt, this applies to what today in general we call religions, as well as to the Church. However, the falsity of this modern dogma can be shown in several fundamental points.

In the first place, there is the insurmountable difficulty of defining the concept of religion with any degree of precision using only modern logic. In the second place, witness modernity's absolute silence concerning the incommensurability of traditions and cultures, which we must always try to understand and value in light of their empirical, historical materialization. The modern dogma substitutes this knowledge with abstract descriptions that unjustifiably assimilate them (a typical example is the use of the phrase, "the three monotheistic religions"). In the third place, the falsity of this dogma is revealed by modern man's inability to imagine and conceive of an Absolute different from the modern Absolute, the latter of which must always present itself as a power opposed to all otherness, including that of creation itself. The Christian Absolute, for example, the God who is the communion of the Father, Son, and Holy Spirit — the God who reveals himself as "Love" because the Son became man "for us men and for our salvation," making us participants in the divine life through the gift of the Holy Spirit — has nothing to do with modernity's conception of the Absolute. Lastly, the dogma of religious violence serves to hide the fact that the two truly religious institutions in the contemporary world ("religious" in the modern sense of the term) — the modern market and state — precisely because they are idolatrous, have since their inception provoked a violence that is both constant and unequalled in recorded history. These institutions have sacrificed, and continue to sacrifice, millions of men, women, and children to their interests — loudly in wartime and silently in a thousand other ways, such as, for example, through the systematic and iniquitous destruction of marriage and the family — just as they tend to sacrifice any institution or group of people that seeks to be free and is not willing to serve those interests.

In the same vein, and even if we appear to be taking a momentary detour from the ideas under discussion, it is interesting to note that — even though Islam has been both an empire and a "religion" from its earliest days, and therefore has always been spread through the use of force — the particular brand of Islam that has sprung up in the twentieth century (commonly called "radical" or "fundamentalist") is more a combination of Enlightenment secularist political ideas and the contemporary world's enormous means of power than it is a simple offshoot of traditional Islam.[4] An adequate empirical knowledge of Islam and its evolution in the contemporary world should suffice to dismantle yet another false assertion of modern mythology: that is, that Islam must accept the Enlightenment in order for a moderate Islam to exist.

Rediscovering Our Identity

Perhaps mentioning Islam in this context is not in vain. It is possible that Islam's stubborn resistance to the assimilation of Enlightenment categories provides an opportunity for Western Christians to reflect in a new way on the social aspects of Christian dogma and on the corporeal nature of the Church. It may provide, further, an opportunity to take stock of our paralysis before the challenges of secular modernity, and of how deeply this secular modernity has taken hold of our minds.

I do not mean to insinuate that the Church should imitate Islam's way of binding the religious community with the political one. But I do wish to

---

4. See John Gray's fascinating book *Al Qaeda and What It Means to Be Modern* (New York: New Press, 2003). And although they come from very different points of view, two other recent books that connect the most troubling developments of present-day Islam to modernity are Paul Berman, *Terror and Liberalism* (New York: W. W. Norton, 2004); and Ian Buruma and Avishai Margalit, *Occidentalism: The West in the Eyes of Its Enemies* (New York: Penguin, 2004).

say that the circumstances in which Divine Providence has placed us invite us to rediscover our Christian identity beyond the problematic modern scenario. Only to the extent that the Church recovers its center outside of this scenario will it be able to truly meet men and women of all traditions with respect and affection, in a way that is distinctively its own and that it can learn only from its Master. In other words, and no matter how paradoxical it may seem, if the Church wishes to be an instrument of peace and coexistence in the melting pot of cultures in which we live, it must relearn to be itself; only to the extent that it is itself will it be able to withstand the pressure to fit into the social and conceptual machine of the modern, secular world.

To relearn to be itself, to relearn to be Christians: in the Christian tradition this movement is called conversion. And conversion is always a grace that must be desired and requested. Even this desire itself is a gift of God, since no one can desire what he has not been given to see, at least in some way.

But this conversion entails certain intellectual tasks that the Church cannot avoid, and that we can only partly explain here. First, the Church must relearn to measure itself more by its own Tradition than by the categories of the contemporary world, of which, in any case, it is already a part. And perhaps in order to do so the Church must be willing to recognize where the Tradition is still alive, to rediscover it, to listen to its code of conduct and suggestions, and to consent to be surprised by it. Out of its experience, therefore, the Church could make an intelligent critique of secular society and could recover its theological tradition, beginning with a strong Christology and ecclesiology. Faith in the Trinity, above all, is charged with meaning for the capacity to love and to welcome what is "different" — multiplicity — as a positive, without this entailing the negation or destruction of unity. Lastly, it is crucial to recover the category of sacrament as a central Christian category, not only for the Christian faith, but also for ontology, so that the instrumental logic described above can be replaced with what we could call a "sacramental logic." This substitution must occur in the relationships between the various members of the Church, and in the Church's relationship with all human beings, with all of creation. Indeed, everything is a sign of Christ, and "in Him all things hold together." Furthermore, everyone is someone whom Christ has loved unto death. This implies that the idea of the supreme rationality of "interest" must be replaced with that of the supreme rationality of "gratuitousness."

In being true to itself, in public and in private, and in any and all circumstances, the Church will be constantly exposed to the historical verification of its life as the testimony to a fulfilled humanity. Indeed, this is the definitive test of every tradition, recognizable by all, whatever their religious or cultural background. The testimony of the true God, accessible to all, is the testimony of a humanity that does not need to censor any part of its makeup as rational and free, as desiring truth, beauty, and goodness. It is the testimony to the fulfillment, as grace, of that humanity.

Only this testimony will allow the Church to show that some of the most authentically human ideals of Enlightenment modernity have been realized in the Church's historical "flesh" and not in a utopia (although the Church could in no way bring about this modernity). These ideals include the unreserved recognition of the value and meaning of reason and freedom, and the hope for a limitless communion — one that does not stifle differences — in our common humanity.

Interculturality and Christian Mission in Today's Society

Massimo Borghesi

An adequate understanding of the relationship between Christianity and cultural processes requires revisiting the history of that relationship as it has unfolded over the course of the last decades. This will allow us to overcome a kind of habitual abstraction in dealing with this issue, and at the same time to point out the extent to which ideology has, over the last forty years, settled into both the concept of culture and that of the Christian "mission" in the world.

Multiculturalism: Scrutinizing Two Models

Between the late 1950s and early 1960s, Europe hosted a lively debate on "decolonization." Marked by the writings of Frantz Fanon (*Les damnés de la terre,* 1961) and Claude Lévi-Strauss (*Race et histoire,* 1952; *Tristes tropiques,* 1955), the *querelle* between Western and "other" cultures took the form of criticism of the anthropological-cultural primacy of the West.[1] Decolonization was accompanied by a rediscovery and validation of indigenous traditional cultures, of membership in an ethnicity, of the difference between "whites" and "non-whites." Between the late 1960s and early 1970s, the process of differentiation became radicalized in the encounter with Marxism. The critique of the West turned sour. The *internal* protest that grew up in

---

1. See Massimo Borghesi, "L'Occidente e l''altro': Tra estraneità e integrazione," *Il Nuovo Areopago* 2 (2001): 81-96.

European and American universities provided concepts for delegitimizing the Western, capitalist, and imperialist model, perceived as the outcome of an arrogant humanism that presumed to standardize and unite the world under itself. Breaking up this pseudo-unity was a stage in that process that, in a revolutionary light, saw the subaltern cultures of Africa and Latin America rise to be factors of global class struggle. The culture of the 1970s was permeated by the effort to differentiate itself from the universalist, Christian-Enlightenment cultures that had marked the postwar reconstruction period after 1945 — a period characterized by the primacy of the person, which was ratified by the Universal Declaration of Human Rights. From feminism, to homosexuality, to the Afro-American culture of Malcolm X, to the demands of indigenous culture in the Latin American world of the 1980s and 1990s, to the radical Islam of the 1990s and into the third millennium, the opposition to Western unification led, as a result, to an un-unifiable multiculturalism.[2] It is both an internal multiculturalism and an external one, which, in the case of Islam, takes the shape not of particularism, but of a universalism that opposes the "Christian" universalism.

With this movement to delegitimize the West, culture became a tool of conflict, the assertion of a dialectical, antagonistic identity that pitted itself against the seduction of "integration" offered by "the system." Every "tribe" celebrated its own negative identity, its irreducible otherness, its being *outside* social laws and conventions. The multiculturalism of the 1970s, masked in part by the universalism of Marxist doctrine, was a story of rejection of the West.

Marx, Nietzsche, and Freud, the "masters of suspicion," were, together with Heidegger, the authors of the crisis of the "sunset of the West." This sunset had to do with humanism, the centrality of the individual person, and, with it, Christianity. Thus multiculturalism's protest against the West also implicated the Christian model. It protested the Christian mission in the world, in "underdeveloped" countries, a presence that, in the modern era, would have accompanied and sanctioned both imperialism and colonization. The history of Christian mission came to be reread, negatively, as part of a broader history of oppression, of violent uprooting of indigenous cultures, of intolerant mentalities. Rigorously unsaid was the aspect of lib-

2. This incompatibility has to do not only with the identities of those who believe themselves to be oppressed, but also, as is the case with xenophobic movements, with the identity of the oppressors as well. On the apartheid and the South African transition during the 1980s and 1990s see *Il Nuovo Areopago* 2 (2001), dedicated to the theme "Multiculturalismo: Il caso Sudafrica."

eralization, of solidarity, and of consensus that the Christian missions have represented in the history of oppression of peoples.

The picture we have briefly outlined underwent changes starting in the 1980s and 1990s. With the decline of Marxism between 1989 and 1991, the conflictual aspect that multiculturalism had assumed gave way to a "polyphonic" vision, to the idea of a "cultural blend" — a blend of race-religion-ideology by which the world seemed to be a point of convergence for a multiplicity of diverse voices. This was a vision that fed as much upon the globalization scenarios that accompanied the period following 1989 as it did upon the New Age mysticism that defined the 1990s. This was because the New Age movement, which was at the doors, operates under the banner of spiritual unification, peace, and harmony. On this view, the world moves toward a holistic perspective, toward a "uni-totality," in which the distinctions that inform our cultural tradition — human/divine, body/soul, spirit/matter, man/woman, good/evil, West/East — are overcome.

The New Age finds an ally in postmodern thought, according to which, after the sunset of ideologies and the end of the strong truths of metaphysics and religion, the world can arrive at an era of tolerance and peace. In order to achieve this, it is enough to dissolve the conflictual aspect of multiculturalism, depriving identities of their dialectical pathos.[3] If there are no "truths," if monotheism is totalitarian, there is space left only for a soft polytheism, fluffy and "aesthetic." The aesthetic society is a world without conflicts, that is, without truth. Its shape is given by "virtuality," by a lightening of reality, by getting past the "letter" of every sacred text. In the hermeneutic space of "spiritual" interpretation, diversities dissolve; they are reassembled in new shapes. Life becomes metamorphosis, the continuous testing of changeable faces. Diversity, like the veil of maya, is the appearance of a river that knows no borders.

September 2001: Return to the "Clash of Civilizations"

The transition from the 1970s to the 1990s, from a conflictual multiculturalism to one that was soft and iridescent, was destined to change again after

---

3. The American philosopher Richard Rorty offers an interesting example of this perspective in his critical dialogue with the Indian scholar Anindita N. Balslev. See the latter's *Cultural Otherness: Correspondence with Richard Rorty* (Shimla: Indian Institute of Advanced Study, 1991).

September 11, 2001. The collapse of the Twin Towers in New York City represented the return to the conflictual vision of cultures — a return for the West, not in general. It cannot be said that radical Islam, which grew up in the war against the USSR in Afghanistan, Chechnya, and what was formerly Yugoslavia, had fallen asleep in the rancor resulting from the first war in Iraq. It was simply not of concern to the Western world, dominated as the West was by dreams of globalization. After 9/11, however, the world seemed once again divided, marred by conflict and war. The rediscovery of Islam in an anti-Western role led to the "clash of cultures" so astutely diagnosed by Samuel Huntington in his 1996 book *The Clash of Civilizations and the Remaking of World Order.* Huntington's book overturned the thesis expressed by Francis Fukuyama in his 1992 book *The End of History and the Last Man,* which surmised that after 1989 the world had launched itself toward the end of conflict, toward a progressive homologation according to the Western economic, legal, and political model. The data disproved this theory, and for Huntington it became evident that the planet was propelling itself not toward a "one-dimensional" world, but toward a pluralism of positions with competing and incompatible ideals.

The end of Marxism did not mark the advent of a "new world order" led by the West, but the rise of countries with ancient cultural traditions (China, India, Japan), which had been hidden by the global clash between East and West and were now returned to the foreground.[4] This return was favored by the economic development of states and nations that had previously been far underdeveloped. Wealth, according to Huntington, brings with it self-esteem, the proud affirmation of one's own identity and roots. In this way, economic globalization, far from ushering in a unified world, instead favors the rediscovery of those cultures eclipsed by the worldwide success of the West. It is a matter of truly historical civilizations, namely, the Chinese-Confucian, Japanese, Hindu, Islamic, Western, and Latin American.

Despite being marked by Christianity, the West, which includes Europe,

---

4. This return to particular "roots," traditions, and attachments is also *internal* to the West. See the case of Quebec's autonomy in Canada, which is the focus of Charles Taylor's essay "The Politics of Recognition," in *Multiculturalism and "The Politics of Recognition": An Essay,* ed. Amy Gutmann (Princeton, NJ: Princeton University Press, 1992), pp. 25-73. This text has been collected, along with Jürgen Habermas's *Kampf um Anerkennung im demokratischen Rechtsstaat* (Frankfurt: Suhrkamp, 1996), in the Italian volume *Multiculturalismo: Lotte per il riconoscimento* (Milan: Feltrinelli, 2002). Cases analogous to that of Quebec include those of the Basque countries and Catalonia.

North America, Australia, and New Zealand, includes for Huntington neither South America nor Eastern Europe, which is permeated by Orthodox Christianity. Huntington has a tendency, that is, to define the Western sphere by the scope of Christianity of Protestant imprint, a Christianity that receives a Catholic imprint in the degree to which it has passed through an adequate process of secularization. Thus, after the fall of the Iron Curtain, new, invisible barriers were to mark the boundaries between states and nations. In the sunset of ideologies, the world that emerges appears dominated by the clash between "civilizations." But this clash is not what Huntington actually hopes for. Contrary to those (and they are many) who continue to cite his work as an example of a position that favors a climate of war, it should be pointed out that the author's concern, starting from a pessimistic view of the present, is that of one who warns against positions that could directly or indirectly lead from a latent clash to a declared one. For Huntington, "Western belief in the universality of Western culture suffers three problems: it is false; it is immoral; and it is dangerous."[5] It is false because it is not true that the world is westernizing. It is immoral because "imperialism is the necessary logical consequence of universalism. . . . As Asian and Muslim civilizations begin more and more to assert the universal relevance of their cultures, Westerners will come to appreciate more and more the connection between universalism and imperialism."[6] Third, "Western universalism is dangerous to the world because it could lead to a major intercivilizational war between core states and it is dangerous to the West because it could lead to the defeat of the West."[7]

Huntington's position becomes clearer in its unique characteristics. Attentive to a global framework in which U.S. hegemony is in decline, a framework marked by an equilibrium between powers-civilizations, the author shares the perspective of multiculturalism without accepting either the dialectical version of the 1970s or the postmodern one of the 1990s. Civilizations are incompatible "closed worlds," and precisely for this reason it is necessary to limit their dialectic as much as possible. While a relativist regarding what is external, Huntington is not one with respect to what is internal. In order to remain cohesive, each civilization has to maintain a certain uniformity, to oppose the multiculturalism that leads to its disintegration.

5. Samuel Huntington, *The Clash of Civilizations and the Remaking of World Order* (New York: Simon & Schuster, 1996), p. 310.

6. Huntington, *Clash of Civilizations*, p. 310.

7. Huntington, *Clash of Civilizations*, p. 311.

"Multiculturalism at home threatens the United States and the West; universalism abroad threatens the West and the world."[8] For the author, "a multicultural world is unavoidable because global empire is impossible. The preservation of the United States and the West requires the renewal of Western identity. The security of the world requires acceptance of global multiculturality."[9]

He outlines, then, the idea of the world as the cohabitation of civilizations irreducibly marked, as in the West, by the primacy of the individual or, as in Asia, by the primacy of the community. Among these "closed worlds," Huntington also includes "Western" Christianity as separate from the Greek Orthodox, Latin American, African, Middle Eastern, and Eastern varieties. This view is analogous to that of the American theoconservative with one difference: for Huntington the Western model should not be exported, but rather protected. In any case, Christianity is identified with a "civilization," closed within the terrain of a determined culture. In this Huntington is loyal to the multiculturalist perspective, which, in both its optimistic and its pessimistic iterations, identifies Christianity completely with the West. This fails to take into consideration the idea of mission, the idea that what is specifically Christian is the capacity to open and invigorate "other" cultures. This "opening," from within the geopolitical view of the world divided into "civilizations," seems impossible. Moreover, it seems dangerous, able to disrupt the difficult equilibrium that characterizes the emerging multipolar world.

In updating the political vision of Henry Kissinger to fit the framework of the end of the millennium, Huntington wants to block a reality in motion, not to interfere in the domestic context of the "civilizations of power," and to respect customs and mentalities even if they are radically different from those of the West. There is wisdom in this. But in one point his reflection is lacking: in the failure to acknowledge the possibility that precisely a Christianity that is not simply "Western" could play a role in overcoming the "clash of civilizations." This is a possibility that the Roman pontificate has already demonstrated, preventing the conflict between the West and the Islamic world from assuming the form of a return to the Middle Ages, of a crusade between Christianity and Islam.[10]

8. Huntington, *Clash of Civilizations,* p. 318.
9. Huntington, *Clash of Civilizations,* p. 318.
10. On problems related to the topic of multiculturalism, see Franco Crespi and Roberto Segatori, eds., *Multiculturalismo e democrazia* (Rome: Donzelli, 1996); Javier Prades, "L'uomo tra etnia e cosmopolitismo: Fondamenti antropologici e teologici per il dibattito sulla multiculturalità," *Il Nuovo Areopago* 1 (2001): 5-32; Carmelo Vigna and Stefano Za-

The Christian Mission from the 1970s to the 1990s: Two Contrasting Models

As we have seen, the topic of cultural pluralism assumed a different meaning in the transition from the 1970s to the 1990s. During this period, multiculturalism, permeated by Marxism, assumed a decidedly anti-Western tone. The Christian mission was rejected as a form of imperialism, a way, overt or covert, to impose the eurocentric perspective on underdeveloped and developing countries. In this anti-Western view, "mission becomes the mere presumptuous attitude of a culture that imagines itself to be superior, that tramples upon a whole multitude of religious cultures in the most shameful fashion, thus, it is held, depriving those peoples of what is best: their own heritage. Thence comes the imperative: Give us back our religions, as the right ways for the various peoples to come to God and God to them; where these religions still exist, do not touch them!"[11] Such a perspective plainly leads to the delegitimization of the very idea of mission. It is not the abuse of mission that is called into question, its violent imposition where violent imposition occurred, but rather it is mission itself as the communication of Christian truth and love that is taken as problematic. It can now survive only as a practice, as human advancement, an advancement separated from every truthful dimension and generally modulated according to categories belonging to Marxist doctrine. Mission comes to coincide with the process of liberating oppressed peoples from the yoke of rich countries, with the liberation of the masses from the powerful, of the working classes from capitalist exploitation.

In the climate of the 1970s, the preferential option for the poor and the (just) struggle against all forms of discrimination and violence underwent the reduction of a perspective that belonged itself within the Marxist framework of worldwide class struggle. Christian witness thus lost its quality of *gratuitousness* and became ideology and political militancy. The reign of God became an earthly reign, the reign of Caesar, the reign of might and power.

---

magni, eds., *Multiculturalismo e identità* (Milan: Vita e Pensiero, 2002); Leonardo Allodi, *Globalizzazione e relativismo culturale* (Rome: Studium, 2003).

11. Joseph Ratzinger, *Truth and Tolerance: Christian Belief and World Religions,* trans. Henry Taylor (San Francisco: Ignatius Press, 2004), p. 73, published in Italian as *Fede, Verità, Tolleranza: Il Cristianesimo e le religioni del mondo,* trans. Giulio Colombi (Siena: Cantagalli, 2003), p. 76. For a critical take on the Christian mission in the early 1970s see *Communio: Strumento internazionale per un lavoro teologico* 15 (1974), dedicated to "La missione alle genti."

The globalization of Christianity, its secularization, was the cost of its legitimization. By adhering to Marxism, the Christian backed out of the modern "compromise" between church, nobility, and middle class. It was released from its bond to the conservative, and in this way could contribute to the progress of the world. The cost was renunciation of faith in Jesus Christ as the only Savior. Christ became the inspiration of a practice that found its interpretative criteria elsewhere — in the Hegelian-Marxian dialectic. Under these criteria, salvation is brought about humanly by means of a method that finds in Christianity only the occasion of a stimulus for generosity and devotion. Such generosity, however, should not be extended to the class enemy, the ideological adversary. The world remains strictly divided between Jews and Greeks, slaves and freemen, men and women. Christian love can do nothing about it.

Following this "practicist" notion of mission, the "dialogical" version came about in the 1980s and 1990s. In the global shift that followed the fall of communism, multiculturalism passed from its "dialectical" form to its "dialogical" one. In the New Age climate, differences faded away, became frail. Pluralism tended toward a secret monism, a mysticism of the One that transcends the diversity of the dialoguing perspectives. Thus, within a theological framework that undergoes historical changes, Christian mission passed from human advancement, fueled by a "theology of revolution," to dialogue with the cultures and religions of the world.

This vision tends to be articulated from two perspectives. One affirms a pluralist theology of religions in which dialogue stems from the fact that Christianity is not the whole truth. In the second, it follows as a consequence of the first that the non-Christian religions represent not only fragments of truth, but also "means of salvation." This reading finds important frames of reference in the work of John Hick and Paul Knitter.[12] Both perspectives

12. See the following works by John Hick: *God and the Universe of Faiths: Essays in the Philosophy of Religion* (New York: St. Martin's, 1973); *Problems of Religious Pluralism* (London: Macmillan, 1985); *An Interpretation of Religion: Human Responses to the Transcendent* (New Haven: Yale University Press, 1989); *Philosophy of Religion,* 4th ed. (Englewood Cliffs, NJ: Prentice-Hall, 1990); *A Christian Theology of Religions: The Rainbow of Faiths* (Louisville, KY: Westminster John Knox, 1995). Hick is also coeditor, with Paul F. Knitter, of the work *The Myth of Christian Uniqueness: Toward a Pluralistic Theology of Religions* (Maryknoll, NY: Orbis Books, 1987). From Knitter see: *No Other Name? A Critical Survey of Christian Attitudes toward the World Religions* (Maryknoll, NY: Orbis Books, 1985); *One Earth, Many Religions: Multifaith Dialogue and Global Responsibility* (Maryknoll, NY: Orbis Books, 1995); *Jesus and the Other Names: Christian Mission and Global Responsibility* (Maryknoll, NY: Orbis Books, 1996); *Introducing Theologies of Religions* (Maryknoll, NY: Orbis Books, 2002).

depend to a fundamental degree on the Kantian structure of the authors' thought, which distinguishes between a divine, unknowable *noumenon* and the phenomenal images of it that we may have. In this way the various religions become the raiment of a profound truth that defies every characterization. Religions, including Christianity, represent symbols and metaphors of a divine Reality that is never truly *revealed*. Religious pluralism therefore gains a transcendental justification: a single divine *noumenon* calls for many religious phenomena. This does not mean that all religions have equal importance. But the differentiation between them cannot be conducted on the doctrinal plane, but must be carried out on the practical one. This differentiation never leads to a definitive result, since, at the level of experience, it is not possible to establish whether Christianity is superior to Buddhism or Hinduism. In reality Hick does not believe in the dogma of Chalcedon, in the concrete incarnation of the Word in Jesus of Nazareth. His is a "Christology of the Spirit," in which Jesus is "divine" because he is *one* of the representatives of God's love in the world. He is not the fullness of divinity, but simply one of the manifestations of God's reality. Religious pluralism is realized by means of the relativization of Christianity.

In analogous terms Paul Knitter bases his "dialogical" conception of faith on the fact that "the Christian's experience does not say clearly and certainly that Jesus is the *only* Savior meant for all. To experience Jesus as the only Savior would require experience and knowledge of other religions to the extent that one could say that in no other religion do believers make similar claims about their founders or teachers, or that in no other tradition are there religious figures who affect people's lives similarly to the way Jesus has transformed Christians' lives."[13] Knitter grounds the need for interreligious dialogue on the reduction of the figure of Christ. This dialogue takes the place of Christian mission understood as the communication of the fullness of Revelation.

> If there are other ways by which the Divine "saves" and transforms, other ways that are important not just for their own people but for all humankind, then the dialogue is not just a "holy competition" in which the various "one-and-only" claims try to find out who is right. It will be a dialogue in which, yes, the religions do have to confront and correct each other; but

---

For an analysis of the positions of Hick and Knitter see Karl-Heinz Menke, *Die Einzigkeit Jesu Christi im Horizont der Sinnfrage* (Freiburg: Johannes Verlag, 1995); "Il cristianesimo e le altre religione," *La Civiltà Cattolica* 1 (1996): 107-20; Ratzinger, *Fede, Verità, Tolleranza*, 121-31.

13. Knitter, *Theologies of Religions*, p. 58.

it will be one in which they cooperate rather than compete. If God is revealing and saving in many religions and not just in one, then the dialogue will be one in which the religions, by listening to each other, learn more of this God who is always more than any one of them could ever know.[14]

This leads the author to theorize an overcoming of the New Testament language of Jesus as "the one-and-only": "If we grant that there are two sources for a Christian theology of religions — both the Bible and the dialogue with other religious believers — then we can, or must, ask whether it is possible to understand this one-and-only language differently than Christians have in the past."[15]

Like Hick, Knitter therefore leans toward the overcoming of the "model of accomplishment": Christ as the truth of every religious position. In the words of Schillebeeckx, cited by the author, "There is more religious truth in all the religions together than in one particular religion. . . . This also applies to Christianity."[16] From this angle, dialogue changes from a tool into the very method of salvation: salvation becomes "dialogical." Knitter finds philosophical grounds for this position in a *perspective* notion of truth in the postmodern sense and, at the same time, in a *relational* concept of the self. The perspective truths of the various religions expand in the dialogical community into a "unitive pluralism." The conclusion is that "to be Christian or Hindu, one must be part of this wider religious community. Today, so it seems, one must be religious *interreligiously*."[17] In this way Knitter leaves behind the figure of the "anonymous Christian" theorized by Karl Rahner in a famous essay of 1961,[18] a figure that maintains the centrality of Christ as the

14. Knitter, *Theologies of Religions*, p. 59.

15. Knitter, *Theologies of Religions*, p. 59.

16. Edward Schillebeeckx, *Church: The Human Story of God*, trans. John Bowden (New York: Crossroad, 1991), p. 166, quoted in Knitter, *Theologies of Religions*, p. 8.

17. Knitter, *Theologies of Religions*, p. 10.

18. Karl Rahner, "Das Christentum und die nichtchristlichen Religionen," in *Schriften zur Theologie*, vol. 5 (Einsiedeln: Benziger, 1962), pp. 136-58. Rahner's position was criticized by Henri de Lubac in *Paradoxe et mystère de l'Église* (Paris: Aubier, 1967) and by Hans Urs von Balthasar in a note to the third edition of *Cordula oder der Ernstfall* (Einsiedeln: Johannes Verlag, 1968). For de Lubac, "that 'anonymous Christians' will be found in diverse milieux where, one way or another, the light of the gospel has penetrated, no Christian could possibly still deny. Even that he might find it elsewhere, by virtue of some secret operation of the Spirit of Christ, this also may be admitted. In any case no one has the right to declare the grace of the redemption his own personal prerogative.

"To hold, however, because this is so, for an 'anonymous Christianity' spread throughout the world, would not be logical, though it might sound so. Neither would it be logical

final cause of every religious expectation, and moves in the direction of a salvific polytheism. Dialogue becomes the locus of salvation, of the pull toward the One who, in the Eastern-Indian sense, transcends the phenomenal manifestations of individual religions. The mysticism of the One does not eliminate religious pluralism, but it relativizes the contents and the methods. The religions, Christianity included, are all beams from the same star, which, in its splendor, evades any "revelation."

Mission and Interculturality after 9/11

The events of September 11, 2001, represented, as mentioned above, the return of an adversarial vision of contemporary history, the denial of the great hopes that followed the fall of the Berlin Wall. This adversarial vision has swept away the optimistic and pacifistic framework that underlaid interreligious dialogue during the New Age years. In the sudden self-enclosure of religions into geopolitical, monocultural blocs, the West has found itself to be "Christian" once again in contrast to other worlds that press at its doors from without and threaten Western civilization from within. In a hypothetical return to the Middle Ages, Christianity and Islam again confront one another with a language that does not scorn the call to arms. After years of dialogue, in the era of "globalization," we see a return to monothematic cultures that are closed and impenetrable. In the Christianity-Islam dialectic, the alternative is between Huntington's viewpoint, which is aimed at not disrupting the sphere of influence of the respective civilizations, and that of the American theoconservatives, who are convinced that they can impose upon the Islamic world the ethical-political model of the West. The "dialogical" version of mission disappears from the horizon, just as the "soteriological" conception of religions as so many modes of salvation is thrown into crisis.

Fundamentalism and radical Islam, in their bloodiest aspect, show the limits of a viewpoint that, in its uncritical form, accepts every religious expression as a manifestation of a good and just life. On the contrary, in the threatening call to the "God of armies" religion risks looking like a road to

---

to conclude, as is still done, to an 'implicit Christianity' which it would be the sole concern of apostolic preaching to render explicit — still essentially unchanged. All of which would be as much as to say that the revelation we owe to Christ was no more than the surfacing of something that had always existed." Henri de Lubac, *The Church: Paradox and Mystery*, trans. James R. Dunne (Staten Island, NY: Alba House, 1969), pp. 87-88.

perdition, the accomplice of the nihilism that it should reject. A shift has thus occurred from an optimistic vision of the non-Christian forms of religion to a profoundly pessimistic one. In parallel, Western ideology, after years of being discredited and delegitimized, tends to present a *cultural* superiority of Christianity over every other position. In both the dialogical version of Christianity and the conflictual one, however, the character of mission in the Christian sense is forgotten. The idea that Christianity is the precious pearl that every person, atheist or religious, is secretly seeking has made itself scarce. Scarce is the desire to communicate a Reality whose Presence changes the world. Under this profile we can observe how human advancement and dialogue, the two versions of mission from the years 1970-2000, have often been modes of throwing Christian mission off track, forms of flight from serious Christianity precisely due to its absence. Both social advancement, centered on the primacy of practice, and dialogue as conceived by Knitter have functioned as replacements.

These replacements went from being instruments — however contingent and imperfect — of mission to being methods of salvation, loci of change in the world. Given this, however, it is necessary to clarify — even at a time when both ideas appear obsolete and out of fashion — that human advancement and dialogue are fundamental modes of expression of the Christian mission. It is important to reinforce this point today when the lack of both concern for the poor and desire for reconciliation is severely problematic. A Christian mission without charity, which includes social charity — that is, justice — is not fully Christian. Similarly, a mission without the valorization of all that is true in the human nature, historically-sociologically-culturally, is mere fundamentalism. Mission presupposes the "religious sense," the desire for the divine immanent in every person.[19] In this way mission requires human advancement as much as it does dialogue. They are the means through which is communicated *id quod maius cogitari non potest.*

However, human advancement and dialogue are not the only means of such communication. Martyrdom, as an extreme form of witness to the Truth, has for Christianity an even higher value. Nevertheless, charity and dialogue are the normal ways through which the Christian encounters other people. Through them is communicated to the human person what he is missing — the "point" that, once manifested, gives a new form to everything, enhances and purifies. Without this point, culture outlines mere sketches,

---

19. Cf. Luigi Giussani, *Il senso religioso* (Milan: Rizzoli, 1997); translated by John Zucchi as *The Religious Sense* (San Francisco: Ignatius Press, 1990).

incomplete profiles. It is what Kierkegaard calls the "Archimedean point," the point inside and outside the world given by the divine Person of Christ. This point opens; it opens the closed-mindedness of the world. Not only cultural closed-mindedness, marked by contrasting civilizations, but also religious closed-mindedness. The world, as Romano Guardini so astutely observed, tends to close itself, to celebrate in religious terms, in the multiple figures of the gods, its own absoluteness.[20]

The self-closure of the world (political, social, and cultural) is always a closure of the "religious" type, a closure that is overcome by those — the "just" among the peoples — who yearn for the unknown God. In front of this closure, the dynamic of the Christian presence is that of favoring encounter between cultures, of favoring interculturality. "This is exactly what the Christian sees as foreshadowed in the wonder of Pentecost, in which there is not one single language (single civilization) prescribed for all the others, as in Babylon (the type of cultures of achievement and of power), but unity comes to pass in multiplicity. The many languages (cultures) understand each other in the one Spirit. They are not abolished; rather they are brought together in harmony."[21] Already in antiquity this integration, not between a "precultural" Christianity and culture, but within a Christianity that receives from Israel the purified elements of the Egyptian-Hittite-Sumerian-Babylonian-Persian-Greek culture, originates as an interculturality.

> With this in mind, we should talk, no longer about "inculturation," but about a meeting of cultures, or . . . about "interculturality." For "inculturation" presupposes that, as it were, a culturally naked faith is transferred into a culture that is indifferent from the religious point of view, so that

20. See Massimo Borghesi, *Romano Guardini: Dialettica e antropologia* (Rome: Studium, 2004), pp. 161-95; Massimo Borghesi, "'Sacralità' del mondo e 'apertura' cristiana in Romano Guardini," in *Secolarizzazione e nichilismo: Cristianesimo e cultura contemporanea* (Siena: Cantagalli, 2005), pp. 167-80.

21. Ratzinger, *Truth and Tolerance*, p. 82. This is a major difference between Christianity and Islam. As Rémi Brague writes: "Here, it seems to me, appears a decisive difference between the Arabic and the European transmission of ancient heritage. It is situated without doubt, first of all, on the linguistic level. The fundamental phenomenon was that of the presence or absence of a continuity of language. Latin and Greek survived Christianity, which expressed itself by their means. In Islamized regions, on the contrary, Arabic caused Greek to disappear and progressively relegated Syriac and Coptic to the rank of purely liturgical languages or regional dialects." Rémi Brague, *Eccentric Cultures: A Theory of Western Civilization,* trans. Samuel Lester (South Bend, IN: St. Augustine's Press, 2002), p. 94; originally published as *Europe, la voie romaine* (Paris: Criterion, 1992).

two agents that were hitherto alien to each other meet and now engage in a synthesis together. But this depiction is first of all artificial and unreal, because there is no such thing as a culture-free faith and because — outside of a modern technical civilization — there is no such thing as religion-free culture.[22]

Christianity favors interculturality because man is one. "A meeting of cultures is possible because man, in all the variety of his history and of his social structures and customs, is a single being, one and the same."[23] The human being is touched by truth.

The fundamental openness of all men to others, and the agreement in essentials to be found even between those cultures farthest removed from each other, can only be explained by the hidden way our souls have been touched by truth. But the variety, which can even lead to a closed attitude, comes in the first instance from the limitation of the human mind: no one can grasp the whole of anything, but many and varied perceptions and forms come together in a sort of mosaic, suggested by the way that each is complementary with regard to the others: in order to form the whole, each needs all the others. Only in the interrelating of all great works of culture can man approach the unity and wholeness of his true nature.[24]

This is the truth of the dialogical theology of religions, the limit of which, however, lies in its not understanding the role of Christianity, which is not one religion among others, but is the "Archimedean point" that, on the one hand, opens cultures up to one another, favoring interculturality, and on the other hand, relativizes them, taking away their potential absoluteness. Christianity desanctifies, that is, secularizes — as Augustine notes in *De civitate Dei* — both politics and religion. It does not deny the religious yearning contained in the various religions, but it demythologizes the form. This demythologization is forgotten by that current of theological thought that sees all religions as means of salvation.

Such an inclusive theology leads, on the one hand, to sanctioning a nonintegrable polytheistic pluralism and, on the other hand, to not differentiating between the various forms of religious expression. Given this tendency, essential points become obscured. The first is that not all religions

22. Ratzinger, *Truth and Tolerance*, p. 64.
23. Ratzinger, *Truth and Tolerance*, p. 64.
24. Ratzinger, *Truth and Tolerance*, p. 65.

understand themselves to be means of salvation. The Homeric religion, the world of myth, does not foresee the theme of salvation of the soul. The second essential point is that the many religions offer models that are at odds with one another — they do not come together in unity. Buddhism's vision of the world, reality, and the person is, on some points, antithetical to that of Christianity. The third point is that religions frequently present, within their own traditions, contradictory instead of homogeneous aspirations. The fourth is that some religions, founded upon bloody practices such as human sacrifice, stoning, and cannibalism, can hardly be presented as avenues leading to God.

The problem that emerges from an articulated reflection on this topic is that one cannot automatically conclude that all religions are means of salvation from the (correct) idea that the Spirit transcends the visible bounds of the church and that Christ died for all humankind. Such automatism precludes and places limits on the free action of God who, directly touching the human heart, has no need of the religious mediation of cults and rites in order to act. As Ratzinger observes: "Anyone who sees in the religions of the world only reprehensible superstition is wrong; but also . . . anyone who wants to give only a positive evaluation of all religions, and who has suddenly forgotten the criticism of religions that has been burned into our souls not only by Feuerbach and Marx but also by such great theologians as Karl Barth and Bonhoeffer, is equally wrong."[25] The fire of religious criticism was also present in the Fathers, who perceived clearly the revolutionary character of Christianity, a character that with "the Christian rejection of the gods signifies much rather a choice to be on the side of the rebel, who for the sake of his conscience dares to break free from what is accustomed."[26] Following this line of thought, Ratzinger wonders: *"How do we know that the theme of salvation should only be tied to religions?* Do we not have to approach it, in a far more discriminating manner, from human existence as a whole? And should not the highest respect for the mystery of God's activity always be our guide?"[27]

The fact that in its first centuries the church found its antecedents in the Greek enlightenment, that is, in philosophy that was critical of religion and its rites, ought to give us food for thought. "Those patristic texts about the 'sowing of the word' (and similar concepts and images), which are nowadays

25. Ratzinger, *Truth and Tolerance,* pp. 65-66.
26. Ratzinger, *Truth and Tolerance,* pp. 21-22.
27. Ratzinger, *Truth and Tolerance,* p. 53 (emphasis added).

taken as evidence for the power of salvation in other religions, did not originally refer to religions at all but to philosophy, to a 'pious' enlightenment,
which is what Socrates stands for, at the same time active both in enlighten-
ing people and in seeking after God."[28] This "enlightenment" critique of religions explains why Christianity, during the Roman Empire, was viewed as
a form of atheism for its rejection of the *pietas* and the rites of the public
religion. Nevertheless, as Ratzinger observes, this critique does not entail
the denial of man's religious quest. "Thus Christianity has a quite singular
position in the spiritual history of mankind. We could say that it lies in Christianity's not dividing enlightenment from religion but in combining them in
a structure in which each has repeatedly to make the other purer and more
profound."[29] Historically, Christianity was initially supported by philosophy
in its deconstruction of myths and rites. Later, however, it recognized the
translatability of the gods, the possibility of recovering the places of worship
and the ceremonies in the new context of the feasts of saints and martyrs. In
this way it passed from destruction to transformation. Sacred sites were allowed to remain as such, and the intention to honor the divine was taken up
and transformed according to a new meaning. This recognition was not only
belated, built upon the remains of ancient paganism, but was in some way
at the beginning of Christianity.

> The speeches in Lystra and Athens (cf. Acts 14:15-17; 17:22-31) are ac-
> knowledged as models for the evangelization of the Gentiles. In these
> speeches Paul enters into "dialogue" with the cultural and religious values
> of different peoples. To the Lycaonians, who practiced a cosmic religion,
> he speaks of religious experiences related to the cosmos. With the Greeks
> he discusses philosophy and quotes their own poets (cf. Acts 17:18, 26-28).
> The God whom Paul wishes to reveal is already present in their lives; in-
> deed, this God has created them and mysteriously guides nations and
> history. But if they are to recognize the true God, they must abandon the
> false gods which they themselves have made and open themselves to the
> One whom God has sent to remedy their ignorance and satisfy the long-
> ings of their hearts.[30]

In this way Paul validates a religious inquiry that crosses the religions, that
is "transversal" to them. "It is the dynamic of the conscience and of the silent

28. Ratzinger, *Truth and Tolerance,* p. 82.
29. Ratzinger, *Truth and Tolerance,* p. 83.
30. John Paul II, *Redemptoris missio,* no. 25.

presence of God in it that is leading religions toward one another and guiding people onto the path to God, not the canonizing of what already exists, so that people are excused from any deeper searching."[31]

The *"Missio ad gentes"*: Islam and the East

There is a mission to carry out in Christian countries that have passed through secularization, a mission in "postsecular societies,"[32] and there is the mission *ad gentes,* aimed at those who have not yet encountered Christianity. Among these latter are the Islamic peoples and the peoples of the East (India, China, and Japan). The situation of Christian communities in Islamic areas is well known. The application of Sharia, or Islamic law based on the Quran, poses grave problems to both freedom of worship and freedom of religion. In Islam, the Muslim has no right to change his or her religion. Conversion to another faith will bring about discrimination and severe penalties. For Christians present in Islamic countries, dialogue and human advancement are often the only permitted expressions of a witness that, otherwise silent, carries the sign of divine love for mankind.[33] In a general way, the dialogue between the church and Islam, by opposing the "clash of civilizations," helps traditional Islam resist fundamentalism and radicalism. This dialogue provokes Islam to rediscover the link between faith and reason, which, while present in medieval Islamic philosophy, has long been lost.[34]

The church, on the other hand, can and must ask that Islam — and first of all, Turkey, which hopes for entrance into Europe — guarantee religious freedom. The freedom to believe and adhere to a certain religious position is, at base, the only true obstacle preventing Islamists from "inter-culturalizing" in the West and Christians from "inter-culturalizing" in Muslim countries. Nevertheless, on one point Christians and Muslims can al-

31. Ratzinger, *Truth and Tolerance,* p. 54.

32. See Massimo Borghesi, *Secolarizzazione e nichilismo: Cristianesimo e cultura contemporanea* (Siena: Cantagalli, 2006) pp. 3-108.

33. See the interview of Msgr. Giovanni Bernardo Gremoli, apostolic vicar of Arabia, "Un vescovo cattolico nella culla dell'islam," *30 Giorni* 1-2 (2006): 24-34. On the dialogue between Christianity and Islam, see Elisa Buzzi, ed., *Islam: Una realtà da conoscere* (Genoa: Marietti 1820, 2001); *Oasis* 1 (2005), 2 (2005), and 3 (2006).

34. See Rémi Brague, "Bagliori medievali della filosofia islamica," *Oasis* 3 (2006): 90-94.

ready agree: the veneration of the figure of Mary. The Madonna is highly venerated in Islam. In the Quran the name of Mary appears directly sixteen times, while in twenty-three cases it is associated with the name of Jesus, who, nevertheless, is denied divine filiation. It is thus possible that Mary could serve as a bridge between Christianity and Islam.[35]

In addition to Islam, the *missio ad gentes* is directed to the East — Confucian China, Buddhist and Hindu India, Shinto Japan — as expressed, for example, in John Paul II's encyclical *Redemptoris missio:* "Particularly in Asia, *toward which the Church's mission* ad gentes *ought to be chiefly directed,* Christians are a small minority."[36] The 1999 apostolic exhortation *Ecclesia in Asia* looks to the East, as does Ratzinger. In his book *Truth and Tolerance* he writes that "there is no doubt that the question Islam poses for us deserves detailed attention. But it is not within the scope of this book, which is limited to the (to my mind) more fundamental choice between the mysticism of identity and the mysticism of personal love."[37] The model of the ideal that truly opposes Christianity is not the Islamic one — Islam grows through births not through new conversions — but the Eastern one. This is an idea that Ratzinger shares with Romano Guardini. The mysticism of identity, the spiritual monism of India, resolves religious multiplicity in the phenomenal appearance of the invisible One. This is the model that underlies the theology of religions of Hick and Knitter. It is a model that fascinates the West: the New Age spirituality of the postmodern. For this model, the Christian difference, the *Verbum caro,* is resolved into one of the possible phenomenal manifestations of the divine. The East grasps the figure of Christ in this way, emptying the Incarnation of its reality and its salvific claim. It is the *Unknown Christ of Hinduism* of Raimundo Panikkar.[38] Apart from differences of form and doctrine, the religions coincide at the existential, ontic-intentional level. What they seek is total union with the Absolute. Here religious unity becomes a unity in the interiority that excludes the historicity of the Christian event. Mysticism pits itself against the Incarnation. In this is manifested the problem posed by the dialogue between Christianity and Eastern culture. The Buddhist and Hindu East, differently from Islam and also from the Confucian tradi-

---

35. See Giulio Basetti-Sani, *Maria e Gesù figlio di Maria nel Corano* (Palermo: ILA Palma, 1989).

36. John Paul II, *Redemptoris missio,* no. 37 (emphasis added).

37. Ratzinger, *Truth and Tolerance,* p. 85 (emphasis added).

38. Raimundo Panikkar, *The Unknown Christ of Hinduism* (London: Darton, Longman and Todd, 1964).

tion,[39] is mystical. Salvation occurs in the internal sphere, not in the relationship with something "external." This "exteriority," as Emmanuel Lévinas has amply shown, is the mark of the biblical position, and the Christian position in particular. Guardini writes:

> It is this law of the incarnation, according to which the invisible and unknown God does not manifest himself in the abyss of our souls, as absolute mysticism demands; nor through the supreme elevation of thought, as the philosophers wish; nor in the effort of moral ambition and detachment from the world, as the autonomous ascetic claims — but in the human face and in the word of Christ. . . . The revelatory word of Christ becomes clear only when I accept my neighbor, the thing, and destiny. The Christian existence is not something absolute, in the philosophical sense, nor something defined by mystical detachment or asceticism in systematic terms, but is something historical.[40]

Christianity communicates itself through *personal* encounters, in the contingency of space-time circumstances. It is the event of an affection that

39. The problems posed by a Christian presence in China do not first of all depend on traditional culture, but rather on the government's ideology and policies. On the Christianity of present-day China see Gianni Valente, *Il tesoro che fiorisce: Storie di cristiani in Cina* (Rome: Associazione Amici di 30 Giorni, 2002); Gianni Valente, "Anche a Shangai c'è qualcosa di nuovo," *30 Giorni* 7-8 (2005): 80-93.

40. Romano Guardini, "Christliches realismus," in *Unterscheidung des Christlichen: Gesammelte Studien 1923-1935* (Mainz: Matthias-Grünewald-Verlag, 1963). Likewise Ratzinger, following Guardini, observes how "faith is based on our meeting something (or someone) for which our capacity for experiencing things is inadequate. It is not our experience that is widened or deepened — that is the case in the strictly 'mystical' models; but something *happens.* The categories of 'encounter,' 'otherness' (*alterité:* Lévinas), 'event,' describe the inner origins of the Christian faith and indicate the limitations of the concept of 'experience.' Certainly, what touches us there effects an experience in us, but experience as the result of an event, not of reaching deeper into ourselves. This is exactly what is meant by the concept of revelation: something not ours, not to be found in what we have, comes to me and takes me out of myself, above myself, creates something new. That also determines the historical nature of Christianity, which is based on events and not on becoming aware of the depths of one's own inner self, what is called 'illumination.' The Trinity is not the object of our experience but is something that has to be uttered from outside, that comes to me from outside as 'revelation.' The same is true of the Incarnation of the Word, which is indeed an event and cannot be discovered in one's inner experience. This coming to us from outside is scandalous for man, who is striving after autonomy and autarchy; for *every* culture it is a presumption" (*Truth and Tolerance,* pp. 88-89). For a similar perspective see Luigi Giussani, *Un avvenimento di vita, cioè una storia* (Rome: Il Sabato, 1993).

exalts the personal dimension. The dialogue between Christianity and Eastern culture can and must validate the *religious* experience of the East, its *unitive* point of view, but it must also be placed in relation to the *personal* God, one in three. This is a relation through which the human person also becomes an "I," terminal of an essential relationship with the divine "You." The reality of the person, of the personal love of God for man, which finds its supreme manifestation in Christ, is the shocking news that Christianity communicates to the world.

War and the American Difference:
A Theological Assessment

Stanley Hauerwas

America is assumed to be different, because Christianity is still thought to thrive in the United States. Whereas Christianity is allegedly dying in Europe, it seems alive and well here, which confirms for many the contention that there is an inherent link between Christianity and democracy. For it is assumed not only that America is a Christian nation, but also that it is the paradigmatic exemplification of democracy.

In *A Secular Age* Charles Taylor tries to explain this presumed difference between America and Europe. At least one of the reasons that may account for the difference, Taylor suggests, is that America never had an *ancien régime* in which the church legitimized a hierarchical social order. Also at work may be the different role that elites play in determining general attitudes toward belief and unbelief. For example, the skepticism of academic elites in British society had more effect in England because elites have more prestige in British society than elites in America.

The primary reason for the American difference, according to Taylor, is the development of a common civil religion that allowed Americans, as

This essay was originally written for the seminars held in Milan and Treviso (Italy) during the academic year 2007-2008 and organized by the Foundation for Subsidiarity. It has been previously published in Stanley Hauerwas, *War and the American Difference: Theological Reflections on Violence and National Identity,* by Baker Academic, a division of Baker Publishing Group, © 2011, pp. 3-12, and is used here in a slightly different form with kind permission.

well as immigrants in America, to understand their faiths as contributing to a consensus summed up by the motto *E pluribus unum.* This is in marked contrast to Europe, where religious identities have been the source of division either between dissenters and the national church, or between church and lay forces. In America, religious difference, which is even more varied than in Europe, is subordinated to "one nation under God." Religious people may find they are in deep disagreement about abortion or gay marriage, but those disagreements are subordinated to their common loyalty to America.[1] Their subordination also includes their faith in God; that is, whatever kind of Christian (or non-Christian) they may or may not be, their faith should be in harmony with what it means to be an American.

Taylor observes that this difference also accounts for the respective attitudes Europeans and Americans have toward national identities. Europeans generally are quite reticent about national identity, which Taylor attributes to the European memory of the First and Second World Wars. He observes that war, even war that seems "righteous," now makes most Europeans uneasy. Yet that is not the case with Americans. Americans' lack of unease with war may stem from their (incorrect) belief that there are fewer skeletons in the American closet than in the European closet. But Taylor thinks the reason for the American support of war is simpler. "It is easier," Taylor observes, "to be unreservedly confident in your own rightness when you are the hegemonic power."[2]

Taylor is right to recognize that America's unrivaled power in the world gives Americans a sense of confidence about our role as the "world's policeman," but he does not *articulate* — to use one of his favorite words — how American civil religion (our assumption that we are a "religious nation") relates to the fact that war for most Americans is unproblematic.[3] War is a moral necessity for America because it provides the experience of the *unum* that makes the *pluribus* possible. War is America's central liturgical act necessary to renew our sense that we are a nation unlike other nations.[4] World War I was the decisive moment because it was that war that finally healed the wounds caused by the American Civil War.

1. Charles Taylor, *A Secular Age* (Cambridge, MA: Belknap, 2007), pp. 522-27.

2. Taylor, *A Secular Age,* p. 528.

3. For Taylor's emphasis on the significance of being articulate for locating our lives morally, see his *Sources of the Self: The Making of Modern Identity* (Cambridge, MA: Harvard University Press, 1989), pp. 92-107.

4. I develop this account of war in my essay "Sacrificing the Sacrifices of War," first published in the *Criswell Theological Review* 4.2 (2007): 77-96, but also included in part 2

This is well documented by Richard Gamble in his book *The War for Righteousness: Progressive Christianity, the Great War, and the Rise of the Messianic Nation*. Gamble provides ample evidence to show how liberal Protestants justified the First World War as redemptive for the nation and church. For example, Lyman Abbott, a well-known progressive Protestant who had sought to reconcile Christianity with evolution, argued that America as a Christian nation must be willing to be self-sacrificial in service to other nations. Therefore America rightly opposed "pagan" Germany because Germany is a society in which "the poor serve the rich, the weak serve the strong, the ignorant serve the wise." By contrast, America is a society of "organized Christianity" in which the "rich serve the poor, the strong serve the weak, the wise serve the ignorant."[5]

Harry Emerson Fosdick, the exemplar of Protestant liberalism, even suggested that returning troops would present a special challenge to the nation and the churches since the soldiers would have learned the meaning of self-sacrifice through the experience of the war.[6] They also would have experienced the potential of cooperative action through the regenerative power of devotion to a higher cause. Accordingly, the returning soldiers would challenge reactionary views of society and the church because they would expect to remake their world in accordance with the lessons they learned from the war.[7] War, in short, was seen as the laboratory for the more egalitarian social policies that advocates of the Protestant social gospel so desperately desired.

Christianity and democracy in America were and continue to be, through the experience of war, inextricably linked. Arthur McGiffert, then president of Union Theological Seminary, argued that religion was necessary "to promote and sustain democracy." Religion, according to McGiffert, had to dispose of its "egoistic and other-worldly character" by becoming socially re-

---

of my *War and the American Difference: Theological Reflections on Violence and National Identity* (Grand Rapids: Baker Academic, 2011). The significance of the American Civil War is crucial in order to understand the liturgical significance of war in American life. For example, see my essay "Why War Is a Moral Necessity for America or How Realistic Is Realism?" *Seminary Ridge Review* 9.2 (2007): 25-37.

5. Richard Gamble, quoting Abbott in *The War for Righteousness: Progressive Christianity, the Great War, and the Rise of the Messianic Nation* (Wilmington, DE: Intercollegiate Studies Institute, 2003), p. 155.

6. Harry Emerson Fosdick, "The Trenches and the Church at Home," *Atlantic Monthly* 123.1 (1919): 22-33.

7. Gamble, *War for Righteousness*, p. 211.

sponsible. "The religion of democracy," he warned, "must cease to minister to selfishness by promising personal salvation, and must cease to impede human progress by turning the attention of religious men from the conditions here to rewards elsewhere."[8] Such was the lesson to be learned from war.

I call attention to how Americans understood the theological and moral significance of World War I because I think we fail to appreciate what Taylor identifies as the American civil religion if we do not take the American understanding of war into account. For example, Taylor observes that the traditional American synthesis of "civil religion," associated with a nondenominational Christianity with a strong connection to civilized order, is still, unlike its British counterpart, in its "hot" phase. That it is so, however, has everything to do with the American experience of war as constitutive of the substance of our civil religion.

Even political theorists as insightful as C. B. Macpherson can miss the significance of war for American civil religion. Macpherson identified two versions of liberal democracy, which he argues shape American democracy but are in conflict with one another. In the first, a capitalist market society is assumed to be compatible with democratic processes. This form of democracy, no matter how much the rise of the welfare state modifies it, remains dominant — particularly in America, and various balance-of-power models from American political science have given renewed theoretical legitimacy to it.

Macpherson associates the other version of liberal democracy with John Stuart Mill's attempt to moralize liberalism by arguing that a liberal society must be one in which all the members of the social order are equally free to realize their capabilities. From Macpherson's perspective liberal democracy, particularly the democracy of the United States, has tried to combine both forms of liberalism.[9] Thus at times "liberal" means *the stronger can dominate the weak as long as they follow market rules,* while at other times it means *the attempt, usually through state agency, to achieve freedom for all to develop their capacity.* As a result, American politics cannot help but appear incoherent, as different and contradictory policy alternatives are put forward in the name of "freedom."[10]

8. Quoted in Gamble, *War for Righteousness,* p. 214.

9. C. B. Macpherson, *The Life and Times of Liberal Democracy* (Oxford: Oxford University Press, 1977), p. 1.

10. Thus Alasdair MacIntyre's now classic description in *After Virtue: A Study in Moral Theory,* 3rd ed. (Notre Dame: University of Notre Dame Press, 2007) of the inability in liberal societies to know what might count as an argument.

For example, one defense for abortion is the right of an individual to have control over her body, but it is still assumed that laws against suicide make sense in the name of preventing harm. While some portions of the American society think it legitimate to appeal to their religious convictions to address such issues, others see this as a threat to the consensus that makes America work. Thus Taylor's observation that, even though the Protestant character of the original American civil religion has been broadened to include "all faiths" or "no faiths," there is still a strong "religious" character to American public life. That such is the case is confirmed by the very existence of secularist and liberal believers who seek a more secular America.[11]

I agree with Macpherson that both forms of liberalism shape American life, but the tension between them can go unnoticed exactly because America is so wealthy and has the common moral experience of war. Of course wealth, as it turns out, makes war necessary; yet Americans assume that we never go to war to sustain our wealth, because they understand war as a moral enterprise commensurate with our being a democracy. From such a perspective, the military adventures prompted by September 11, 2001, were absolutely necessary for the moral health of the republic. That America must fight an unending war against terrorism means Americans have a common enemy that unites us.

If I am right about the place of war for sustaining the American difference, as a Christian I wish America as a nation were more "secular" and the Christianity of America were less American. Put differently, I wish America were more like Europe, for I fear that the American version of Christianity cannot provide a political challenge to what is done in the name of the American difference. In short, the great difficulty is how to keep America, in the proper sense, secular.

In order to elaborate this observation I think it helpful to call attention to Mark Lilla's important book *The Stillborn God: Religion, Politics, and the Modern West*. Lilla begins his book by giving voice to a sentiment raised after September 11, 2001, and occasioned by the Bush presidency. He (and many on the Left) had assumed that battles over revelation and reason, dogmatic purity and toleration, divine duty and common decency, had been relegated to the scrap heap of history. So people like Lilla "find it incomprehensible that theological ideas still inflame the minds of men, stirring up messianic passions that leave societies in ruin. We assumed that this was no longer

---

11. Taylor, *A Secular Age,* p. 528.

possible, that human beings had learned to separate religious questions from political ones, that fanaticism was dead. We were wrong."[12]

Lilla seeks, therefore, to defend "the great separation," that is, "to develop habits of thinking and talking about politics exclusively in human terms, without appeal to divine revelation or cosmological speculation."[13] Lilla understands this separation to be an extraordinary achievement because political theology is a "primordial form of thought" that for millennia provided the well of ideas and symbols for organizing society and shaping moral lives. In the West, Christianity was the source of political theology even though the political theology Christianity represented could not help but create political societies that were and are inherently unstable. The instability results from the Christian presumption that believers are in the world but not of it. For example, Christians have always had trouble making sense of an empire they accidentally acquired.[14]

Lilla argues it was Hobbes who found the way, after a millennium of Christian political theology, to discuss religion and the common good without making reference to the nexus between God, man, and the world.

---

12. Mark Lilla, *The Stillborn God: Religion, Politics, and the Modern West* (New York: Knopf, 2007), p. 3.

13. Lilla, *Stillborn God*, p. 5. Charles Taylor, in a very interesting review of Lilla's book, argues that Lilla's understanding of political theology fails to do justice to the natural law justifications of early modern thought that did not appeal directly to revelation or to premises drawn from revelation. According to Taylor, Lilla's argument depends on his view of political theology (suggested later in his book) that a genuine secular politics presumes a mechanistic understanding of the cosmos. Taylor thus challenges Lilla's presumption that "the great separation" has ever been quite the achievement Lilla assumes. Taylor's review is available as *"The Stillborn God:* Two Books, Oddly Yoked Together," *The Immanent Frame,* Social Science Research Council, January 24, 2008, http://blogs.ssrc.org/tif/2008/01/24/two-books-oddly-yoked-together/.

14. Lilla, *Stillborn God*, pp. 42-45. Lilla observes that although Christianity "is inescapably political, it proved incapable of integrating this fact into Christian theology. The political organization of medieval Europe, tottering on that theological ambivalence, could not have been more perfectly arranged to exacerbate the conflict inherent in all political life.... Perhaps if Christianity had seen itself as the political religion it really was, presenting the pope as an earthly sovereign with full authority over secular matters, some bloodshed could have been avoided. But living as a Christian means being in the world, including the political world, while somehow not being of it. It means living with a false consciousness" (pp. 85-86). Lilla associates this instability in Christian political theology with the dialectic between transcendence and immanence at the heart of the incarnation. For such an astute reader of Barth, it is surprising that Lilla fails to understand that what is meant by such a dialectic must be christologically determined.

Hobbes was able to do so because he, anticipating Feuerbach, had the wisdom to turn questions about God into questions about human behavior; to reduce that behavior to psychological states; and then to portray those states as artifacts of desire, ignorance, and the material environment.[15]

For Hobbes the gods are born out of fear of death, poverty, and calamity; but Hobbes knew better than to try to deny such fear. Rather he focused fear on one figure alone, the sovereign. Such a sovereign — Hobbes called him an "earthly God" — could ensure that his subjects should fear no other sovereigns but him. No longer would there be a tension between church and crown because now the sovereign would make clear that salvation depended on obedience to himself.

Lilla thinks Hobbes's great achievement, this great separation that is crucial for the art of living in a liberal democratic order, is secured by three developments. The first is the intellectual separation made possible by the scientific revolution, in which a now mute natural world is separated from its Creator. As a result, investigations into nature can be separated from thoughts about God. Second, the crucial distinction between the public and the private was developed, relegating religious convictions and practices to the latter. To be sure, Lilla acknowledges, Hobbes made the sovereign responsible for public worship, but not for actually mounting an inquisition to determine if citizens really believed "Jesus is the Christ." Third, perhaps less obviously but equally consequential, is Hobbes's argument for separating academic inquiry from ecclesiastical control. One of the achievements of Hobbes's project can be seen in theology's becoming, as it has in modernity, but another academic discipline relegated to divinity schools.[16]

Though Hobbes is often thought to legitimate a violent understanding of politics, that is, human existence as a war of all against all, Lilla argues that Hobbes is actually trying to limit the violence that is unleashed by political theology. For when war is undertaken in the name of God, there can be no limit to killing, because so much is allegedly at stake. That is why human beings who believe in God commit acts in war that no animal would even commit. Animals kill only to eat and reproduce, but humans fight to get into heaven.[17] Hobbes, on Lilla's reading, is the first great realist in international affairs. After Hobbes, war at least has the potential to be humanely limited because it can be fought for selfish reasons.

15. Lilla, *Stillborn God,* p. 88.
16. Lilla, *Stillborn God,* pp. 89-91.
17. Lilla, *Stillborn God,* pp. 84-85.

According to Lilla's argument, Locke and Hume provided softer accounts of Hobbes's Leviathan but nonetheless remained fundamentally Hobbesian. Like Hobbes, they wanted to protect modern man from the superstition and violence associated with political theology by developing liberal habits of mind. In particular Locke thought it possible and necessary to liberalize Christianity itself, which Lilla suggests bore fruit in the work of Rousseau, Kant, and Protestant liberals such as Schleiermacher and Troeltsch. Yet Lilla judges the attempt of Protestant liberals to ground religion in human experience to be a failure because

> it failed to inspire conviction about the Christian faith among nominal Christians, or attachment to Jewish destiny among nominal Jews. Once the liberal theologians succeeded, as they did, in portraying biblical faith as the highest expression of moral consciousness and the precondition of modern life, they were unable to explain why modern men and women should still consider themselves to be Christians and Jews rather than simply modern men and women.[18]

Such is the dilemma of Christians in America. To the extent that Christians try to be "political" by playing by the rules set down by "the great separation," they cannot help but become unintelligible not only to their neighbors but, more importantly, to themselves. I think this helps account for the strident rhetoric of the Religious Right in America. Though claiming to represent a conservative form of Christianity, the Religious Right is politically a form of Protestant liberalism. The Religious Right makes a fetish of this or that belief (e.g., the substitutionary account of the atonement they take to be the hallmark of Christianity), but by doing so they play the game determined by the great separation — that is, Christianity becomes primarily a matter of "belief."

Yet secular people in America fear the Religious Right, because they think that the rise of the Religious Right and Islam threatens the "great separation." Thus Lilla ends his book by reminding those who, like him, are committed to Hobbes's great achievement that they are the exception. They cannot expect other civilizations to follow the path of the West. But according to Lilla, the West has made the choice to protect individuals from the harm they can inflict on one another in the name of religion. It has done so by securing fundamental liberties and by leaving the spiritual destinies of

18. Lilla, *Stillborn God,* p. 248.

each person in his own hands. In short, Americans have chosen to keep our "politics unilluminated by the light of revelation. If our experiment is to work, we must rely on our own lucidity."[19]

But Lilla's account of the great separation does not explain how a country allegedly shaped by Hobbes and Locke is, particularly in reference to war, nevertheless a nation that understands itself in religious terms.[20] Americans are said to be the beacon of hope for all people. They must be ready, therefore, to make sacrifices, for example, to go to war for the good of the world. In short, Lilla does not explain why it is very hard to keep the secular "secular" in America. Even though the church has been relegated to the "private" realm, the nation is still conceived and legitimated in salvific terms. It is not Christians and Muslims that challenge the great separation, but rather it is "America."

Lilla's sense that Hobbes's achievement may be threatened is widely shared by others in America. For example, in his book *Education's End: Why Our Colleges and Universities Have Given Up on the Meaning of Life*, Anthony Kronman sounds themes very similar to Lilla's. The university, as Lilla suggested, is the key agent for sustaining the great separation. Kronman acknowledges that Protestant piety had shaped the early universities in America, but he argues that after the Civil War, universities were organized to sustain a secular and humanistic account of life. Students would be initiated into secular humanism by reading the great texts of the Western tradition, and through such reading they would learn "that it is possible to explore the meaning of life in a deliberate and organized way even after its religious foundations have been called into doubt."[21]

As a result of this humanistic emphasis in the universities, those in the humanities came to believe they had the competence and the authority to lead students in a disciplined study of the human condition, in order that students might pursue their own personal search for meaning. Their pedagogy assumed that no fixed conception of the end of human life or of a single right way to live could be sustained. For, according to Kronman, there simply is no "vantage point that we can ever occupy from which our lives can be seen as a whole."[22] Secular humanism does not require that God be rejected

19. Lilla, *Stillborn God*, pp. 308-9.

20. See, for example, Michael Northcott, *An Angel Directs the Storm: Apocalyptic Religion and American Empire* (London: I. B. Tauris, 2004).

21. Anthony Kronman, *Education's End: Why Our Colleges and Universities Have Given Up on the Meaning of Life* (New Haven: Yale University Press, 2007), p. 74.

22. Kronman, *Education's End*, p. 34.

or even thought to be irrelevant to life, as long as such judgments are left to the individual.

Kronman acknowledges that death is the most determinative challenge that confronts the secular humanist. "We all die, and know we will, and must adjust ourselves to the shadow which the foreknowledge of death casts over the whole of our lives."[23] Yet death also forces us to recognize that whatever meaning life may have depends on us. Accordingly, for Kronman, life for the secular humanist is self-contradictory. The secular humanist seeks to abolish the limits that give his longings meaning; that is, he seeks to be in control. Yet in the attempt to seize control, he comes to recognize that without the limits he seeks to overcome, the ends he seeks could not exist.[24]

Sounding very much like Lilla in his account of Hobbes, Kronman argues that religion, drawing on our fears, encourages us to revalue the limits of life by accepting those limits as an occasion for gratitude rather than rebellion. The smug cosmopolitan observers of this religious revival think this development to be shallow and mindless. Kronman thinks such an attitude fails to recognize that the problem is not the death of God but the death of man. The university's task is to preach the rebirth of a humanism that is more honest and honorable than anything religion can offer.[25]

Kronman's understanding of secular humanism assumes what Lilla calls "the great separation," thus confirming Lilla's contention that the university is the crucial institution to sustain liberal social orders. Yet Kronman fears that the secular university has lost its way by becoming a research university beset by the demands of the politically correct. I certainly think the humanities have lost their centrality in the modern university, but I think that loss is due much more to the humanism Kronman advocates. For once the "great separation" is accepted, a Hobbesian world cannot be avoided — that is, a death-determined world committed to the defeat of death. In such a world, the university cannot help but become the home of technologies designed to increase our power over fate. In the process, we are fated by our creations.

23. Kronman, *Education's End,* p. 76.

24. Kronman, *Education's End,* p. 232.

25. Kronman, *Education's End,* p. 243. Kronman is more than ready to declare that any "religion" at some point must demand a sacrifice of the intellect because a religion finally insists that at some point thinking is not adequate to questions of life's meaning. So every religion in a basic sense must be fundamentalist because the answers it is prepared to give to life's questions are anchored in its own convictions (pp. 198-99). Kronman does not supply the necessary philosophical defense of his understanding of rationality.

Such a world, and the universities that serve it, must go to war in an effort to defeat those forces that threaten our security. Americans are determined to live in a world of safety even if we have to go to war to make the world safe. That project is often justified, according to Kronman, in the name of individual freedom and toleration; democratic government; respect for the rights of minorities and for human rights generally; a reliance on markets as a mechanism for the organization of economic life; and the acceptance of the truths of modern science and the ubiquitous employment of its technological products as aspirational goals all should want. According to Kronman, "To be openly opposed to any of these things is to be a reactionary, a zealot, an obscurantist who refuses to recognize the moral and intellectual authority of this ensemble of modern ideas and institutions."[26] I have little doubt that Kronman believes this, but that he does so means he simply cannot see what the rest of the world sees, namely, that this is an ideology for a culture of death.

Kronman and Lilla are to be commended for their willingness to advocate secular humanism as a moral, educational, and political project. They seem to assume, however, that the secular humanist will be more peace-loving, and I find it hard to locate any evidence that would support such a conclusion.

By calling attention to Lilla and Kronman I hope to have helped us see that if we as Christians are to reclaim the political theology required by the truthfulness of Christian convictions, we will need to begin by doing theology unapologetically. In particular that means Christians must reclaim theology as a knowledge central for the work of any university worthy of the name "university." That will require, at least in America, a recovery of the church as a polity capable of challenging the presumption that the state is the agency of peace. In short, if my analysis concerning the American difference is close to being right, it should make clear that a commitment to Christian nonviolence is the presumption necessary for the church to reassert its political significance.

In *Veritatis splendor* John Paul II claimed that there is an inseparable connection between truth and freedom, which, if broken, results in totalitarianism.[27] America is a society built on the assumption that freedom must precede truth. Therefore America is presumed to be the alternative to totalitarianism. However, if my account of the American difference is correct, I think this presumption needs to be reexamined, particularly in light of the way war sustains American political life.

26. Kronman, *Education's End*, pp. 172-73.
27. John Paul II, *Veritatis splendor*, August 6, 1993.

Multiculturalism in Britain:
The Case of the Recent Debate over Sharia

John Milbank

The Background of the Debate in Great Britain

In the first two weeks of February 2008, a rather bitter furor ensued in the United Kingdom in the wake of a radio interview and a lecture delivered by the archbishop of Canterbury.[1] Perhaps no archbishop of Canterbury in the last one hundred years has been in such trouble as Rowan Williams after these two interventions. The reason that I focus on this incident is that I think it casts an interesting light upon issues having to do with multiculturalism in Britain and an even stronger light upon issues concerning the relation between universal reason and tradition. These issues arise with respect to the practical reasoning that goes on in the sphere of law.

It is important first of all to understand something of the background to the question of multiculturalism in Britain. In many ways, historically, Britishness is very flexible; it is much less racially defined than the identity of any other European nationality.[2] Successive waves of immigrants have come into Britain and become British in a very short time. This is partly because British identity is associated with certain attitudes of mind, certain life-stances. It also has to do with a postimperial legacy in which England, Scot-

1. Rowan Williams, "Civil and Religious Law in England: A Religious Perspective," Temple Festival Series Lecture, Royal Courts of Justice, London (February 7, 2008). See also "Multiculturalism: Friend or Foe," Address, Toynbee Hall, London (May 16, 2007).

2. See Krishan Kumar's excellent *The Making of English National Identity* (Cambridge: Cambridge University Press, 1983).

land, Wales, and Ireland were swallowed up in a bigger project that transcended ethnicity and local cultural identity. In many ways it is hard for continental Europeans to recognize that really there isn't a British nationhood — there is only an English, Welsh, Scottish, or Irish nationhood. Thus Britishness is something of a construct, and in the wake of empire it has tended to break down — now Scots, much more than they used to, overwhelmingly define themselves as Scottish, and the Welsh to a lesser degree likewise. But this has left the English in something of a dilemma, and it has also meant that immigrants have become worried about whether they fit so easily into "Englishness" (or "Scottishness" or "Welshness") as they do into "Britishness." It is also true that most of the waves of immigrants into Britain from former British colonial territories like the West Indies or Kenya were very British in outlook to begin with, and if they have become more aware of a separate identity, that is partly because of the racism they have received from the English. Particularly, I am frightened by many Anglican churchgoers, who have often failed to welcome their own — to the latter's infinite distress and alienation. And so if those alienated later formed a separate cultural identity, it was somewhat in reaction to that situation. In the case of immigrants from the Indian subcontinent, however, there is also the presence of a Hindu subculture and to an even greater degree a Muslim subculture.

In the wake of a certain breakdown of British identity and of a breakdown of British working class identity, one is seeing a kind of ghettoization of British urban culture, with people increasingly living inside ethnic or cultural groups. And the government has become worried about this situation, although until recently it was taking a multiculturalist approach to it — perhaps government leaders had been listening far too intently to academics, which is often a bad idea! Concisely stated, the multiculturalist policy held that these groups all have their own unique cultures and that they all ought to be respected.

Recently, however, people have started to realize that this policy does not help when cultures are interacting with each other, because then the question arises, on what basis are they going to interact? Increasingly, one may find a situation where people are not identifying very strongly with the country in which they now live. Indeed, if one were to visit London now, he would discover that it is quite extraordinary compared to any other European city — full of people who are in a sense scarcely aware that they are in England at all. And people coming, say, from the north of England to London increasingly return home and shake their heads and say that their capital city is just like a foreign country and that they cannot recognize it as part of England anymore.

More recently, the New Labour government quite clearly switched direction and decided that everybody must take on some dimension of Britishness, even if groups continue to possess their own separate cultures. Former prime minister Gordon Brown issued multiple statements to the effect that British values are unique and that such uniqueness is what truly matters. He set up a commission to discover just what these important British values really are — apparently they are very important, but we need a committee to specify them!

The Intervention of Archbishop Williams

Now I believe all this is an important backdrop to the archbishop's speech, because there seems, at least on the face of it, to be an element of the speech still attached to the old multicultural strategy more associated with Tony Blair than with Gordon Brown's "British values" policy. Sure enough, immediately after Rowan Williams's now notorious speech, Brown issued an injunction saying that everybody in Britain must adhere to British values. Williams's speech — which is a very interesting, quite complicated address (that belongs to a wider series of interlinked lectures) — is concerned with the issue of the operation of religious law in Britain. The setting for this concern, however, is much broader — Williams is really bothered about the threats to group rights, and, more specifically, the threats to the rights of religious groups. In the background is the situation in which Catholic adoption agencies in Britain have had to close down because they refused to comply with the government requirement that all adoption agencies accept homosexual couples on an equal basis to heterosexual couples. There has also been a great deal of agitation for all doctors to be forced to perform abortions in England as a condition of being doctors. Therefore, many people fear a decline of the idea that one can opt out of something conscientiously on account of the attitudes of the group to which one happens to belong.

Given these realities, Rowan Williams, in a rather MacIntyrean kind of way, is asking the political process and the law to take account of the narratives in which people situate themselves and of the reasons they give for their own actions. The problem, of course, is in determining on precisely what kind of public basis we do this. Do we do it on a Christian basis, do we do it on a secular basis, or do we do it on a kind of pan-religious basis?

I think this is the problem that some of Pope Benedict XVI's remarks also open up: if we are taking religious traditions seriously, does this mean we are taking all religious traditions equally seriously? There is a sense in which if one takes tradition seriously then one has to commit to a particular tradition — because simultaneous commitment to a plurality of often-conflicting traditions would be no traditionalism at all. The pope and the late Luigi Giussani are right about the importance of a founding event, but there is a sense in which it is Christianity uniquely that founds itself upon an event as opposed to a long historical process or the law; stressing the event is perhaps explicitly Christian. By comparison, Judaism stresses God's long fidelity to a people, including the giving of a law, and Islam stresses simply the revelation of a law that then gives rise to a new history. This contrast is very relevant to the following considerations.

In Rowan Williams's speech, there is a mixture of basing things on secular arguments, on specifically Christian arguments, and on arguments that have to do with religiosity in general, and this triplicity may be a key to why he said what he did and then got into such an awful lot of trouble. What specifically and ostensibly got him into trouble was his saying that Sharia, Islamic law based on the Quran, ought to be extended in England, and indeed that its extension is inevitable. It is clear that he was thinking, *if I am going to demand that Christian attitudes towards life, towards sexuality, and towards many other matters be respected in the public sphere, then I have to hold out my hand to other religious groupings and accept that their social ideas of the normativities of their religious bodies be also taken into public account.* And this means that for Judaism and Islam we have to take on board the fact that law for them is a sacred matter. He did not mention this point, but it is also relevant that for Christians law is relatively more secularized than it is for Judaism and Islam. For these religions it is a more defining, more neuralgic issue,[3] and Williams was trying to respect this.

Here, in fact, some of what he said was more or less uncontroversial. Orthodox Jewish law has been recognized to some degree by British common law for a hundred years in relation to matters like marital disputes. It plays a kind of subsidiary but complementary role, although it is interesting that only recently has there had to be a clarification concerning whether

3. See Rémi Brague, *The Law of God: The Philosophical History of an Idea,* trans. Lydia G. Cochrane (Chicago: University of Chicago Press, 2007). Brague makes the point well about Christianity secularizing law, yet he also undertreats the issue of canon law and wrongly extends this thesis towards a secularization of the ethical as such.

one could be considered "not divorced" under Jewish law but "divorced" under public law. This sort of outright contradiction has not really arisen in relation to Catholic canon law because the latter does not usually claim any formal state recognition of its jurisdiction — but in the Jewish case there was an instance in which it was as if for the British State somebody was at once divorced and not divorced. But this anomaly has now, it seems, been sorted out.

However, Williams appeared to resurrect just this specter. For he seemed to suggest that, were Sharia officially recognized, people could opt for different jurisdictions when it came to financial matters, or to matters of marriage and divorce, and it was this suggestion that caused all the controversy. He was not just talking about, say, a Sharia court trying to sort out the arguments between a couple before they go before a British court — the British government makes no objection to such proceedings (although even such modest proposals appear to have run into trouble in Canada). What he instead seemed to suggest was that sometimes, in a divorce proceeding, for example, one would be able to choose between two different systems. And because he said one would still have the right to appeal against the Sharia ruling, he effectively suggested that the two systems operate with two different sets of principles. It was this that caused an absolutely furious reaction, and perhaps understandably.

Since then Williams has almost had to retract this proposal — possibly because it effectively accords coercive power to a Sharia court. Besides, although it is true that an Islamic woman could appeal against the ruling of such a court, in effect, because of social coercion, she would not be likely to do so, even though Sharia is far less favorable to women than is British public law. Thus many people, notably many Muslim women, were very worried about the degree of plurality that Rowan Williams was actually entertaining.

A Different Understanding of Pluralism: Organicist or Liberal?

Arguably, he was confusing two different senses of pluralism. One is the sense very compatible with Catholic social teaching and ideas of subsidiarity (which he notably seems sometimes to edge away from as too linked to central coordination). In other words, it is a critique of the absolute sovereignty of the center. For this mode of political "pluralism," which he obliquely invoked, one should disperse sovereign power to several localities and even sometimes to corporate bodies like businesses or cooperatives, or to hospitals, schools, and universities. But such a "corporatist" model (using this term in the broadest possible sense), because it is essentially *organic,* doesn't really involve any conflict of jurisdictions. Even if, in a more modern version of this model, one includes the roles of different church denominations and other bodies committed to their own idiosyncratic worldviews, then to a degree one grants them rights, because to some extent one accepts that they are contributing to the common social good, even if one dissents from some aspects of their views and actions.

This reflection may indicate one reason why things have now become very difficult. For in the past there was a tacit consensus that, say, a Baptist church was contributing to social morality and solidarity. Today, however, this consensus is failing because we now have a much more drastic mode of secularization and a growing popular and public view that the church is the enemy of certain supposed sexual and bio-sexual rights. I also think that Rowan Williams effectively appeared to confuse the older but now threatened sense of pluralism (which I have just invoked) with something *somewhat* more like a multiculturalist, postmodernist, cultural-studies sense of pluralism in which one declares that the other is utterly other, we can't judge the other, we have to let those who are other do their own thing.

Of course the problems with this second sense of pluralism are crude and obvious. What does one do if the other wants to sacrifice babies? And Williams didn't adequately deal with that problem. For really we can only accept Islamic otherness up to the point at which it begins to conflict with our very firm sense of the dignity of women — to give what I think is a crucial example in relation to this issue.

I would also argue that, by suggesting a kind of liberal group pluralism — in other words, by conferring on groups inalienable rights as if they were corporate individuals — what Williams was not facing up to (in the wake of his intellectual heroes here — Lord Acton and the Anglican monk John Neville Figgis)[4] is that liberalism *always* favors the individual over the group and it *cannot have* any strong notion of group personality. A "realism" at the group level (the group is more than the sum of its parts) will always be outflanked by a "nominalism" at the individual level, since the very idea of a

---

4. John Emerich Edward Dalberg Acton, *Essays on Freedom and Power* (London: Thames and Hudson, 1956). See, for example, page 80, where he asserts, with quite breathtaking anachronism, that Adam Smith's "doctrine of freedom and self-reliance, which is the foundation of political economy" is already to be found in the New Testament! John Neville Figgis, *Churches in the Modern State* (London: Longmans, Green, 1913).

priority of groups over the political whole *already* suggests a contradictory "nominalism" (the groups themselves are so many unrelated atoms) that is also mythical, because groups no more entirely "precede" the political whole than do Locke's supposedly contracting, isolated individuals.

Acton and his followers were all rather confused about this because they were trying to combine a British Whig with a Catholic and Germanic pluralist-organicist legacy. But the latter (as in Otto von Gierke) remained more coherently Aristotelian and Thomist: even though sovereignty is dispersed, "social" groups are still from the outset positioned by a certain "political" unity, however inchoate. This thesis is *not* the same (and this may be the key to the theoretical confusion) as the post-Bodin notion of a single sovereign center. The crucial point here is that in the premodern era, social subgroups (feudal manors, universities, guilds, monasteries) were *also* conveyers of dispersed, sovereign political power — there were manorial courts, for example. The Actonian model, however, tries to make merely *social* groups prior to *political* unity. But this is, after all, simply to buy into a modern liberal political model ("liberal" in the sense of contractarian individualism, not of constitutionally limited government; Williams, in the wake of Acton and Figgis, appeared to fudge this distinction). Indeed it is to buy into a Bodin- and Hobbes-inspired notion of absolute sovereignty — because the monopolization of all absolute law and coercive power will still be needed to adjudicate between heterogeneous groups, just as much as it will be needed to adjudicate between the warring desires of individuals. Just for this reason the key promoter of "left-liberal pluralism," Harold Laski, eventually logically defected towards a Fabian-Marxist state socialism as the better guarantor, as he now supposed, of equal, individual freedom of choice.[5] It is notably only an incorrigible eccentric like the late and remarkable David Nicholls who tries to maintain a logically defeated, liberal pluralist legacy.[6] By comparison, though, a more truly Catholic, Gierkean, and Thomist (for Aquinas was absolutely no Whig, as Acton imagined!) organicist pluralism can sustain a more logical resistance to individualist liberalism, since it has no postulate of either individuals or groups existing "before" the political, while equally (in a tradition that is at once Aristotelian and Augustinian) it does not posit (as do Hobbes and Locke) a political that precedes society and societies.

---

5. Harold Laski, *Liberty in the Modern State* (Harmondsworth: Penguin, 1937); Bernard Zylstra, *From Pluralism to Collectivism: The Development of Harold Laski's Political Thought* (Assen: Van Gorcum, 1968).

6. David Nicholls, *Three Varieties of Pluralism* (London: Macmillan, 1974).

However, this organicism does *not* rule out elements of a more heterogeneous pluralism and tolerance of differing groups. This is because, as already explained, political society as a whole need not entirely agree with the premises of the Baptist church — or the Muslim *Ummah* — to be able nonetheless to accept that they are performing certain social roles that contribute to the cohesion of the political whole. Now *quite often* Rowan Williams seems to be indicating something like this, but he needs to make it clearer. Too often he speaks in a tone of Actonian incoherence — and this can give shelter to language that has a "multiculturalist" resonance. Perhaps we need from him less "Whig socialism" (whose incoherence Laski's trajectory long ago exposed) and more "Tory socialism" of the Ruskinian variety — or "Red toryism," whose logic lies close also to the traditions of Cobbett, Chesterton, and Belloc and is really more authentically Catholic.

The Actonian version of group personality falls between nominalism and realism into metaphysical incoherence by treating a group as a fully-fledged unit "prior" to its looking towards the political whole and therefore towards the human whole. For even if one sees the human whole as represented more by a religion than a state, this is only because a religious group like Islam or the church *is* a kind of superpolity.

Hence to have a notion of group personality you need a teleological ethics — you have to be able to say that a certain group is aiming for a goal, for a collective character that fits into a wider sense of what its role is as a group. And so to repeat: even if this group is the Baptist church, and even if one is a Catholic or an agnostic and one does not agree with the antisacramental or religious ideas assumed by Baptists, one could still say that relatively speaking the group is pursuing certain social goals that we as a society recognize as compatible with our sense of human dignity and as promoting it. It is a bit like the idea that pacifists can opt out of a war. We let them do this because we implicitly say to ourselves that their hyperbolic respect for human life actually affirms a basic principle of our society. So in a way a pacifist is not a rebel; in a way a pacifist is all too loyal a subject, all too devoted (albeit woodenly) to the undergirding principles of law, and so in consequence we let pacifists have their rights of conscience. Similarly, up to now, with attitudes towards abortion. If you were coming from a secular pro-abortion point of view (which of course I don't share) you would be saying we don't agree, but respect for human life in principle is something that we *do* agree about, and so we accept that anti-abortion doctors should not be required to perform abortions.

The trouble, however, is that when a more virulent *and, we must con-*

cede, more consistent liberalism arises — one that no longer has any sense of a "thick" notion of what constitutes human dignity, a notion that goes beyond respect for the individual will and material happiness — then all this breaks down. Thus many in the secular press in Britain are now saying that nobody has the right to opt out of laws, that one should know that if one refuses to perform an abortion this is potentially threatening to women and their rights.

The problem, then, is that if one tries to make a liberal argument for group rights, one will always have to favor the individual who appeals over against the group's collective head. There are secular lawyers now, legal theorists, working on the idea that churches should be legally censored if they do not accept women priests, for example. This is a serious possibility on the horizon, and though I am actually in favor of women priests for theological reasons, I am *not* in favor of the idea that such a change could be imposed by the state. Other secular theorists are even arguing against any rights of religious freedom, on the basis that any notion of a special right to religious freedom in excess of general, individual freedom of opinion in some way accords to religion (and so to "unreason") a public dignity and a public role, and gives license to a certain authority of religious government over religion's members. Indeed the liberal logic here is impeccable — if ironic, since religious liberty is part of the founding story of liberalism. Because this is so, the idea that a group is given a right, if this idea is based on merely liberal principles, can always be overwritten by the rights of the individual will that is much more fundamental for liberal doctrine. And for this reason, liberalism *cannot* defend corporate religious freedom. Liberalism is nominalist, just as it is voluntarist, and it is clear that William of Ockham already had liberal contractarian attitudes, denying any ideas of the common good.[7] Thus the paradigmatic individual within liberalism is always going to be the individual person possessing a free will, and this is why a liberal approach to group rights and the rights of religious bodies breaks down.

It seems Rowan Williams's "depth mistake" therefore is to have somewhat confused and conflated (or at least to have appeared to do so) these two senses of pluralism — "organicist" and "liberal," for convenient shorthand. Furthermore, basing the argument on a kind of general respect for religious points of view will not work. Religions are just too different from

---

7. This genealogy has often been traced, most recently and overwhelmingly by André de Muralt. See his *L'unité de la philosophie politique: De Scot, Occam et Suarez au libéralisme contemporain* (Paris: Vrin, 2002).

each other. For example, ironically, if one reads about the history of Islam, one will find nothing like an endorsement of organic pluralism in its history. Islam is actually a very individualistic religion. Sharia applies to matters between individuals, and apart from that there is a very strong central state with the caliph commanding absolute sovereign power.[8] In fact, Islam is proto-modern in its political ideas, and it may well be that it helped in the Middle Ages to shape Western political modernity. It is just for this reason that if one does believe in something like a kind of group pluralism, something like the idea of subsidiarity, something like the idea that we need to break down state sovereignty, such beliefs are only truly undergirded by various forms of Christian metaphysics and especially Catholic metaphysics.

Counter to this, one might say that in a way it is common sense to recognize that people exist in groups and that they are not primarily individuals. Now this is indeed common sense, but — and here comes a Chestertonian point! — it is only Catholic Christianity that actually rescues a common sense that has been destroyed by a secular, liberal nominalism that appears to have a more rigorous abstract reason on its side. In this case, as in others, there is a strange fit between Christianity and the human condition, and this is why I think that only an outlook informed by Christianity enables one to respect something like group rights in this sort of way, including the group rights of other religious faiths.

To give one example of this: Rémi Brague has recently indicated that Christianity is constitutively "liberal" in a way that Islam is not.[9] This is because the New Testament fully accepts the Old, builds upon it, and reads it in a certain way, while the attitude of Christians to the Quran, which came later, has to remain open and problematic. The possibility remains that Christians can see the Quran as true up to a point, even if defective. For Christians, Islam can be seen as less than the full truth. But the Quran, on the other hand, sees both the Old and the New Testaments as distorting an original "Islamic" revelation once given to Abraham. Therefore it cannot possibly see Judaism and Christianity as, *in their very fullness,* less than the entire truth, but must, on the contrary, view *all* of their specificity as distorting a pure, Abrahamic monotheism, which is simply that disclosed by

8. See Sayyed Mohammed Khatami, *La religion et la penseé prises au piège de l'autocratie* (Paris: Peeters, 2005); Aziz Al-Azmeh, *Muslim Kingship: Power and the Sacred in Muslim, Christian, and Pagan Polities* (London: I. B. Tauris, 2001).

9. Rémi Brague, *Du Dieu des Chrétiens et d'un ou deux autres* (Paris: Flammarion, 2008).

the Quran itself. So whereas Christianity can regard Islam in general as but lacking, Islam must see Christianity in its entire positive specificity as a distortion and concealment of the truth. There is no possible parity and reciprocity here.

Reactions to Williams's Speech

My contention that it is in fact only Christianity that can defend a group pluralism is indirectly confirmed by the reactions to what Williams said. *Nobody* understood his "religion in general" argument. There were two responses. Overwhelmingly, people said that the law of Britain is secular and universal and based on the Enlightenment, but to a surprising degree also, people rang up the media and said, British law is based on Christian-Jewish ideas that are from the Bible. This is only half true (much of it winds back to dark, Germanic forests!), but it is very interesting that they said that, that even many nonchurchgoers made this claim.

What was even more surprising was that, for the most part, moderate Muslim opinion (including the dubiously moderate Tariq Ramadan, who more or less stabbed Rowan Williams in the back here) said, we don't want more Sharia, we like the fact that law is somewhat secularized in Britain, suggesting that many British Muslims have already started to conform to a more Christian sense of the secularization of law — or even that this secularization was part of what they found attractive about Britain in the first place. Which is very interesting. The only Muslims who welcomed Williams's cautious endorsement of Sharia were people who were either clearly extremists (a classification which may include up to 90 percent of London's Muslim youth) or who could be suspected of a kind of creeping extremism — the kind of people who want to legitimate polygamist marriage, for example. Also, Muslim reactions sometimes expressed, in effect: we are glad that Christianity is the legacy on this island because, if one is going to be nonsecular, one must be committed to one religion or another and not to religion in general, and the commitment to Christianity does give us a certain protection against totally unlimited, dominant secularity.

Thus my conclusion about the archbishop's speech is that, fine and probing as it is in many ways, he seemed somewhat to confuse pluralism in an organicist or subsidiarist sense with pluralism in a multiculturalist sense. Also, he failed to stress that if one wants to link reason to religious tradition, one actually does have to have a specific religious commitment. Otherwise, if one merely tries to coordinate neutrally between different religions, one must fall back into a secular, pluralist position. As Phillip Blond has frequently declared, *something always rules,* and it is never merely formal but is always substantive in some way, however disguised. Perhaps, therefore, Rowan Williams did not declare boldly enough that we need to think specifically out of our Christian tradition.

One also needs to stress that there is a link between Christianity and universalism, that Christianity is *not* simply one more "difference" or "otherness" that must be respected. In the wake of Alain Badiou's book on St. Paul and the emergence of universalism from the Christian event, we have left this sort of postmodernism behind, both on the secular side and on the Christian side.[10] For in a sense, Enlightenment universalism is only the bastard child of the Christian quest for universalism. And as a matter of fact, the Christian sense of universalism is precisely what protects the idea of a pluralism of centers of power in a good, subsidiarist sense. It is the Christian primacy of the personal that has given rise to the idea that Christians will form free associations for specific purposes within Christendom. Hence the Middle Ages witnessed the sustained growth of different kinds of free associations that helped to make Europe a corporation of corporations. Moreover, because these different entities — feudal manors, cities, guilds, monasteries, mendicant orders, lay fraternities, universities, and so on — all had to relate to each other, this period also witnessed the growth of constitutionalism, or of "liberalism" in the good and proper sense.

Far more important (to my mind) for comprehending the peculiarity of European approaches to politics than the abstract, liberal notions of the Enlightenment is this long-term legacy of medieval, Catholic constitutionalism. Why is it that Hungary can leap into democracy without much experience and Russia cannot? Because Hungary once belonged to Latin Christendom. Therefore it seems there are real reasons to think that genuine pluralism is in the end protected by this specifically Christian tradition.

This means that we *cannot be content,* as Williams sometimes implies we can, with simply thinking of the church as one more social body prior to the political that exercises a continuous, negative critique of the political.[11] For such contentment downplays the Pauline and Augustinian claim that the

10. Alain Badiou, *Saint Paul: La fondation de l'universalisme* (Paris: Presses Universitaires de France, 1997).

11. Rowan Williams, "Europe, Faith, and Culture," Lecture, Anglican Cathedral, Liverpool (January 26, 2008).

church (*ecclesia* — which implies in Paul something like "the ruling council of the cosmopolis") is itself a superpolity that is not more particular than the state but is rather more universal than the state in its very concretion, and that within this superpolity are protected many diverse but collaborating individuals and subgroups.

In consequence, according to the strange, gothic logic of personalism, individuals and subgroups are at once "more" and yet at the same time "less" than the social whole, since in belonging to Christ we are gradually raised to equal and unique sonship with him; since also in pursuing the natural, political end we exceed this as persons in the direction of a supernatural end. It is hard to see how anything other than a christological logic and the logic of grace could underwrite this "double excess" that allows at once collectivism and the integrity of the individual, and co-ordinates the two.[12]

In a nutshell: European politics is actually, indeed literally (in theological terms, which take the metaphor literally), based upon the idea of the body of Christ. It is because Europeans as individuals and as social groups have considered themselves to be personal more-than-parts of the body of Christ that they have tended to develop notions of free and independent but collaborating institutions — sometimes equal with each other, sometimes hierarchically embedded. And curiously enough, in a certain inchoate way, it seems that many Muslims — great numbers of whom are now also coming to an appreciation of the Jesus of the Gospels — recognize that as well.

12. See John Milbank, *The Word Made Strange: Theology, Language, Culture* (Oxford: Blackwell, 1997), pp. 268-92.

Knowing the Truth through Witness: The Christian Faith in the Context of Interreligious Dialogue

Javier Prades

We live in a context that is both multicultural and multireligious. In this historical context, Christianity does not renounce the claim to truth of its announcement for the salvation of humankind (cf. Acts 4:11-12), and Christians carry out this task of announcing salvation by testifying to the Fact of Christ. They maintain that their proposal is reasonable, that is, that it can be grasped by any person because it is a credible proposition. Therefore they have always been ready to give reasons for their hope to those who ask (cf. 1 Pet. 3:15).

In order to show the reasonableness of this undertaking, we must first recover the legitimacy of the philosophical and religious question of truth, and must do so in a time that seems to preclude a priori the existence of truth. Second, we must clarify the original nature of Christian witness. Finally, we must be able to prove that witness is an adequate mode of knowing and transmitting the truth. We will begin with the first question.

The Question of Truth in the Context of the Dialogue between Faith and Religions

Fragmentation of Meaning and the Return of the Sacred

The proposal of truth has become increasingly problematic in Western culture: "What runs through the multiplicity of expressions of the present age is the inclination to put in parentheses, and ultimately to drop, any common reference to the truth. . . . It is no longer considered plausible, let alone de-monstrable, in terms of the individual elements of a personal, lived experi-ence as they are knit together among themselves."[1] It is no longer thought possible that there is room among common interests for the determination of the ultimate criteria of judgment, to the point that this impossibility be-comes a prohibition to which an individual must conform in order to live in relationship with the rest of society.

In this context, which assumes the fragmentation of meaning, there is a simultaneous growth of interest in religious expressions. This return of the sacred does not by itself assure that the cultural climate will change, because many manifestations of the "wild sacred" do not oppose the disappearance of truth but actually reinforce it. Under what conditions could the interest in religion, unexpected until a few decades ago, be favorable to the cause of truth? That is to say, what is the link between truth and religion?

George Steiner, along with many others, has asserted the legitimacy of the ultimate question of "why," which cannot be erased without the enact-ment of unacceptable censorship.[2] And Hans Urs von Balthasar recalled that the philosophical question surrounding the meaning of being — why does being exist rather than nothing? — becomes a religious question in reference to the human person: what is the meaning of that singular being who won-ders about the meaning of existence?

This, in fact, is the question of salvation, and it has always been posed by religions, which inquire about the meaning of the world and the person. Philosophy, which asks the fundamental questions, and religion, which won-ders about the significance of the world and the person, objectively converge on that ultimate level. The reference to the truth is part of the truly religious question, and every true philosophy wonders about the ultimate questions, which we might call religious.[3] Thus, religion does not exist in the abstract,

1. Sergio Ubbiali, "La religione e le religioni: Trascendenza, fede, e pluralismo," in *Unicità e universalità di Gesù Cristo: In dialogo con le religioni,* ed. Massimo Serretti (Cinisello Balsamo: San Paolo, 2001), pp. 113-47, at 133 (our translation).

2. George Steiner, *Errata: El examen de una vida,* trans. Catalina Martínez Muñoz (Madrid: Siruela, 1999), p. 207; originally published as *Errata: An Examined Life* (London: Weidenfeld and Nicholson, 1997).

3. Hans Urs von Balthasar, *Epilogo* (Milan: Jaca Book, 1994), p. 100; translated into English by Edward T. Oakes as *Epilogue* (San Francisco: Ignatius Press, 2004). On the ob-jective overlap of the religious question with the highest-level questions posed by reason, see John Paul II, *Fides et ratio,* no. 33. In depth, for this paragraph, see Angelo Scola, "Gesù Cristo: Religioni e testimonianza," in *L'attuale controversia sull'universalità di Gesù Cristo,* ed. Massimo Serretti (Rome: Lateran University Press, 2002), pp. 5-13.

but has historically always appeared in the concrete form of different religions, and therefore the issue of the relationship between religion, religions, and truth is unavoidable.

The Christian faith refers intrinsically to the question of truth (the question of foundation). Therefore, it has never excluded the religious dimension as an ingredient of theological faith, *fides* — recall the classic debate *de vera religione* that once introduced apologetics manuals. This is one reason why faith must face the religions. But there is a deeper, theological reason why it must do so: faith asserts that God himself was incarnate, and as a consequence, that it is possible for human freedom, which is always historically situated, to meet him in history, where religions coexist. One can understand well the calls of the Church's magisterium to dialogue with religions not only for tactical reasons — to facilitate a coexistence based on good will — but as an intrinsic dimension of the evangelical mission.

The Faith-Religions Relationship Calls Us to Rethink the Question of Truth and Freedom

In interreligious dialogue, Catholic theology cannot limit itself to merely classifying the different ways of understanding the religious phenomenon according to the well-known typology of models: exclusivity, inclusivity, pluralism.[4] These typologies, even if they reflect real differences in the way each religion participates in christological salvation, cannot fully explain the originality of the historical revelation of Christ with respect to the religious experiences of humanity.

One of the critical reasons for this insufficiency is philosophical in nature: these models owe much to a modern conception of *intentionality*, characterized by a marked "gnoseologism." In this view, the relationship of man with the truth is reduced to a conceptualistic expression of representative knowledge: in the process of knowledge, "the assertion of the truth is the fruit, representative in nature, of a mere conceptual operation. And action is the execution of this foreknown ideal, the putting-into-practice."[5] This theory inevitably derives from an idea of reason as "separate" (abstract and absolute) and bears as a consequence the great effort to integrate knowledge and freedom. If modernity considers both the dignity of knowledge and that

---

4. For an overview of such models see Serretti, *L'attuale controversia*.
5. Scola, "Gesù Cristo," p. 9 (our translation).

of freedom to be indispensable achievements, this "intellectualist" theoretical model makes it nearly impossible to explain the link between knowledge and freedom. Indeed, reason rests "upon evidence of connections of knowledge that are indifferent to freedom, which is conceived as unsettling [for knowledge]. Nonetheless, by an inevitable push-back, the supreme argument for the legitimization of the public system of reason remains its congruence with the individual dignity of consciousness."[6]

In such an understanding of reason, faith is relegated to the sphere of pure sentiment; it is external to reason and juxtaposed to it in accessing the divine truth. The theologies that derive from this contemporary dualism cannot but find themselves at an impasse when they must position faith in relation to religions. The solutions that come from these theologies range from the rigid repetition of doctrine to a hermeneutic relativism. In the obvious diversity of these positions we can nevertheless recognize that same modern root, which is incapable of explaining either the originality of the event of Christ or the relationship between truth and freedom. These positions fail to propose a theoretical model capable of communicating the original claim of Christian revelation: the claim that gives truth value to a historical Fact freely decided by God and addressed to our historical freedom. God the Father did not want to communicate himself to humankind through an idea, but chose to manifest himself through his incarnate Son. Jesus Christ, sent by the Father, freely decided to let himself be known (revelation), passing through the free act of the individual person, who receives him thanks to the gift of the Spirit (faith). This encounter between the individual person and the Truth takes the modality of *witness*, understood in its deepest sense as an intrinsic characteristic of the free act that refers intentionally to reality.

The theological proposal regarding revelation and faith must be reconsidered from both the epistemological and ontological points of view. This task requires us to take seriously the constitutive *difference* in which humankind lives, where the role of a person's free decision is crucial to his accessing the truth. It is not that the truth is the result of man's decisions — it is not that man can produce truth; nonetheless, the truth, transcendent and absolute, needs the act of that decision to attest to itself.[7] Unlike the contempo-

---

6. Pier Angelo Sequeri, "Coscienza credente e mediazione della testimonianza," in *La testimonianza in H. U. von Balthasar: Evento originario di Dio e mediazione storica della fede*, ed. Marcello Neri (Bologna: EDB, 2001), pp. 7-20 (our translation).

7. Cf. Joseph Ratzinger, *Introducción al cristianismo*, 5th ed. (Salamanca: Sígueme,

rary understanding, intentionality has a practical configuration that corresponds to the (symbolic) way in which the foundation offers itself in history to the act of human freedom. It has to do with understanding in depth that being *(esse)* is the event that originally awakens the decision of freedom, manifesting itself (anticipating itself, promising itself) in every being *(ens)*. Being is the event that turns toward the freedom/faith in every being (as the place of difference), in which appears that which is. Faith fits into this context as correlate of the question put forth by the event, according to a conception of evidence that is broader than the conceptualistic one. Within this ontological perspective, the mediating act of freedom through which the individual decides his or her humanity constitutes the place where the transcendent foundation is communicated.[8]

In keeping with the ontological renewal mentioned above, we may observe that recent studies on religion see religious rites as a way of knowing truth.[9] In ritual action, which is typical of religion, human beings recognize their proper way of accessing truth. The affirmation of truth is accomplished only when one personally takes up the content of the rite in the decision to adhere to it. The ritual gesture, interrupting the ordinary course of actions, distances man from asserting that the truth is a product of his own abilities. Differently from ordinary actions in which man himself produces the effect, ritual action allows man to put into action that decision that manifests the original meaning of his acts. In these ritual gestures, which always have some particular character but are of universal import, man's decision about himself includes the determination of his destiny: man recognizes the existence of an Other who comes before him and is irreducible to the sum of all people, in such a way as to make possible man's experience of being truly himself. It is typical of ritual action to restore the unity of personal existence with the origin, the foundation — a unity that must

---

1982), p. 123; translated into English by J. R. Foster as *Introduction to Christianity* (San Francisco: Ignatius Press, 1990).

8. Cf. John Paul II, *Fides et ratio,* nos. 80, 48, 83, 99; cf. Angelo Scola, Gilfredo Marengo, and Javier Prades, *La persona humana: Antropologia teologica,* 2nd ed. (Milan: Jaca Book, 2006); Hans Urs von Balthasar, *Teológica,* vol. 1, *Verdad del mundo,* trans. Lucía Piossek and José Pedro Tosaus (Madrid: Encuentro, 1997), translated into English by Adrian J. Walker as *Theo-logic: Theological Dramatic Theory,* vol. 1, *Truth of the World* (San Francisco: Ignatius Press, 2000). Ubbiali describes a hermeneutic that is not relativistic, but open to ontology, "La Religione," p. 137.

9. Ubbiali, "La Religione," pp. 125ff.; *Il mondo del sacramento: Teologia e filosofia a confronto,* ed. Nicola Reali (Milan: Paoline, 2001).

be continually renewed, because it never fully coincides with the result of the concrete decision that has been made. What happens paradigmatically in ritual action could be extended to all the daily actions of the individual until it informs his or her entire life (as we see in a unique way in Christianity, in the Eucharistic action). Keeping in mind the philosophical and religious rethinking mentioned above, Christian revelation claims to respond, in an absolutely gratuitous way, to this structure of truth, which all religions seek, but nevertheless fail, to fully realize.

What Does It Mean to Witness to the Christian Faith?

According to Christian revelation, "every single person can adhere to the original and transcendent foundation only in the act of a free decision in favor of the event that accomplishes the evidence of that phenomenon. This event is Jesus Christ."[10] He, in his singularity of being the incarnate Son of God, claims to fulfill the universal (eschatological) fullness of God's revelation; that is, he claims to refer to the original foundation. In this way he historically makes real the ultimate meaning of man and of the world — as a response to the religious question of salvation — giving himself to the concrete historical freedom of the individual human being.

The category of witness explains well the encounter between man and reality — witness understood as freedom's response to the foundation.[11] The importance of this was rediscovered in postconciliar theology: "Faith in a revelation that occurred historically is communicated by means of witness. Therefore, witness is one of the central concepts of Christian theology."[12] Indeed, whether in the singular case of the freedom of Jesus who responds to the Father, being the Son of God, or in the case of Christians who live the Word, the sacrament, the communion, and the authority through the gift of the Holy Spirit, we find ourselves faced with the testimonial structure of revelation, of faith, and of faith's transmission. Only when witness is placed in this philosophical-theological intersection does it become decisive for expressing the irreducible novelty of the Christian Fact, and only here does it point to a specific way of dialoguing with religions and with cultures. In-

10. Scola, "Gesù Cristo," p. 9 (our translation).
11. Cf. Balthasar, *Verdad del mundo,* pp. 92, 172-86.
12. Klaus Hemmerle, "Verità e testimonianza," in *Testimonianza e verità: Un approccio interdisciplinare,* ed. Piero Ciardella and Maurizio Gronchi (Rome: Città Nuova, 2000), pp. 307-23, particularly 307 (our translation).

deed, only at this intersection is witness free from the reductive preconceptions with which it is often conceived, and which render it useless for its foundational task. It goes without saying that witness is able to recover the existential dimension of faith, in that it expresses a personal decision that engages life through an affective bond. In this way witness corrects the intellectualist drift of a faith that identifies with the repetition of correct doctrine. Still, we must be careful not to lose the theoretical richness of the relationship between witness and truth, which we touched on above and will return to later. Witness is not limited to a sort of biographical self-referentiality on the part of the believer, but instead refers back to divine revelation. Even if Christian testimony always involves the witness, we must not forget that the witness "refers to that irreducible reference [Jesus of Nazareth] as the ultimate end of the gesture on which he is focused, and explicitly aims to render him the proper beginning and fulfillment of the act of faith to which he desires to attain."[13] Since it is by nature truth-bearing, witness cannot be identified with merely manifesting the evidence of faith's good effects (in the form of a good example), or with the lived conviction of its existentiality. Its task is not limited to offering a relevance that involves our affection, as if it had to compensate for an evidentiary defect in revelation. Witness has the claim of efficaciously conveying the truth of Christ.

Some Aspects of Witnessing as a Process for Knowing the Truth

The ethical or sentimental reduction of witness is an inevitable consequence of the difficulty of recognizing it as a way of knowing the truth. The serious negative implications of this weakness for the Christian faith are evident to everyone. The trouble comes from the impoverishment of revelation in transmission compared with this revelation's original nature, but it also has ancient philosophical roots. Further, the mistrust of witness as a philosophical category has, at different moments of Western culture, affected the relationship between truth and Christianity. These two elements influence one another in turn.

Bearing in mind this turbulent philosophical-theological history, we must welcome the attempts made since the 1970s to again take up witness as a theoretical category — attempts made not infrequently by Christian thinkers. To mention just a few of these: From Germany, we can point to

13. Sequeri, "Coscienza," p. 12 (our translation).

Klaus Hemmerle and his 1970 essay "Truth and Witness."[14] In Italy, the famous 1972 conference in Rome remains a watershed; the conference proceedings contain all of the great names of international thought of the day.[15] There is no doubt that Francophone scholars have been particularly attuned to this problem: authors like Paul Ricoeur, following Jean Nabert and, more recently, Jean-Luc Marion, suggest a revival of this topic.[16] In the Anglophone world, too, some interesting thought has developed, starting, for example, from the classic contraposition between Locke-Hume and Thomas Reid on evidentialism and the principle of credulity.[17] Let us take a synthetic look at some of the problems inherent to the truth-bearing value of witness. In this way we will address, albeit provisionally, the third question we opened at the beginning of this chapter.

Suspicion about Witness as a Method of Knowing

Mistrust toward witness as a way of knowing the truth finds its roots long ago in Aristotelian thought. Aristotle's *Rhetoric* looks at proofs or means of persuasion, that is to say, the techniques of persuasion that reach not a necessary judgment, but a probable one. In that text Aristotle considers witness among the "extra-technical" proofs, exterior to the argument of the orator. Therefore whoever uses witness is not a true master, because it occupies an inferior place, given its exteriority to the argument itself.[18]

In the modern epistemological tradition, authors like Descartes, Locke,

---

14. Hemmerle, "Verità" (our translation).

15. Enrico Castelli, ed., *La testimonianza,* atti del convegno indetto dal Centro internazionale di studi umanistici e dall'Istituto di studi filosofici (Rome: Istituto di Studi Filosofici, 1972). Giuseppe Angelini et al., *L'evidenza e la fede,* ed. Giuseppe Colombo (Milan: Glossa, 1988). Andrea Milano, *Quale verità? Per una critica della ragione teologica* (Bologna: EDB, 1999).

16. Paul Ricoeur, "L'herméneutique du témoignage," in Castelli, *La testimonianza,* pp. 35-61; Jean Nabert, *Le desir de Dieu* (Paris: Cerf, 1996), pp. 263-380; Edmond Barbotin, *Le témoignage,* 2nd ed. (Brussels: Culture & Vérité, 1995); Jean-Luc Marion, *Étant donné: Essai d'une phénoménologie de la donation,* 2nd ed. (Paris: Presses Universitaires de France, 1998), 302-5; "Le témoignage: Perspectives analytiques, bibliques et ontologiques," *Philosophie* 88 (2005).

17. Cf. C. A. J. Coady, *Testimony: A Philosophical Study* (Oxford: Clarendon Press, 1992); Jennifer Lackey and Ernest Sosa, eds., *The Epistemology of Testimony* (Oxford: Oxford University Press, 2006).

18. See Aristotle's text and commentary in Ricoeur, "L'herméneutique," p. 40.

and Kant express their suspicion of witness as a legitimate source of knowledge, in line with the concept of "separate" reason described above.[19] But within the discussion of the truth of Christianity, what began as mistrust would become a denial of the truth value of witness. It is Spinoza who criticizes the contradiction of a "historical revelation of the Absolute" to the extent that when a witness speaks of particular historical events, reason tending to universal truth is not called upon to take this into consideration. Spinoza considers contradictory the claim of prophets and holy authors that they find universal and eternal truth in particular changes they have witnessed. This divorce between testimonial mediation and universal reason, summed up in Spinoza's position, led philosophy and theology in a new direction, and Claude Bruaire has labeled it as the root of many forms of irreligiousness in our day.[20] In keeping with this diagnosis, Xavier Tilliette points to the famous eighteenth-century polemic between truth of reason and truth of fact as the root of the modern opposition between reason and witness.[21] For Lessing and the Enlightenment thinkers, the Christianity of reason could do without witnesses to the historical facts because the doctrine justifies itself. Indeed, having reached the rational maturity of Christianity one can relativize its historical origin, and along with it the testimony of prophecies, miracles, gestures, resurrection. It is evident that an understanding of testimony reduced completely to ethics or to a purely exterior confirmation of a doctrine fully grasped by intellectual means not only renders testimony superfluous, but inclines toward a much more serious reduction of the understanding of truth itself and of the nature of Christianity.

Testimony as a Way of Knowing Truth

Ricoeur helpfully introduces our description of witness because he intends to address *in recto* the Enlightenment objection to Christianity, that is, its objection to the possibility that purely contingent events could testify to the absolute. Do we have a right to invest a moment in history with an absolute

19. Cf. Roger Pouivet, "L'épistémologie du témoignage et les vertus," *Philosophie* 88 (2005): 11-27, particularly pp. 12-13; Stéphane Chauvier, "Le savoir du témoin est-il transmissible?" *Philosophie* 88 (2005): 46.

20. Cf. Claude Bruaire, "Témoignage et raison," in Castelli, *La testimonianza,* pp. 141-49.

21. Cf. Xavier Tilliette, "Témoignage et vérité: Valeur et limites d'une philosophie du témoignage," in Castelli, *La testimonianza,* pp. 89-100.

character?[22] The French author replies, following Nabert, that a philosophy of witness will be possible only where the question of the absolute is meaningful. To ask oneself the philosophical question about witness means to ask oneself about testimony to the absolute, or more precisely, about absolute testimony to the absolute.[23] Witness appears to be connected to what he calls "the original affirmation," that is, the interior act by which each person reaches a certain ultimate idea of him or herself.[24] He considers both the *example* and the *symbol* insufficient for this process to occur in the historical condition of the individual. The former is insufficient because it ends up becoming a rule, a law, or moral sublimity; evil opens up an abyss that cannot be closed by calling on the law but demands instead an event in which, through contingent facts, one can assert that the unjustifiable (evil) is overcome here and now: there is a need, therefore, for "absolute actions."[25] Neither is a *symbol* sufficient, for it lacks historicity and concreteness, even if it does not vanish as rapidly as an *example,* because it "gives to think." The philosophical issue of witness consists, according to the French philosopher, in wondering if we can clothe a moment in history with the absolute; that is, if we can blend into one the interiority of the original affirmation and the exteriority of absolute actions, within the ambit of a human life marked by unjustifiable evil.

To this end Ricoeur proposes the identification of a double exegesis in a single articulated process, like the two foci of an ellipse: the act of historical understanding of the signs given by the absolute, and the act of consciousness of oneself. The signs brought about by the absolute in history (the prophets of Israel, the Church kerygma) are the signs through which the consciousness recognizes itself. How does this process work?

22. Ricoeur, "L'herméneutique."

23. Not everyone concedes this immediate connection between testimony and the absolute. The validity of knowledge derived from testimony is discussed in the various fields of the natural, social, and legal sciences, even explicitly apart from its relationship with the absolute. See the essays of Pouivet and Chauvier cited above. The description of what Ricoeur calls the "philosophical problem" of witness could perhaps be reserved to experiences of spiritual value, where the supporting elements are historical immanence and transcendence. Cf. Barbotin, *Le témoignage,* pp. 35ff.

24. Cf. Ubbiali, "La Religione," p. 122; Barbotin, *Le témoignage,* p. 40.

25. For Nabert and Ricoeur the problem of evil is decisive in describing the nature of witness. The only response to remorse for an offense that is no longer reparable is that the victim share the suffering of the guilty party: this is possible only by the witness of people who, in their lives, attest to the presence of the absolute, by which they can measure their own being.

For the French philosopher, the witness given by historical signs implies both the free gift of something to be interpreted as the manifestation of the absolute, and the inevitable request or need for interpretation. This process of interpretation of signs coincides in action with the process of the interpretation of the self, in such a way that the progress of the consciousness toward itself involves paying closest attention to the historical signs of the absolute. The deepest interiority of the act corresponds to the greatest exteriority of the sign, not because of the weakness of witness, as Aristotle thought, but because of the historical and finite character of consciousness. Reflection cannot by itself produce the unity of the two poles, but it can recognize them and verify that they are not heterogeneous.[26] In the method of witness the act of absolute manifestation is inseparable from an adhesion that implies a choice, in correlation with acts of judging. In witness one recognizes the expression of a freedom that one desires for oneself. What for the individual is still only an idea can be recognized in the witness as historically existent: another exists who is simultaneously free and real. This recognition is not possible except through an act of the same kind, that is, the interior act of freedom itself.

The Ricoeurian attempt incites the task of exemplifying and deepening the unity of the two aspects — interior and exterior — of the single interpretive process, and with this unity its ontological and truth-bearing elements. In particular, we may wonder how the sign is grasped by the individual, and how the individual carries out the process of interpreting both the sign and the self.

The thought of Luigi Giussani, who describes the Christian encounter with great educational value and without technical claims, brings to light some aspects of the truth-bearing process inherent to Christian witness.[27] He describes the encounter with the witness using the metaphor of a *spark*. The spark ignites when the individual intuits immediately that the witness brings something true for the individual himself. This intuition moves the individual by the inevitable dignity of the truth — which Giussani calls correspondence with the complex of needs that make up the human condition

---

26. Ricoeur warns that if we accept objectified awareness as the epistemological way to judge self-awareness, the result will be a horrible *metábasis eis allo genòs* ("L'herméneutique," p. 58). See also Sequeri, "Coscienza," p. 8; Hemmerle, "Verità," p. 320.

27. See Luigi Giussani, *Certi di alcune grandi cose (1979-1981)* (Milan: Rizzoli, 2007), pp. 204-28; Luigi Giussani, *Il Senso Religioso* (Milan: Rizzoli, 1998), particularly chapters 1, 5, 10, and 12; translated into English by John Zucchi as *The Religious Sense* (Montreal: McGill-Queen's University Press, 1997).

— and awakens in him a "poverty of spirit," which strips and exposes his heart. "The spark . . . is the glittering of a new awareness of the origin of the self . . . of a different and new sentiment of oneself. But the sentiment of oneself is always due to an original phenomenon; the sentiment of oneself depends on the image we have of our origin, of the origin of the 'I.'"[28] This original image of the "I" — Giussani continues — is transformed when the "I," becoming interested in what he or she has encountered, through an "attractiveness" coming from outside, is brought to a new discovery of him or herself. This is how the decision is made to adhere to the external reality that has unveiled the depths of the self, and it leads in a new way to a relationship with God that was already given to the "I" in its original image, and that now seems profoundly new: "The decision is generated only by the discovery that the 'I' is attracted by an Other, that the substance of my 'I,' the substance of my being, my heart, is identical to 'being attracted by an Other.'"[29] The depth of this encounter — no longer only the exterior encounter with the witness, but simultaneously the interior encounter — is what Giussani speaks of as *conception:* "It is truly a conception of the self that comes from this profound embrace between my 'I' and the Other, whose attractiveness I discover, accept, and recognize."[30] Giussani's approach, although sketched just briefly, provides valuable elements for understanding the truth-bearing value of witness. It converges both with the renewed ontological understanding of intentionality and with the description of ritual actions, which operate as premises for an understanding of witness and, as Ricoeur insisted, remain subordinate to neither "absolute knowledge" nor hermeneutical relativism.

In light of the foregoing, we can indicate multiple elements that suggest a possible development: (1) The decisive role of the evidence of Someone who fills the individual's intuition in the experience of correspondence through a sign (recall what was said above about conceiving every being as the place of difference).[31] (2) Because it deals with evidence that has not been intellectualistically reduced, it is the unity between the experience of

28. Giussani, *Certi di alcune grandi cose,* p. 215 (our translation).

29. Giussani, *Certi di alcune grandi cose,* p. iv (our translation). It is no coincidence that Augustine realized that he was attracted by a beauty as new as it was original: "Late have I loved you, beauty so ancient and so new! Late have I loved you" (*Confessions* 10.27.38).

30. Giussani, *Certi di alcune grandi cose,* p. 218 (our translation).

31. The donation is not simply one of a meaning to be interpreted, but, in the ontological terms used above, it is a donation of being as an event that originally calls forth the decision of freedom, manifesting itself in every being.

true recognition and affective adherence that decisively reaches a free decision about the self and about the sign. (3) The connection between the interpretation of the self and the interpretation of the sign (the witness) occurs inasmuch as the original image of the "I" constitutively implies a relationship with God, which the encounter with the witness does not eliminate but radically renews. This understanding of witness is rooted in the understanding of elementary experience, where man discovers "I-am-You-who-makes-me." Before the divine Witness, man comes to say "I-am-You-who-come-to-meet-me." (4) The interpretation of witness does not originally depend on the problem of evil, inasmuch as it begins from the consistency of creaturely experience, which was not erased by original sin. Nor does it underestimate the importance of the redeeming Witness, that is, he who places the absolute action of the victory of mercy over unjustifiable evil. (5) The result of the decision is an assimilation so profound that we can speak of a "conception" of the "I," which Johannine and Pauline language identifies as a "new birth" or "new creation." The new interpretation of the "I" is profoundly interpersonal and dialogical. It can also be highly dramatic because everyone can defend him or herself in front of recognized evidence.[32] (6) On this understanding of witness we can articulate a "nuptial" conception of life as vocation, in dialogue with the Mystery of God through every lived experience.

Some Concluding Remarks

Our multicultural and multireligious world is marked by the apparent impossibility of proposing the truth. The rebirth of religion is not in itself decisive for overcoming this situation. The question of the truth-bearing value of religion and philosophy needs to be recovered.

In this context, the Christian originality is to announce a definitive truth for the world and for humankind. Faith must compare itself with religions on the grounds of truth and freedom.

Because the modern conception of reason as *separate* makes it difficult to articulate truth and freedom, there is a need to rethink the ontology, on

---

32. In his conversion, Paul Claudel describes the "spark" that immediately leapt out, and the battle that lasted four years, between the force of that evidence of the truth and his materialistic philosophical convictions, as well as his anti-Catholic sentiment. See "Ma Conversion," in *Oeuvres en prose* (Paris: Gallimard, 1965), pp. 1008-14.

the one hand, and the ritual nature of religions, on the other, as means of accessing the truth.

Christian revelation claims to attribute truth value to a historical Fact freely decided by God and addressed to our historic freedom.

Christian witness is an essential dimension of revelation. It cannot be reduced to pure self-referentiality, nor to an affective supplement for missing evidence; rather, it addresses a precise term of reference: Jesus Christ and the Triune God.

Witness means that the individual decides about him or herself in relationship with the absolute and in interpreting the historical sign that awoke the initial attraction; it involves his or her adherence (unity of consciousness, affection, and freedom) to such an extent that he or she can then speak of a new conception of the "I."

Multiculturalism and Civil Community inside the Liberal State: Truth and (Religious) Freedom

David L. Schindler

The liberal state is severely limited in its capacity to deal adequately with the problem of multiculturalism. The limitations stem from its inability to permit persons from the world's major religious traditions really to participate in its public (economic, political, academic, and cultural) institutions,[1] except insofar as it succeeds in assimilating these persons into its own liberal understandings of freedom, reason, and religion. Such a suggestion, of course, can only seem counterintuitive, since it appears to call into question the hallmark of the liberal state: *its unique capacity precisely to tolerate differences* of the most radical sort among its citizens.

We need therefore to qualify carefully what it is we mean to argue. To that end we begin with some definitions and general observations.

Liberalism and the Purely Juridical Idea of Statecraft

By the "liberal state" I mean the modern state conceived as an essentially juridical order: a state that takes its purpose to be the protection of rights

---

1. There is an inevitable intertwining of the public and the private. The term "public" applies in a strict sense to institutions officially sponsored by the state, but of course extends to all institutions in society, even "private" ones, insofar as these institutions are subject to state laws and regulations — for example, those relative to matters of sexual or gender discrimination, to government funding of research in universities, and the like.

even as it understands rights principally in the negative terms of immunity from coercion. The juridical state understands itself to be about implementing procedures necessary for adjudicating fairly between competing exercises of freedom by individuals in society, as distinct from defending, or calling to mind in an explicit way, any truth to which these individuals might already-anteriorly be "bound" *qua* human. Such a state thus tends toward displacing the notion of the common good by that of public order. In its Anglo-American version (in contrast to its Continental versions), this displacement does not intend the establishment of a "secularist" truth. On the contrary, this state declares itself incompetent in matters of truth bearing on the nature and destiny of the person. In the phrasing of John Courtney Murray, America's constitutional order embodies "articles of peace" in contrast to "articles of faith." America's liberal state insists that it is peculiarly able to promote genuine freedom — is most able to secure *all* persons' rights — because it advances *no* person's truth, *no truth about the person at all.* Rather than eliminating the question of truth, the juridical state (of Anglo-American liberalism) intends merely to transfer truth claims beyond the sphere of the *state,* in order to ensure the unencumbered freedom of citizens to engage in the search for truth in the distinct sphere of *society.*

Needless to say, this is a powerful argument. Let me emphasize from the outset that the liberal intention to protect the dignity of all human beings in their reality as free and rational subjects must be embraced without reservation. Furthermore, liberalism is correct that realization of this intention requires a limited state and thus a distinction between state and society. Liberalism is also right that church and state must be kept separate, in accord with the principle enunciated by Pope Gelasius I in the fifth century.[2]

My argument means to call none of this into question. What it does mean to call into question is liberalism's tethering of its defense of individual subjectivity and freedom to the purely juridical idea of statecraft. The problem is that liberalism takes the *limited* state to be just so far and of necessity a *juridical* state, whose only proper purpose is to protect rights conceived

---

2. As these statements should make clear, the argument advanced in the present paper is not meant to criticize democracy tout court, but only its meaning as articulated reductively in terms of the idea of the juridical state with its juridically conceived rights. In a word, it is important to resist reducing the meaning of democracy and of modernity to the rendering of both given by "purely" juridical liberalism. The critique of liberalism in the present article explicitly affirms the intrinsic importance of freedom and subjectivity *in* the defense of truth, and thus sustains the distinct contribution of modernity, but it does so nevertheless precisely by rejecting the liberal reading of both freedom (and subjectivity) and statecraft.

as negative in their object and content: such that, in enforcing the right to religious freedom, for example, the state claims to remain in principle empty of any positive conception of truth regarding either freedom or man's relation to God.

I take the liberal-juridical state's claim that it remains empty of, and hence indifferent toward, substantive conceptions of the human being to be at once (theoretically) incoherent and (practically) unrealizable. My argument in the present forum is limited to demonstrating that the apparently easy assumption of the purely juridical state's greater effectiveness, if not perfect consistency and complete effectiveness, in securing freedom masks profoundly urgent problems. My proposal is that we can reasonably compare the liberal and nonliberal ideas of statecraft in terms of each one's real capacity to protect the freedom and dignity of *all* citizens *over the long run* only insofar as we come to terms with the problems inherent in the idea of the purely juridical idea of statecraft.

The argument to follow, then, attempts to bring into relief what is an ineliminable and in fact dangerous paradox lying at the heart of the liberal state. The liberal state's peculiar defense of freedom at once really does (in one sense) maximize the spread of freedom even as (in another sense) it hiddenly enforces a deep and pervasive unfreedom. The liberal state's peculiar defense of limited coercive power at once really does (in one sense) result in the restriction of such power even as (in another sense) it hiddenly promotes the ever-increasing expansion of this power. In a word, the liberal-juridical state embodies a confused, reductive, and dualistic understanding of the relations between state and society and state and church.

To express this paradox in more concrete, substantive terms: the liberal state with its primarily juridically conceived rights inclines *per se* toward an undermining of its own intention to protect equally the freedom and dignity of all human beings. Indeed, it embodies a hidden dynamic for nothing less than what Joseph Ratzinger/Benedict XVI has termed a "dictatorship of relativism," and thereby for what *Evangelium vitae* notes as the tendency in today's democratic societies toward a "totalitarianism" marked by "the supremacy of the strong over the weak."[3] My intention is to show how and why this is so, in terms of the issues evoked by the phenomenon of multiculturalism.

---

3. John Paul II, *Evangelium vitae,* encyclical letter on the value and inviolability of human life, March 25, 1995, nos. 20 and 23.

Multiculturalism

What is meant by multiculturalism? The term "culture" derives from the Latin *cultus,* which means in turn cultivation, tending or caring for, education, or indeed reverence for or worship of God; and the dictionary, in one of its many definitions, describes "culture" generally as "the customary beliefs, social forms, and material traits of a racial, religious, or social group." Consistent with these meanings, but with a more precise focus, John Paul II in *Centesimus annus* says that "man is understood in a more complete way when he is situated within the sphere of culture through his language, history, and the position he takes towards the fundamental events of life, such as birth, love, work and death. At the heart of every culture lies the attitude man takes to the greatest mystery: the mystery of God. Different cultures are basically different ways of facing the question of the meaning of personal existence."[4] Indeed, the pope goes on here to say that "when this question is eliminated, the culture and moral life of nations are corrupted."[5]

Thus, when we refer today to the problem of multiculturalism, we have in mind the increasing plurality of cultures within Western society relative to the question regarding the meaning of personal existence — relative to the attitude assumed in the face of the mystery of God, and in this context also relative to the meaning of birth, love, work, and death. Multiculturalism takes form most pertinently in the multiplicity of the great world religions, the major religious traditions of Judaism, Christianity, Islam, and so on. The issue, then, is how a significant sense of community in public economic, political, academic, and cultural institutions can be sustained among persons who coexist within a single state or global order — that is, without such persons being forced, as a condition of their participation in such institutions, to change their fundamental beliefs, especially their beliefs regarding the nature of truth and freedom, in a way that undermines their dignity as free and intelligent subjects.

Now the juridical state, conceived as a protector of rights that is devoid of any truth claim, undergirds the assertion that liberal states can accommodate this problem of multiculturalism better than those states that still consider themselves somehow directly concerned with the truth regarding the nature and destiny of man. Unlike other, more traditional (e.g., premodern)

---

4. John Paul II, *Centesimus annus,* encyclical letter on the hundredth anniversary of *Rerum novarum,* May 1, 1991, no. 24.

5. John Paul II, *Centesimus annus,* no. 24.

states, the juridical state, according to its defenders, sets no a priori restrictions regarding the truth held by any of its members. Rather, it merely insists that members of society — including, most pertinently here, individuals formed in nonliberal religions and cultures — make the case for the truths in which they believe via the free and reasonable sort of dialogue fostered *de jure* by the juridical state. Once again, and in sum: the juridical state is considered uniquely effective in the face of the problem of multiculturalism because only the juridical state *unconditionally* respects the freedom and just so far the dignity of every human person — that is, it respects freedom and dignity *irrespective of the "truth" that any person espouses, including the truth about God.*

Liberalism's peculiar response to multiculturalism is thus to insist that, as the necessary condition for securing public-political community in a multicultural world, we must enshrine (constitutionally) ever less truth. Instead, we must enshrine ever more formal-procedural notions — as distinct from concrete, substantive truths regarding the nature and destiny of man. We must do so because differences in the understanding of precisely such truths serve to fragment community — often to the point of violence — in the first place. The juridical state insists, in a word, that those participating in its public institutions should (therefore) share in common the (empty) form and not the substantial content of freedom and reason, most especially as these latter bear on ultimate truths about religion and God.[6]

Now, any legitimate criticism of the liberal argument to remove truth claims from the public sphere bears a responsibility to meet the argument's main burden, which is to promote the building of civil community. A genuinely comprehensive community, however, will be one that is truly inclusive of nonliberals — such as adherents of at least some of the world's major religious traditions — as well as liberals, and of the most defenseless as well as the strong. What the problem of multiculturalism can help us see, then — contrary to the assumptions of liberalism and nearly all contemporary expectations — is that such human community is realizable not by (constitutionally) bracketing truth as the only (realistic) way to protect freedom, but by coming to regard freedom itself as *intrinsically a matter of* truth. We must see that there is no freedom rightly understood except as a matter of truth

---

6. This sort of approach to resolving the problem of pluralism is given in its classic expression in John Courtney Murray's "articles of peace" reading of (American liberal) constitutional order. See especially his *We Hold These Truths: Catholic Reflections on the American Proposition,* 2nd ed. (New York: Sheed & Ward, 1986).

— even as, correlatively, there is no truth rightly understood except as a matter of freedom.

But what can this mean? As noted, the modern state recoils from the question of truth: the modern state's juridical form stems not in small measure from the conviction that disrespect unto violence issues precisely from the variant claims to truth, especially those claims relative to God held by the different religions (or churches). And yet the gospel tells us that the truth will make us free (John 8:32), and indeed that it is only by standing in the truth that we are really free in the first place. This suggestion of the gospel that the bond between truth and freedom is indissoluble, I wish to argue, retains its cogency — in both its theological meaning and its distinctly philosophical implications — even within modern statecraft and even as modern states face the problem of multicultural claims to truth. How so?

What I have to say in the present forum can only be a first step into the thicket of issues evoked by this question. But it is a step that nonetheless seems to me necessary, given the profundity of what is at stake for the future of humanity.

Multiculturalism, Liberalism, and the Mutual Relation of Freedom and Truth

My proposal, then, is that the problem presented by multiculturalism in the context of the liberal state is in principle susceptible to resolution only insofar as freedom is understood as a matter of truth, and truth as a matter of freedom. The problem of multiculturalism, in a word, can be resolved as a matter of principle only insofar as we recognize freedom in its truth as an *order of responsiveness to and respect for the other,* an order first established and elicited *by* and *in relation to God.*

What we are terming here a resolution *in principle,* however, is obviously not synonymous with a historically realized resolution. For the intrinsic relation being asserted between freedom and truth, as well as the original and abiding relation of freedom and reason to God, implies substantive notions of freedom, truth, and God scarcely held in common among the liberal and nonliberal traditions now coexisting within the modern state. Indeed, it is just such notions that are most disputed and apt for fracturing community. We thus seem to be back to square one — to an obvious preference for the juridical state with its official emphasis on procedural rather than substantive notions.

Now I do mean to argue that we can begin to resolve the problem raised by multiculturalism only insofar as we recognize the mutual inherence of freedom and truth, and indeed the rootedness of both in God. The first point, however, is to see that in today's multicultural environment we can no longer avoid the *question* regarding the mutual relatedness of freedom and truth, and regarding the original and abiding relation of freedom and truth to God. In fact, it is *just this question* that is provoked *above all* in the meeting between liberal and nonliberal (i.e., major religious) traditions. Liberal societies, when confronting issues involving the meaning of human existence, most basically invoke freedom; the major religious traditions, on the contrary, most basically invoke truth, including especially the truth about God. This fundamental difference has grave implications for the possibility of any true public encounter among cultures within a liberal state.

The essential condition for realizing civil community among adherents of liberal and nonliberal traditions now living side by side lies in fostering a community of dialogue that permits the voice of each tradition to speak and be listened to in its integrity, apropos of what it is that is emphasized respectively in each tradition — here, freedom for liberals and truth (about God and man) for nonliberals.

Once this is said, however, it may again seem evident that the liberal-juridical state provides the precise (constitutional) conditions wherein this sort of dialogue and examination of questions is most encouraged and can most readily take place. The liberal state, in promoting the freedom to search for the truth that it (putatively) does not yet know, encourages private institutions and individuals to raise questions and take up dialogue, while the more traditional (premodern) approaches to statecraft, in promoting the truth that they already know, appear necessarily to restrict just such questions and dialogue in favor of what is given in the tradition.

With this, however, we come to the main burden of what I now mean to propose, which is that the liberal state's claim of ignorance in the matter of truth is profoundly misleading. The fact of the matter is that liberal freedom, in its inner logic as such, albeit unwittingly and indeed contrary to the express intentions of those who espouse such freedom, carries a claim of truth about the nature of freedom and intelligence — in relation to God.

The problem of multiculturalism inside the liberal state is thus properly conceived not first as a matter of the liberal tradition's *freedom* relative to nonliberal traditions' *claims of truth,* but of the liberal tradition's *claim of truth about freedom* relative to nonliberal traditions' *claims of truth about freedom.*

To show the implications for a multicultural society of the truth claim masked within the juridical state, I will first show how this liberal claim about freedom, even as it really does "liberate" in one sense, is nevertheless innerly coercive. Its coercive nature is such that it tends — *de jure* and not merely *de facto* — toward the elimination of genuinely mutual public communication, and thus of the civil community that presupposes such communication; and that it tends at the same time toward an unwitting "supremacy of the strong over the weak." I will then show how at least one version of a nonliberal claim of truth, rightly understood — and here I will consider Catholicism — in principle sustains this mutual communication and supports the weakest among us. How can this double assertion be credibly defended?

Liberalism as Dogmatic Closure

The dogmatic closure endemic to liberalism derives from the fact that the juridical state harbors an implicit claim of truth about the nature of freedom (and of reason and God) *inside its announced (public, constitutional) incompetence* in matters of truth. To be sure, the juridical state insists that what it is doing is precisely *deferring* these claims to private individuals' and institutions' exercise of freedom and intelligence. But that is just the point: this intended deferral *eo ipso* takes freedom, for public-constitutional purposes,[7] to be an act of choice quite apart from its objective content, an act that is thereby assumed to be structurally indifferent to any content to which it may (or may not) eventually elect to bind itself (privately). Freedom is assumed to consist first and most properly in the *act of choosing* an order of truth to which freedom would — eventually — be bound.

---

7. The qualifier is important. The state claims that it does not really know what freedom is and that it leaves this for private argument; but it treats freedom simply as an act of choice, as an option in the face of objective contents yet to be chosen, because this seems an obviously innocent way of proceeding. My point is that this is already a definite view of freedom officially favored by government and built into the interpretation of all laws and government regulations. The liberal state thus officially endorses a notion of freedom as a structurally indifferent act of choice — as distinct from an act of choice that is already anteriorly ordered, for example, by virtue of its constitutive relatedness to the other, the world, and God. The problem here, of course, is invisible to those Catholics who already have assumed with liberalism that truth is an object of choice and that the nature of both truth and freedom remains the same whether one understands truth simply as the object of an exercise of freedom or as in some significant sense an immanent presupposition of such an exercise.

Now, to be sure, the capacity to choose is necessarily presupposed in any adequate conception of freedom. The point here concerns rather the original indifference of the act of choosing as assumed by the juridical state, an indifference that misses freedom's anterior *participation* in an order of truth that has always already been *given* to freedom as an immanent — indeed *constitutive* — condition of its exercise.

Thus officially presupposing that it embodies no truth about the nature of freedom — of reason, of religion and God — and that it thereby remains equally open to all claims of such truth, the juridical state never explicitly acknowledges (nor *can* it ever acknowledge, nor, *a fortiori,* need it ever give an account for) any such truth about freedom as inherent in its own structure. On the contrary, this state officially acknowledges itself, and can acknowledge itself, only as an *instrument* of whatever truth about freedom is established privately — as the guarantor of the process of free debate among the multiple private "factions" (James Madison). The juridical state, in short, presumes itself to be always an instrument and never an educator regarding the true nature of freedom.

What I am proposing is that liberalism's vaunted claim to have separated procedural form cleanly from substantive content expresses a dualism (between form and content), which, paradoxically, is itself a confused sort of substantive content. The juridical state's privileging of instrumental process *eo ipso* invests the state with the *substance* of instrumentalism. In its insistence that it is merely an instrument in the service of substantive content and thus not itself an educator regarding the truth of things, the juridical state as such — notwithstanding its expressly contrary intention — becomes an educator on behalf of instrumentalism as the sole substantive "truth" that is constitutionally, and in this sense publicly, permitted and indeed promoted in civil society. But we need now to clarify how this is so.

What is meant by instrumentalism? Recall what was said above about the juridical state's conception of freedom as a primitively indifferent act of choice. This primitive indifference is what establishes the human act as instrumentalist: the human act is construed as an originally *empty* act *whereby* something is first engaged by the will and the intelligence. Which is to say, the other — the world, God — that is engaged by freedom is originally a matter of indifference to the will and the intelligence. The other lacks an inherent worth that makes an *anteriorly given,* thus ineliminable and non-arbitrary, demand upon the will and the intelligence.[8] Though this needs

8. For further exposition of "freedom of indifference" against the backdrop of the Chris-

more elaboration than can be provided here, this original indifference, hence purely instrumental character, of the human act can be expressed in the order of intelligence in terms of a reduction of reason to a matter primarily of technical-managerial power,[9] and in the order of religion in terms of a reduction of religion to a matter primarily of positivism. Thus liberalism's (putatively) purely juridical state, precisely from within its abiding intention of incompetence with respect to claims of truth about the meaning of man, orders society publicly and constitutionally in terms of what is a voluntaristic idea of freedom, a purely technical idea of reason, and a positivistic idea of religion and God. The juridical state, in a word, in the name of avoiding substantive truth about the nature of man, unconsciously embodies a "substantively" instrumentalist truth about the nature of man — one which, *prima facie,* is at odds with the alternative notions of freedom, reason, and religion in (at least some of) the various traditional religious cultures.

As we have already suggested, the juridical state's (blindly) imposed "substantive" instrumentalism undermines what are apparently its most distinctive and attractive capacities: free dialogue among peoples with differing worldviews, a limited state, the separation between church (religion) and state, and the protection of the weak. In the case of dialogue: it is indeed true that virtually limitless dialogue is promoted; the problem is that the dialogue tends to be instrumentalist in nature, that is to say, ordered not toward truth as its end but only toward an interminable *process* of dialogue that takes for granted notions of indifferent freedom, technical reason, and positivist religion. Participants in public dialogue may insist on alternative notions of freedom, reason, and God, but such assertions tend now to have legitimacy only as public expressions of arbitrary private opinion. Which is to say, such notions, for purposes of the public-constitutional ordering of society, are always preempted by the substance of instrumentalism.

Hence the paradox: a kind of relativism is unconsciously imposed on society by the state, even as the illusion is continuously upheld by the state that it is vigorously encouraging society's dialogue in search for the truth.

---

tian tradition, see Servais Pinckaers, *The Sources of Christian Ethics,* trans. Mary Thomas Noble (Washington, DC: Catholic University of America Press, 1995), pp. 242ff.; and D. C. Schindler, "Freedom Beyond Our Choosing: Augustine on the Will and Its Objects," *Communio* 29.4 (Winter 2002): 618-53.

9. The world, in other words, appears originally as an indifferent object: without inherent meaning or worth in itself and thus without an original, inner claim on the intelligence. Hence the spontaneous inclination of the intelligence is toward the world as an object available for manipulation in the interests of the knower.

The state, everywhere inside its jurisdiction, is always already enforcing a monolithic "truth claim" — that, paradoxically, of relativism.

The "limited state," or the state-society distinction, is subject to the same paradox: however much the juridical state may insist on a division of powers, on subsidiary-local institutions of government, and the like, it nonetheless of its inner logic imposes its juridical concept of political order with the paradoxical consequences just noted. Its unconscious truth claim on behalf of instrumentalism is precisely *unlimited* (within its jurisdiction: throughout all its branches and subsidiary institutions). The distinction between state and church (religion) also proves a thin veneer over a hidden truth claim: the juridical state's instrumentalist freedom and intelligence, as we have seen, entail, not an explicit proscription of definite religions, but rather the (hidden) promotion of positivist religion (akin, roughly, to what American founding father James Madison terms a "sect"). Thus, the freedom of religion (of the church) to proclaim and defend its truths about God and man and the world is recognized with respect to the public-constitutional order — but only insofar as it configures its claims to what can be supported by a voluntarist freedom and a technical intelligence.

Finally, regarding protection of the weak in the face of the strong: instrumentalist freedom and intelligence imply an original indifference to the other that renders the other without any inherent — that is, constitutively and not merely contractually given — dignity *as* other. Those who are not useful and cannot assert their rights through an exercise of their own freedom — the unborn, human embryos subject to destruction in scientific research, the terminally ill — have no publicly-constitutionally recognized worth; rather, their rights are contingent on the good will of those who are able to exercise their freedom and choose to enact laws to protect these vulnerable ones. The juridical state is therefore vulnerable to an inversion of democracy into a totalitarianism of the strong over the weak.

The liberal-juridical state, like all states in human history, thus governs on the basis of a truth claim, even as, unlike other states, it denies that it does so — indeed, insists that its uniqueness lies precisely in its ability, by virtue of restricting itself to a (putatively) empty idea of the human act, to avoid claims of truth. The instrumentalist notions tacitly affirmed by the juridical state fundamentally oppose those defended in (at least some) world religions.

The relevant question, then, even in the case of the modern liberal state, is not whether the state can avoid ordering society in terms of a truth claim, but *which* truth can best promote freedom, genuine dialogue, and protection for the weak.

Catholicism and Multiculturalism

Of course, the present argument in its Catholic context takes us to the question of how we are properly to read Vatican II's *Dignitatis humanae.* The key, it seems to me, is to understand that this document does not embrace the juridical idea that freedom has replaced truth as a main concern of statecraft. What the document affirms, rather, is a deepened sense of freedom as integral to the truth rightly conceived — and an idea of statecraft that incorporates this newly integrated sense of the mutual internality of truth and freedom.

Commemorating the fortieth anniversary of *Dignitatis humanae,* Benedict XVI stated that "religious liberty derives from the special dignity of the human person";[10] and that "it is in accordance with their dignity that all men, because they are . . . endowed with reason and free will . . . , are both impelled by their nature and bound by a moral obligation to seek the truth, especially religious truth."[11] In light of this, he goes on to say,

> The Second Vatican Council reaffirms the traditional Catholic doctrine which holds that men and women, as spiritual creatures, can know the truth and therefore have the duty and the right to seek it.[12]
>
> Having laid this foundation, the Council places a broad emphasis on religious liberty, . . . with respect for the legitimate demands of the public order.

In the face of the problem of multiple claims of truth, especially religious truth, Pope Benedict's response is to defend freedom and rights and respect for difference by way of appeal to . . . *truth itself.* The point, then, is that Benedict does not speak of freedom first or most properly in terms of "immunity from coercion," which is to say, he does not adopt the interpretation of *Dignitatis humanae* according to which the document's notion of freedom is primarily juridical — an interpretation that has prevailed among Catholics in Western democracies, certainly including the United States. The legitimate separation of state and church does not entail for Benedict a separation of the state *from the question of truth:* it does not, in a word, entail an embrace of a juridical state.

10. Benedict XVI, *Angelus,* December 4, 2005.

11. Vatican Council II, Declaration on Religious Freedom, *Dignitatis humanae,* no. 2, quoted in Benedict XVI, *Angelus.*

12. Benedict XVI, *Angelus;* cf. Vatican Council II, *Dignitatis humanae,* no. 3.

Recall the statement cited earlier from John Paul II: "When . . . question[s] [regarding the meaning of personal existence are] eliminated, the culture and moral life of nations are corrupted."[13] What I have proposed here is that the juridical state tends toward elimination of these questions, and thus toward corruption, in and through the positivist-instrumentalist content of the freedom, reason, and religion blindly assumed by that state in its constitutional ordering of society. This is a trenchant criticism. My purpose, however, is not to deny the legitimacy and necessity of the liberal intention to promote civil community through a limited state. Rather, I aim to make clear that liberalism cannot realize this intention with consistency, and indeed to suggest at the same time how the world religious traditions — especially notably here, Catholicism — make an essential contribution to the realization of this intention.

13. John Paul II, *Centesimus annus,* no. 24.

Contributors

MASSIMO BORGHESI, Professor of Moral Philosophy, Università degli Studi di Perugia, Italy

FRANCESCO BOTTURI, Professor of Moral Philosophy, Università Cattolica del Sacro Cuore, Milan, Italy

MARTA CARTABIA, Professor of Constitutional Law, Università degli Studi di Milano-Bicocca, Italy

CARMINE DI MARTINO, Associate Professor of Philosophy, Università degli Studi di Milano, Italy

PIERPAOLO DONATI, Professor of Sociology, Università di Bologna, Italy

COSTANTINO ESPOSITO, Professor of History of Philosophy, Università degli Studi di Bari Aldo Moro, Italy

STANLEY HAUERWAS, Professor Emeritus of Divinity and Law, Duke Divinity School

ANTONIO LÓPEZ, Associate Professor of Theology, John Paul II Institute for Studies on Marriage and Family at the Catholic University of America

FRANCISCO JAVIER MARTÍNEZ FERNÁNDEZ, Archbishop of Granada, Spain

CONTRIBUTORS

John Milbank, Professor of Religion, Politics, and Ethics, University of Nottingham, UK

Javier Prades, Professor of Systematic Theology, Universidad Eclesiástica San Dámaso, Madrid, Spain

David L. Schindler, Professor of Fundamental Theology, John Paul II Institute for Studies on Marriage and Family at the Catholic University of America

Angelo Cardinal Scola, Archbishop of Milan, Italy

Lorenza Violini, Professor of Constitutional Law, Università degli Studi di Milano, Italy

Joseph H. H. Weiler, Professor of Law, New York University

Index of Persons

Husserl, Edmund, 20-23, 29, 48-49

Isaac, 112
Isensee, Josef, 108n18

Jesus Christ, 74, 122, 124, 127, 130,
    139-42, 144, 149-51, 179, 181, 182, 189
John Paul II, 76, 147, 149, 162, 177n3,
    180n8, 192, 193, 202
Jonas, Hans, 60, 61, 63, 64

Kant, Immanuel, 65, 77, 123, 159, 184
Kass, Leon, 110n21
Khatami, Sayyed Mohammed, 172n8
Kierkegaard, Søren, 144
Kissinger, Henry, 137
Knitter, Paul, 139-41, 143, 149
Kronman, Anthony, 160-62
Kumar, Krishan, 163n2
Kymlicka, Will, 7

Lackey, Jennifer, 183n17
Ladeur, Karl-Heinz, 102n6
Lanzillo, Maria Laura, 4n3, 53
Laski, Harold, 169
Lessing, Theodor, xii, 184
Lévinas, Emmanuel, 22, 150
Lévi-Strauss, Claude, 132
Lilla, Mark, 156-62
Limbach, Jutta, 107n16
Locke, John, 159, 160, 169, 183, 184
Lollini, Andrea, 98n21
Long, D. Stephen, 121n1
López, Antonio, xvi, 57
Lubac, Henri de, 63n17, 121n1, 141n18
Luhmann, Niklas, 36n12, 108
Luther, Martin, 114

MacIntyre, Alasdair, 12, 121n1, 123,
    155n10
Macpherson, C. B., 155, 156
Madison, James, 198, 200
Malcolm X, 133
Marengo, Gilfredo, 180n8
Margalit, Avishai, 129n4
Marion, Jean-Luc, 183

Maritain, Jacques, 34n7
Martínez, Javier, xvi, 121
Maruko, Tadao, 87n2
Marx, Karl, 65, 79, 133, 146
Mary, 149
Mazzarese, Tecla, 88n3
McGiffert, Arthur, 154, 155
Mead, George Herbert, 8
Menke, Karl-Heinz, 139n12
Merleau-Ponty, Maurice, 26
Milano, Andrea, 183n15
Milbank, John, xvi, 121n1, 163
Mill, John Stuart, 155
Mumford, Lewis, 58n2, 62, 63
Muralt, André de, 171n7
Murray, John Courtney, 191, 194n6

Nabert, Jean, 183, 185
Newton, Isaac, 64
Nicholls, David, 169
Nietzsche, Friedrich, 17, 47, 133
Northcott, Michael, 160n20
Nussbaum, Martha, 96, 97

Ockham, William, 63, 171
Oliver, Simon, 63n14
Oppenheimer, Robert J., 69

Panikkar, Raimundo, 149
Parsons, Talcott, 41
Patruno, Francesco, 106n15
Paul, Saint, 147, 174, 175
Pessina, Adriano, 105n12
Pieper, Josef, 78n57
Pinckaers, Servais, 198-99n8
Plato, 69n35, 74, 75, 78, 79
Poscher, Ralf, 108n19
Postman, Neil, 59
Pouivet, Roger, 184n19, 185n23
Prades, Javier, xiv, xvi, 103n8, 137n10,
    176

Rahner, Karl, 141
Ramadan, Tarik, 173
Ratzinger, Joseph, 34, 35, 65, 66,

www.ingramcontent.com/pod-product-compliance
Lightning Source LLC
Chambersburg PA
CBHW020350270326
41926CB00007B/378